THE
GRIM
READER

———

T H E
G R I M
R E A D E R

Writings on Death,
Dying, and Living On

---

*Edited by Maura Spiegel
and Richard Tristman*

ANCHOR BOOKS
DOUBLEDAY
NEW YORK   LONDON   TORONTO
SYDNEY   AUCKLAND

AN ANCHOR BOOK
PUBLISHED BY DOUBLEDAY
a division of Bantam Doubleday Dell Publishing Group, Inc.
1540 Broadway, New York, New York 10036

ANCHOR BOOKS, DOUBLEDAY, and the portrayal of an anchor
are trademarks of Doubleday, a division of
Bantam Doubleday Dell Publishing Group, Inc.

Book design by Maria Carella

Permissions begin on p. 427

Library of Congress Cataloging-in-Publication Data
The grim reader: writings on death, dying, and living on /
edited by Maura Spiegel and Richard Tristman. —
1st Anchor Books ed.
p.   cm.
1. Death—Literary collections. 2. Bereavement—Literary collections. 3. Grief—
Literary collections. I. Spiegel, Maura. II. Tristman, Richard.
PN6071.D4G75   1997
808.8′03548—dc21   96-48586
CIP

ISBN 0-385-48527-1

CONTENTS

※

PART 2
WHAT WORDS ARE THERE?

꿇

PART 3
GIVE DEATH THE CROWN:
WAR, PESTILENCE, GENOCIDE

❧

PART 4
MAKING ARRANGEMENTS

❧

PART 5
DEATH ISSUES

ॐ

PART 6
A HEALTHY DISTANCE

ॐ

PART 7
RECAPITULATION

IN MEMORIAM B.C. 1925–1994

———————————

And the daughter of Zion is left as a cottage in a vineyard,
as a lodge in a garden of cucumbers. . . .

ISAIAH 1:8

ACKNOWLEDGMENTS

This project is Ted Solotaroff's love child; we thank him warmly for his generous help and encouragement. For advice, assistance, and manifold acts of sustenance, we'd also like to thank Sarah Abramowicz, Alison Akant, Anaheed Alani, Adnan Ashraf, Bonnie Barnes, Jack Barth, Charmaine Beckford, Gila Bercovitch, Georges Borchardt, Clyde Burdios, Amy Carberg, Alex Chachkes, Phebe Chao, Bonnie Costello, Ocie Cureton, Kristin DiSpaltro, Cecily Dixon, Lydia Dreifus, Sandra Dunn, Janice Dutcher, Jill Ferland, Charles Flowers, Ellen Flynn, Kenji Fujita, Joshua Galef, Elyse Goldstein, Jennifer Guilfoyle, Rochelle Gurstein, Robert Hanning, Jonathan Haynes, Debra Hecht, Gina Heiserman, Regan Heiserman, Didi Heller, Ruby Heranandani, Susan Hopper, Donna Joyce, Paul Lazar, Amy Leigh, Philip Lopate, Sandra Massey, Margaret McGrath, Kate Morgan, Daniel Myerson, Cathy Naughton, Scot Nourok, Kevin O'Boyle, Leslie Oleksowicz, Lisa Perkins, Tina Pohlman, Elizabeth Rosen, Jane Rosenman, Rose Schapp, Derek Schilling, Daphne Schmidt, Rebecca Schraffenberger, Carol Slade, Ann Smyth, Virginia Solotaroff, Susan Sontag, Joseph Sparano, Charlotte Spiegel, Jill Spiegel, Lois Taylor, Helen Vendler, Harriet Wald, Estha Weiner, Rachel Williams, Julian Young, Sam Zimmerman, Gina and the family Pollara, David, Jonah, and Jeanette Tristman. And Arthur, Sam, and Kate Heiserman.

PREFACE

The time is past when reading about death was the exclusive passion of the morbid-minded, of those half in love with oblivion. Pursuing, rather than retreating from, the fearful subject has, we now recognize, its fortifying value. Denial, taboo, and shame have been banished in favor of reflection, candor, mutual aid, and acceptance. The battle against the stigma that has commonly attached to fatal diseases (like cancer in the past and AIDS today) is nowadays carried on vigorously in public. The dying, those who care for them, and the bereaved no longer keep to themselves in silent suffering, but seek one another out for community and instruction. And this spirit of facing up, speaking out, listening in turn, has produced a vast new literature.

In these pages we have brought together the best of new writings from various angles on the subject of death and integrated into this company classic statements which have retained their pertinence. In their reckonings with death, writers and thinkers grapple with the indomitable fact and discover emotional resources, insight, and methods of coping unknown to them before the crisis or the terminal illness. And in poems, eulogies, private expressions of grief, love, and loss, letters of condolence, and public words to honor and memorialize, we have sought persuasive forms of consolation.

Those who must comfort the dying or ease their own bereavement will find companionship, we hope, in the authors we have gathered here. For those called upon to eulogize or commemorate we offer affecting models for inspiration as well as memorable quotations. For times when words come hardest we have sought examples of fresh and honest eloquence, and have found these, often enough, in unexpected quarters.

Arranged to invite reflection, to give courage, to stir and educate, *The Grim Reader* means to elicit the pure fascination of its subject at every turn. The reader is engaged in the explosive debates surrounding euthanasia and assisted suicide and is offered perspective, by way of history and anthropology, on personal fears and the public ceremonies that articulate and ease them in near and distant cultures.

Each of these responses to death, uncompromised by denial or deceit, is a beginning in consolation and, though not an easy anesthetic escape, will lessen death's sting at last. That is our premise in collecting the readings that follow. The careful reconstruction of death's history and the hurried journal of its presence, the witty rumination and the catastrophic lament, the tale of the death watch and the polemic against undertakers, even the outburst of comic rebellion—wherever the faces of death are rendered with passion and the accuracy of art, fate comes to a halt, momentarily but sublimely, and to occupy that spot of timelessness is consolation. It does not make us less mortal, nor does it banish fear or grief. It leaves everything in the physical world unchanged. It cures nothing except our understanding.

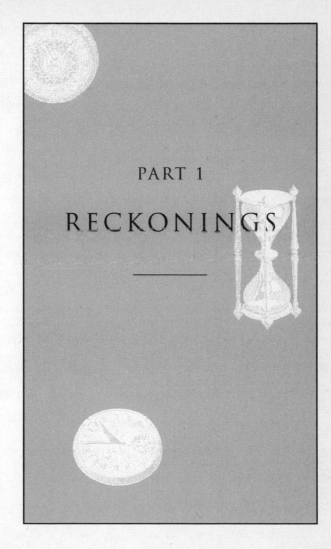

PART 1

RECKONINGS

All creatures recoil from the threat of death, and all creatures die. Man alone, in addition to his moment of perishing, has the lifelong expectation of death to contend with. Only man has mortality. Only man has death on his mind.

With effort, the mind can convert death into something serviceable, if not agreeable. We can acclaim it as the source of all meaning: without it, we should also be without purpose or depth. "Death is the mother of beauty" and, being the very engine of fate, the mother of invention too. Science is our effort to forestall it, culture our hope to live beyond it in other minds. It gives urgency to love and weight to justice, since each depends upon our knowing how scarce and exhaustible a commodity life is. We owe much to death—but, because we owe it ourselves in the end, we do not stop fearing it. Even if we are out of love with life, and death appears by contrast "restful," "easeful," we are not constituted to be wholly fearless in its presence.

The fear of death is most often portrayed as the ultimate fear of the new: it is the "undiscover'd country" Hamlet speaks of, "from whose bourn no traveller returns." Sometimes, though (and increasingly so in modern times), it is frank oblivion, not the unknown, but the unknowing itself, that terrifies, "The sure extinction" of which Philip Larkin writes, ". . . not to be here, / Not to be anywhere. . . ." And sometimes, equivocally, it is the dread of both, "cold obstruction" for the body and its familiar affections, as Shakespeare's Claudio puts it in *Measure for Measure*, "this sensible warm motion to become / A kneaded clod," and hellfire or worse for the severed immortal soul

This notion of psychic survival is not, then, an unmitigated comfort. To skeptics it represents the mere shameless projection of our wish never to die, but it has obviously entailed for those who have taken it seriously a possibility of eternal wretchedness at least as great as any of eternal safety. For a modern person, in any case, it is hard enough to understand what kind of thing the soul might be, let alone to justify a belief in its immortality. Yet if one considers what a powerful force consciousness is, how vastly its inability to contemplate its own disappearance strengthens and complicates a human being's creaturely instinct to survive, it begins to seem easier to accept the eternity of this tenacious faculty than to imagine it extinguished with the death of the body.

Images of a rewarding afterlife perhaps once provided genuine reassurance to the righteous. Such vivid expressions of religious hope seem to entail a contempt for the world as a matter of logic: if the afterlife is going to be good, the loss of earthly life is nothing to bemoan. The New Testament rhetoric that calls life death and death life is only a straightforward expression of a paradox advanced by all religion. Sometimes the blessings of the next world are portrayed in easily recognized earthly terms—the famous "pie in the sky" jeered at by those who would rather attain some contentment here on earth. Yet even where descriptions of the heavenly paradise are most beautiful and enticing, as in the Koran's account of a renewed Eden, its "rivers of milk unchanging in flavor, [its] rivers of wine a delight to the drinkers"—even amid such images of ease and satiety, the text gently reminds the reader that all of this is a "similitude," a sensuous analogy to an otherwise unimaginable condition.

The fact is that immortality is rarely understood to be mortality merely improved upon and prolonged. To attain eternal life, one must indeed "die to this world," as Saint Paul puts it, and that act is unquestionably a sacrifice—of the very matrix of desire and egoism that makes us yearn for life undying to begin with. Most scenarios of deathlessness turn out to be less than lively. Appetite goes, as does all sensual pleasure (except as a "similitude"); politics subside, along with art and its most time-bound manifestation, fashion; curiosity vanishes, having quite literally been satisfied once and for all; initiative is un-called-for, impertinent, and subject to censure.

Despite the diverse myths of afterlife and metempsychosis (not to mention the thrifty if vulnerable idea that the soul, or mind, or spirit, is indestructible), the contrast between life and death remains radical, the touchstone of all antitheses. So radical, indeed, that few authors escape the compulsion to give one of them essential priority over the other. Almost all succumb to one of two powerful metaphors of the relationship of life to death. According to one metaphor— probably the more appealing to intuition, if not to philosophy—death comes to fetch us from this life, more or less as an interloper, a sneak thief who steals into our life and carries us off in secret. We do not so much *lose* our life to this version of death as we are abducted from it, lawlessly and always at the worst moment. Notwithstanding this per-sonal misfortune, life remains the basic state, and the ever robust property of the aggregate of living beings. Life is the true condition of the universe and survives the small disruption of individual deaths essentially undamaged.

According to the other metaphor, our time of life is borrowed, if not out-and-out stolen. It is a diversion, a brief detour around obliv-ion, and we are soon enough back on the real road. Life is the anom-aly, a deviation from the true deathly scheme of things. We may rejoice in it all the same, as in any stroke of good luck—grateful with

Montaigne for whatever terms we get—or we may feel obliged to quell the illicit thing with the hand of cold philosophy, but in either case we know that we have no right to it. When death comes, it is not to abduct but to reclaim. It is received with respect, "the distinguished thing" (as Henry James called it). Death is an officer of nature's law. Once we are nabbed, all alibis are vain; achievement, dignity, identity itself prove counterfeit. It turns out that everyone who enters life does so on forged papers.

Attachment to life is thought, besides, to be unseemly, and, although it is admirable and even heroic for others to labor to preserve one's life, it is at least vaguely dishonorable for one to attempt too much on his own behalf. If life is to be loved, it should be loved heartily, for its lessons and sensations, and not merely for the habit of it. True love of life, as Hazlitt and Stevenson maintain, involves a certain insouciance, even daring, a contempt for its mere dull prolongation. So even in the heart of what might be called hedonism the elevation of life to an absolute value is deprecated. Survivalism reflects the greed of biology and not the generosity of thought: there is no concept of nobility that does not include among its requirements some final disdain for life as endurance. Hence the survivor, even when he has done nothing blameworthy to assure his escape from death, acquires a certain guilt—especially, but not exclusively, in his own eyes. It is as if he bore the responsibility for a vague power—the "vital force," the life instinct—working perhaps unwished-for within him: his very survival is evidence of the rapacity and ingenuity of his ego.

What we regret in the individual, we may yet welcome in the community. Sophocles long ago—when medicine was largely folk-lore—was already marveling at the prowess of the human race in "conquering diseases once thought beyond all cure." "Only against death," he wrote, "has man remained helpless." Yet, given the close connection between disease and death, every inroad against disease appears to be a setback for mortality. The fantasy of parlaying death forestalled into death annulled is sparked for a moment by every bulletin from the laboratory. And yet, though the interesting statistic known as "life expectancy" can be driven upward by the discovery of antiseptics, or antibiotics, or antigens, though we can slow down the aging process and beat back cancer, the contingency of the hour of our death has the peculiar effect of emphasizing the pure necessity of its coming at last.

Human nature is practically defined by this deeply intuited understanding that mortality will forever find a way around our skill. We are afflicted with foreknowledge, of the inevitability of griefs and partings, and of a time when others shall breathe the sweet air in our place. Our sicknesses, whether or not they are unto death, require attention when they occur. But this sad expectation is a kind of ailment written into our liveliest cells: in a sense, it requires continual treatment—a complex protocol, part reconciliation to the inevitable, part defiance of same, part the point-blank viewing of carnal realities, part the free flight of the mind away from them. Nonetheless, this all but impossible balance, vital as it is, turns out to be among the most frequent of human achievements. It has its place in efforts not otherwise companionable: in art and philosophy—whose quarrel is very ancient, Plato says—in ceremony and science. Our most generic name for this facing up to death in our undeniable weakness and impudence is consolation.

————————

WRESTLING
WITH THE FACT

---

*. . . geologic history shows us that life is only
a short episode between two eternities of death,
and that, even in this episode, conscious thought
has lasted and will last only a moment.
Thought is only a gleam in the midst of a long
night. But it is this gleam which is everything.*

HENRI POINCARÉ
The Value of Science

"Transience value is scarcity value in time."

SIGMUND FREUD

ON TRANSIENCE

Though much of the writing of Sigmund Freud (1856–1939) is of a technical nature, expounding his psychoanalytic theory and instructing practitioners of it in technique, Freud was also a literary master who could evoke the psychological mysteries of our common experiences in the most civil and transparent of styles. The fact that our responses appear perfectly natural does not, for Freud, put an end to the need to investigate them. In his 1916 essay "On Transience," he delicately integrates two themes which also crop up repeatedly in his more speculative work: that of the origin of our sense of pleasure, and that of the origin of the pain of loss. He doesn't doubt that we value beauty, and he doesn't doubt that we mourn the loss of what we value, but he suddenly sees a reason to wonder why. In the year following the appearance of this essay, Freud published one of his major technical expositions of the psychology of loss, the seminal paper "Mourning and Melancholia."

Not long ago I went on a summer walk through a smiling countryside in the company of a taciturn friend and of a young but already famous poet. The poet admired the beauty of the scene around us but felt no joy in it. He was disturbed by the thought that all this beauty was fated to extinction, that it would vanish when winter came, like all human beauty and all the beauty and splendour that men have created or may create. All that he would otherwise have loved and admired seemed to him to be shorn of its worth by the transience which was its doom.

The proneness to decay of all that is beautiful and perfect can, as we know, give rise to two different impulses in the mind. The one leads to the aching despondency felt by the young poet, while the other leads to rebellion against the fact asserted. No! it is impossible that all this loveliness of Nature and Art, of the world of our sensations and of the world without, will really fade away into nothing. It would be too senseless and too presumptuous to believe it. Somehow or other this loveliness must be able to persist and to escape all the powers of destruction.

But this demand for immortality is a product of our wishes too unmistakable to lay claim to reality: what is painful may none the less be true. I could not see my way to dispute the transience of all things, nor could I insist upon an exception in favour of what is beautiful and perfect. But I did dispute the pessimistic poet's view that the transience of what is beautiful involves any loss in its worth.

On the contrary, an increase! Transience value is scarcity value in time. Limitation in the possibility of an enjoyment raises the value of the enjoyment. It was incomprehensible, I declared, that the thought of the transience of beauty should interfere with our joy in it. As regards the beauty of Nature, each time it is destroyed by winter it comes again next year, so that in relation to the length of our lives it can in fact be regarded as eternal. The beauty of the human form and face vanish for ever in the course of our own lives, but their evanescence only lends them a fresh charm. A flower that blossoms only for a single night does not seem to us on that account less lovely. Nor can I understand any better why the beauty and perfection of a work of art or of an intellectual achievement should lose its worth because of its temporal limitation. A time may indeed come when the pictures and statues which we admire to-day will crumble to dust, or a race of men may follow us who no longer understand the works of our poets and thinkers, or a geological epoch may even arrive when all animate life upon the earth ceases; but since the value of all this beauty and perfection is mined only by its significance for our own emotional lives, it has no need to survive us and is therefore independent of absolute duration.

These considerations appeared to me incontestable; but I noticed that I had made no impression either upon the poet or upon my friend. My failure led me to infer that some powerful emotional factor was at work which was disturbing their judgement, and I believed later that I had discovered what it was. What spoilt their enjoyment of beauty must have been a revolt in their minds against mourning. The idea that all this beauty was transient was giving these two sensitive minds a foretaste of mourning over its decease; and, since the mind instinctively recoils from anything that is painful, they felt their enjoyment of beauty interfered with by thoughts of its transience.

Mourning over the loss of something that we have loved or admired seems so natural to the layman that he regards it as self-evident. But to psychologists mourning is a great riddle, one of those phenomena which cannot themselves be explained but to which other obscurities can be traced back. We possess, as it seems, a certain amount of capacity for love—what we call libido—which in the earliest stages of development is directed towards our own ego. Later, though still at a very early time, this libido is diverted from the ego on to objects, which are thus in a sense taken into our ego. If the objects are destroyed or if they are lost to us, our capacity for love (our libido) is once more liberated; and it can then either take other objects instead or can temporarily return to the ego. But why it is that this detachment of libido from its objects should be such a painful process is a mystery to us and we have not hitherto been able to frame any hypothesis to account for it. We only see that libido clings to its objects and will not renounce those that are lost even when a substitute lies ready to hand. Such then is mourning.

My conversation with the poet took place in the summer before the war. A year later the war broke out and robbed the world of its beauties. It destroyed not only the beauty of the countrysides through which it passed and the works of art which it met with on its path but it also shattered our pride in the achievements of our civilization, our admiration for many philosophers and artists and our hopes of a final triumph over the differences between nations and races. It tarnished the lofty impartiality of our science, it revealed our instincts in all their nakedness and let loose the evil spirits within us which we thought had been tamed for ever by centuries of continuous education by the noblest minds. It made our country small again and made the rest of the world far remote. It robbed us of very much that we had loved, and showed us how ephemeral was much that we had regarded as immutable.

We cannot be surprised that our libido, thus bereft of so many of its objects, has clung with all the greater intensity to what is left to us, that our love of our country, our affection for those nearest us and our pride in what is common to us have suddenly grown stronger. But have those other possessions, which we have now lost, really ceased to have any worth for us because they have proved so perishable and so unresistant? To many of us this seems to be so, but once more wrongly, in my view. I believe that those who think thus, and seem ready to make a permanent renunciation because what was precious has proved not to be lasting, are simply in a state of mourning for what is lost. Mourning, as we know, however painful it may be, comes to a spontaneous end. When it has renounced everything that has been lost, then it has consumed itself, and our libido is once more free (in so far as we are still young and active) to replace the lost objects by fresh ones equally or still more precious. It is to be hoped that the same will be true of the losses caused by this war. When once the mourning is over, it will be found that our high opinion of the riches of civilization has lost nothing from our discovery of their fragility. We shall build up again all that war has destroyed, and perhaps on firmer ground and more lastingly than before.

Translated by James Strachey.

BERTOLT BRECHT (1898–1956)

ON HIS MORTALITY

1.
Smoke your cigars, go right ahead, the doctor told me,
With or without them everyone's gotta go—obviously.
In the mucous membrane of my eye there are, for example,
    traces of cancer:
Sooner or later they'll be the death of me.

2.
A man need not, of course, despair on that account.
He may yet live long, he really may.
He can fill his stomach with chicken and with blackberries.
It's true he's going to have a bellyache one day.

3.
Nothing can be done about it anyhow, either with drink or
    shenanigans.
Such a cancer grows imperceptibly inside.

It is possible you've already been crossed off the list
At the moment you approach the altar with your bride.

4.

My uncle, for example, still wore well-pressed trousers
When he was marked for the kill.
He looked like life itself, but they were cemetery flowers:
Every hair on his body was ill.

5.

There are people who have it in the family
Only they don't admit it, ever.
They know the difference between pineapple and parsley
But between cancer and a rupture? Never.

6.

My grandfather, on the other hand, knew exactly what he
        was in for
And lived cautiously according to the doctor's fiat
And got to be fifty before he was sick of it.
It should happen to a dog, a life like that.

7.

You and I know: no man is to be envied.
However he lives, each has his cross to bear.
I myself have kidney trouble and
Haven't been allowed to drink for many a year.

Translated by Eric Bentley.

"He who has learned how to die
has unlearned how to be a slave."

MICHEL DE MONTAIGNE

TO PHILOSOPHIZE
IS TO LEARN TO DIE

*Michel de Montaigne (1533–92) tells us that he drafted the spirited essay that
follows a few weeks into his fortieth year, when he had already lived longer
than most of his friends and than Jesus himself. He added afterthoughts to the
essay many times during the next two decades, sometimes enhancing its brave
humanism, sometimes its demure but totally sincere Christianity. It is a kind
of digest of the classical arguments against the fear of death: though on the
whole stoical in disposition—its very title reflects an ancient tradition of
philosophy as consolation—it is blithely inconsistent from the point of view of
systematic thought, being indebted now to the Stoic Seneca, for instance, now
to the Epicurean Lucretius, and to various Platonists, Aristotelians, Cynics,
and Sceptics as well. Yet its every vigorous sentence seems to exemplify a
lesson instinctively Montaigne's: the fear of death may have many sources,
but never mistake the love of life for one of them.*

Cicero says that to philosophize is nothing else but to prepare for
death. This is because study and contemplation draw our soul out of

us to some extent and keep it busy outside the body; which is a sort of apprenticeship and semblance of death. Or else it is because all the wisdom and reasoning in the world boils down finally to this point: to teach us not to be afraid to die. In truth, either reason is a mockery, or it must aim solely at our contentment, and the sum of its labors must tend to make us live well and at our ease, as Holy Scripture says. All the opinions in the world agree on this—that pleasure is our goal—though they choose different means to it. Otherwise they would be thrown out right away; for who would listen to a man who would set up our pain and discomfort as his goal?

. . .

The goal of our career is death. It is the necessary object of our aim. If it frightens us, how is it possible to go a step forward without feverishness? The remedy of the common herd is not to think about it. But from what brutish stupidity can come so gross a blindness! . . . It is no wonder they are so often caught in the trap. These people take fright at the mere mention of death, and most of them cross themselves at that name, as at the name of the devil. And because death is mentioned in wills, don't expect them to set about writing a will until the doctor has given them their final sentence; and then, between the pain and the fright, Lord knows with what fine judgment they will concoct it. Because this syllable struck their ears too harshly and seemed to them unlucky, the Romans learned to soften it or to spread it out into a periphrasis. Instead of saying "He is dead," they say "He has ceased to live," "He has lived." Provided it is life, even past life, they take comfort. We have borrowed from them our "late Mr. John."

Perhaps it is true that, as the saying goes, the delay is worth the money. I was born between eleven o'clock and noon on the last day of February, 1533, as we reckon time now, beginning the year in January. It was only just two weeks ago that I passed the age of thirty-nine years, and I need at least that many more; but to be bothered meanwhile by the thought of a thing so far off would be folly. After all, young and old leave life on the same terms. None goes out of it otherwise than as if he had just entered it. And besides, there is no man so decrepit that as long as he sees Methuselah ahead of him, he does not think he has another twenty years left in his body. Furthermore, poor fool that you are, who has assured you the term of your life? You are building on the tales of doctors. Look rather at facts and experience. By the ordinary run of things, you have been living a long time now by extraordinary favor. You have passed the accustomed limits of life. And to prove this, count how many more of your acquaintances have died before your age than have attained it. And even for those who have glorified their lives by renown, make a list, and I'll wager I'll find more of them who died before thirty-five than after. It is completely reasonable and pious to take our example from the humanity of Jesus Christ himself; now he finished his life at thirty-three. The greatest man that was simply a man, Alexander, also died at that age.

How many ways has death to surprise us! . . . I leave aside fevers and pleurisies. Who would ever have thought that a duke of Brittany would be stifled to death by a crowd, as that duke was at the entrance of Pope Clement, my neighbor, into Lyons? Haven't you seen one of our kings killed at play? And did not one of his ancestors die from the charge of a hog? Aeschylus, threatened with the fall of a house, takes every precaution—in vain: he gets himself killed by a sort of roof, the shell of a tortoise dropped by a flying eagle. Another dies from a grape seed; an emperor from the scratch of a comb, while combing his hair. . . .

. . .

What does it matter, you will tell me, how it happens, provided we do not worry about it? I am of that opinion; and in whatever way we can put ourselves in shelter from blows, even under a calf's skin, I am not the man to shrink from it. For it is enough for me to spend my life comfortably; and the best game I can give myself I'll take, though it be as little glorious and exemplary as you like. . . .

But it is folly to expect to get there that way. They go, they come, they trot, they dance—of death no news. All that is fine. But when it comes, either to them or to their wives, children, or friends, surprising them unprepared and defenseless, what torments, what cries, what frenzy, what despair overwhelms them! . . . If it were an enemy we could avoid, I would advise us to borrow the arms of cowardice. But since that cannot be, since it catches you just the same, whether you flee like a coward or act like a man, . . . let us learn to meet it steadfastly and to combat it. And to begin to strip it of its greatest advantage against us, let us take an entirely different way from the usual one. Let us rid it of its strangeness, come to know it, get used to it. Let us have nothing on our minds as often as death. At every moment let us picture it in our imagination in all its aspects. At the stumbling of a horse, the fall of a tile, the slightest pin prick, let us promptly chew on this: Well, what if it were death itself? And there-upon let us tense ourselves and make an effort. Amid feasting and gaiety let us ever keep in mind this refrain, the memory of our condition; and let us never allow ourselves to be so carried away by plea sure that we do not sometimes remember in how many ways this happiness of ours is a prey to death, and how death's clutches threaten it. Thus did the Egyptians, who, in the midst of their feasts and their greatest pleasures, had the skeleton of a dead man brought before them, to serve as a reminder to the guests.

> Look on each day as if it were your last
> And each unlooked-for hour will seem a boon.
>   [Horace]

It is uncertain where death awaits us; let us await it everywhere. Premeditation of death is premeditation of freedom. He who has learned how to die has unlearned how to be a slave. Knowing how to die frees us from all subjection and constraint. There is nothing evil in life for the man who has thoroughly grasped the fact that to be de-prived of life is not an evil. Aemilius Paulus replied to the messenger sent by that miserable king of Macedon, his prisoner, to beg him not to lead him in his triumph: "Let him make that request of himself."

In truth, in all things, unless nature lends a hand, it is hard for art and industry to get very far. I am by nature not melancholy, but dreamy. Since my earliest days, there is nothing with which I have occupied my mind more than with images of death. Even in the most licentious season of my life, . . . amid ladies and games, someone would think me involved in digesting some jealousy by myself, or the uncertainty of some hope, while I was thinking about I don't remember whom, who had been overtaken a few days before by a hot fever and by death, on leaving a similar feast, his head full of idleness, love, and a good time, like myself; and thinking that the same chance was hanging from my ear.

I did not wrinkle my forehead any more over that thought than any other. It is impossible that we should fail to feel the sting of such notions at first. But by handling them and going over them, in the long run we tame them beyond question. Otherwise for my part I should be in continual fright and frenzy; for never did a man so distrust his life, never did a man set less faith in his duration. . . .

Someone, looking through my tablets the other day, found a memorandum about something I wanted done after my death. I told him what was true, that although only a league away from my house, and hale and hearty, I had hastened to write it there, since I could not be certain of reaching home. Since I am constantly brooding over my thoughts and settling them within me, I am at all times about as well prepared as I can be. And the coming of death will teach me nothing new.

We must be always booted and ready to go; so far as it is in our power, and take especial care to have only ourselves to deal with then. . . . For we shall have enough trouble without adding any. One man complains not so much of death as that it interrupts the course of a glorious victory, another, that he must move out before he has married off his daughter or supervised the education of his children; one laments losing the company of his wife, another of his son, as the principal comforts of his life.

I am at this moment in such a condition, thank God, that I can move out when he chooses, without regret for anything at all, unless for life, if I find that the loss of it weighs on me. I unbind myself on all sides; my farewells are already half made to everyone except myself. Never did a man prepare to leave the world more utterly and completely, nor detach himself from it more universally, than I propose to do. . . .

I want a man to act, and to prolong the functions of life as long as he can; and I want death to find me planting my cabbages, but careless of death, and still more of my unfinished garden.

. . .

People will tell me that the reality of death so far exceeds the image we form of it that, when a man is faced with it, even the most skillful fencing will do him no good. Let them talk; beyond question forethought is a great advantage. And then, is it nothing to go at least that far without disturbance and fever? What is more, Nature herself lends us her hand and gives us courage. If it is a quick and violent death, we have no leisure to fear it; if it is otherwise, I notice that in proportion as I sink into sickness, I naturally enter into a certain disdain for life. I find that I have much more trouble digesting this resolution to die when I am in health than when I have a fever. Inasmuch as I no longer cling so hard to the good things of life when I begin to lose the use and pleasure of them, I come to view death with much less frightened eyes. This makes me hope that the farther I get from life and the nearer to death, the more easily I shall accept the exchange. Even as I have experienced in many other occasions what Caesar says, that things often appear greater to us from a distance than near, so I have found that when I was healthy I had a much greater horror of sicknesses than when I felt them. The good spirits, pleasure, and strength I now enjoy make the other state appear to me so disproportionate to this one, that by imagination I magnify those inconveniences by half, and think of them as much heavier than I find they are when I have them on my shoulders. I hope I shall have the same experience with death.

Let us see how, in those ordinary changes and declines that we suffer, nature hides from us the sense of our loss and decay. What has an old man left of the vigor of his youth, and of his past life? . . .

Caesar, observing the decrepit appearance of a soldier of his guard, an exhausted and broken man, who came to him in the street to ask leave to kill himself, replied humorously: "So you think you're alive." If we fell into such a change suddenly, I don't think we could endure it. But, when we are led by Nature's hand down a gentle and virtually imperceptible slope, bit by bit, one step at a time, she rolls us into this wretched state and makes us familiar with it; so that we feel no shock when youth dies within us, which in essence and in truth is a harder death than the complete death of a languishing life or the death of old age; inasmuch as the leap is not so cruel from a painful life to no life as from a sweet and flourishing life to a grievous and painful one.

The body, when bent and bowed, has less strength to support a burden, and so has the soul; we must raise and straighten her against the assault of this adversary. For as it is impossible for the soul to be at rest while she fears death, so, if she can gain assurance against it, she can boast of a thing as it were beyond man's estate: that it is impossible for worry, torment, fear, or even the slightest displeasure to dwell in her. . . .

What does it matter when it comes, since it is inevitable? To the man who told Socrates, "The thirty tyrants have condemned you to death," he replied: "And nature, them."

What stupidity to torment ourselves about passing into exemption from all torment! As our birth brought us the birth of all things, so will our death bring us the death of all things. Wherefore it is as foolish to lament that we shall not be alive a hundred years from now as it is to lament that we were not alive a hundred years ago. Death is the origin of another life. Just so did we weep, just so did we struggle against entering this life, just so did we strip off our former veil when we entered it.

Nothing can be grievous that happens only once. Is it reasonable so long to fear a thing so short? Long life and short life are made all one by death. For there is no long or short for things that are no more. Aristotle says that there are little animals by the river Hypanis that live only a day. The one that dies at eight o'clock in the morning dies in its youth; the one that dies at five in the afternoon dies in its decrepitude. Which of us does not laugh to see this moment of duration considered in terms of happiness or unhappiness? The length or shortness of our duration, if we compare it with eternity, or yet with the duration of mountains, rivers, stars, trees, and even of some animals, is no less ridiculous.

. . .

Wherever your life ends, it is all there. The advantage of living is not measured by length, but by use; some men have lived long, and lived little; attend to it while you are in it. It lies in your will, not in the number of years, for you to have lived enough. Did you think you would never arrive where you never ceased going? Yet there is no road but has its end. And if company can comfort you, does not the world keep pace with you? . . .

Does not everything move with your movement? Is there anything that does not grow old along with you? A thousand men, a thousand animals, and a thousand other creatures die at the very moment when you die:

No night has ever followed day, no day the night,
That has not heard, amid the newborn infants' squalls,
The wild laments that go with death and funerals.
   [Lucretius]

Why do you recoil, if you cannot draw back? You have seen enough men who were better off for dying, thereby avoiding great miseries. Have you found any man that was worse off? How simpleminded it is to condemn a thing that you have not experienced yourself or through anyone else. Why do you complain of me and of destiny? Do we wrong you? Is it for you to govern us, or us you? Though your age is not full-grown, your life is. A little man is a whole man, just like a big one. Neither men nor their lives are measured by the ell.

Chiron refused immortality when informed of its conditions by the very god of time and duration, his father Saturn. Imagine honestly how much less bearable and more painful to man would be an everlasting life than the life I have given him. If you did not have death, you would curse me incessantly for having deprived you of it. I have deliberately mixed with it a little bitterness to keep you, seeing the convenience of it, from embracing it too greedily and intemperately. To lodge you in that moderate state that I ask of you, of neither fleeing life nor fleeing back from death, I have tempered both of them between sweetness and bitterness.

I taught Thales, the first of your sages, that life and death were matters of indifference; wherefore, to the man who asked him why then he did not die, he replied very wisely: "Because it is indifferent."

Water, earth, air, fire, and the other parts of this structure of mine are no more instruments of your life than instruments of your death. Why do you fear your last day? It contributes no more to your death than each of the others. The last step does not cause the fatigue, but reveals it. All days travel toward death, the last one reaches it. Such are the good counsels of our mother Nature. Now I have often pondered how it happens that in wars the face of death, whether we see it in ourselves or in others, seems to us incomparably less terrifying than in our houses—otherwise you would have an army of doctors and snivelers—and, since death is always the same, why nevertheless there is much more assurance against it among villagers and humble folk than among others. I truly think it is those dreadful faces and trappings with which we surround it, that frighten us more than death itself: an entirely new way of living; the cries of mothers, wives, and children; the visits of people dazed and benumbed by grief; the presence of a number of pale and weeping servants; a darkened room; lighted candles; our bedside besieged by doctors and preachers; in short, everything horror and fright around us. There we are already shrouded and buried. Children fear even their friends when they see them masked, and so do we ours. We must strip the mask from things as well as from persons; when it is off, we shall find beneath only that same death which a valet or a mere chambermaid passed through not long ago without fear. Happy the death that leaves no leisure for preparing such ceremonies!

Translated by Donald Frame.

> ". . . I should not really object to dying
> if it were not followed by death."

THOMAS NAGEL

DEATH

Granted that death is not a good thing, at any rate on the face of it, we may sometimes want more than our reflex against it to tell us why. We may want an actual explanation, something that brings the inferences of the mind into alignment with the instincts of the body. In the following excerpts, drawn from the first chapter of his book Mortal Questions, *the contemporary philosopher Thomas Nagel sorts out all the arguments for and against regretting our mortality with brisk lucidity and—considering the promised end—invigorating wit.*

If death is the unequivocal and permanent end of our existence, the question arises whether it is a bad thing to die.

There is conspicuous disagreement about the matter: some people think death is dreadful; others have no objection to death *per se*, though they hope their own will be neither premature nor painful. Those in the former category tend to think those in the latter are blind to the obvious, while the latter suppose the former to be prey to some sort of confusion. On the one hand it can be said that life is all we have and the loss of it is the greatest loss we can sustain. On the other hand it may be objected that death deprives this supposed loss of its subject, and that if we realize that death is not an unimaginable condition of the persisting person, but a mere blank, we will see that it can have no value whatever, positive or negative.

. . .

I shall not discuss the value that one person's life or death may have for others, or its objective value, but only the value it has for the person who is its subject. That seems to me the primary case, and the case which presents the greatest difficulties. Let me add only two observations. First, the value of life and its contents does not attach to mere organic survival: almost everyone would be indifferent (other things equal) between immediate death and immediate coma followed by death twenty years later without reawakening. And second, like most goods, this can be multiplied by time: more is better than less. The added quantities need not be temporally continuous (though continuity has its social advantages). . . .

If we turn from what is good about life to what is bad about death, the case is completely different. Essentially, though there may be problems about their specification, what we find desirable in life are certain states, conditions, or types of activity. It is *being* alive, *doing* certain things, having certain experiences, that we consider good. But if death is an evil, it is the *loss of life,* rather than the state of being dead, or nonexistent, or unconscious, that is objectionable. (*Note:* It is sometimes suggested that what we really mind is the process of *dying.* But I should not really object to dying if it were not followed by death.) This asymmetry is important. If it is good to be alive, that advantage can be attributed to a person at each point of his life. It is a good of which Bach had more than Schubert, simply because he lived longer. Death, however, is not an evil of which Shakespeare has so far received a larger portion than Proust. If death is a disadvantage, it is not easy to say when a man suffers it.

There are two other indications that we do not object to death merely because it involves long periods of nonexistence. First, as has been mentioned, most of us would not regard the *temporary* suspension of life, even for substantial intervals, as in itself a misfortune. If it ever happens that people can be frozen without reduction of the conscious lifespan, it will be inappropriate to pity those who are temporarily out of circulation. Second, none of us existed before we were born (or conceived), but few regard that as a misfortune. I shall have more to say about this later.

The point that death is not regarded as an unfortunate *state* enables us to refute a curious but very common suggestion about the origin of the fear of death. It is often said that those who object to death have made the mistake of trying to imagine what it is like to *be* dead. It is alleged that the failure to realize that this task is logically impossible (for the banal reason that there is nothing to imagine) leads to the conviction that death is a mysterious and therefore terrifying prospective *state*. But this diagnosis is evidently false, for it is just as impossible to imagine being totally unconscious as to imagine being dead (though it is easy enough to imagine oneself, from the outside, in either of those conditions). Yet people who are averse to death are not usually averse to unconsciousness (so long as it does not entail a substantial cut in the total duration of waking life).

If we are to make sense of the view that to die is bad, it must be on the ground that life is a good and death is the corresponding deprivation or loss, bad not because of any positive features but because of the desirability of what it removes. We must now turn to the serious difficulties which this hypothesis raises, difficulties about loss and privation in general, and about death in particular.

Essentially, there are three types of problem. First, doubt may be raised whether *anything* can be bad for a man without being positively unpleasant to him: specifically, it may be doubted that there are any evils which consist merely in the deprivation or absence of possible goods, and which do not depend on someone's *minding* that deprivation. Second, there are special difficulties, in the case of death, about how the supposed misfortune is to be assigned to a subject at all. There is doubt both as to *who* its subject is, and as to *when* he undergoes it. So long as a person exists, he has not yet died, and once he has died, he no longer exists; so there seems to be no time when death, if it is a misfortune, can be ascribed to its unfortunate subject. The third type of difficulty concerns the asymmetry, mentioned above, between our attitudes to posthumous and prenatal nonexistence. How can the former be bad if the latter is not?

. . .

. . . Suppose an intelligent person receives a brain injury that reduces him to the mental condition of a contented infant, and that such desires as remain to him can be satisfied by a custodian, so that he is free from care. Such a development would be widely regarded as a severe misfortune, not only for his friends and relations, or for society, but also, and primarily, for the person himself. This does not mean that a contented infant is unfortunate. The intelligent adult who has been *reduced* to this condition is the subject of the misfortune. He is the one we pity, though of course he does not mind his condition—there is some doubt, in fact, whether he can be said to exist any longer.

The view that such a man has suffered a misfortune is open to the same objections which have been raised in regard to death. He does not mind his condition. It is in fact the same condition he was in at the age of three months, except that he is bigger. If we did not pity him then, why pity him now; in any case, who is there to pity? The intelligent adult has disappeared, and for a creature like the one before us, happiness consists in a full stomach and a dry diaper.

If these objections are invalid, it must be because they rest on a mistaken assumption about the temporal relation between the subject of a misfortune and the circumstances which constitute it. If, instead of concentrating exclusively on the oversized baby before us, we consider the person he was, and the person he *could* be now, then his reduction to this state and the cancellation of his natural adult development constitute a perfectly intelligible catastrophe.

. . . There are goods and evils which are irreducibly relational; they are features of the relations between a person, with spatial and temporal boundaries of the usual sort, and circumstances which may not coincide with him either in space or in time. A man's life includes much that does not take place within the boundaries of his body and his mind, and what happens to him can include much that does not take place within the boundaries of his life. These boundaries are commonly crossed by the misfortunes of being deceived, or despised, or betrayed. (If this is correct, there is a simple account of what is wrong with breaking a deathbed promise. It is an injury to the dead man. For certain purposes it is possible to regard time as just another type of distance.) The case of mental degeneration shows us an evil that depends on a contrast between the reality and the possible alternatives. A man is the subject of good and evil as much because he has hopes which may or may not be fulfilled, or possibilities which may or may not be realized, as because of his capacity to suffer and enjoy. If death is an evil, it must be accounted for in these terms, and the impossibility of locating it within life should not trouble us.

When a man dies we are left with his corpse, and while a corpse can suffer the kind of mishap that may occur to an article of furniture, it is not a suitable object for pity. The man, however, is. He has lost his life, and if he had not died, he would have continued to live it, and to possess whatever good there is in living. If we apply to death the account suggested for the case of dementia, we shall say that although the spatial and temporal locations of the individual who suffered the loss are clear enough, the misfortune itself cannot be so easily located. One must be content just to state that his life is over and there will never be any more of it. That *fact*, rather than his past or present condition, constitutes his misfortune, if it is one. Nevertheless if there is a loss, someone must suffer it, and *he* must have existence and specific spatial and temporal location even if the loss itself does not. The fact that Beethoven had no children may have been a cause of regret to him, or a sad thing for the world, but it cannot be described as a misfortune for the children that he never had. All of us, I believe, are fortunate to have been born. But unless good and ill can be assigned to an embryo, or even to an unconnected pair of gametes, it cannot be said that not to be born is a misfortune. (That is a factor to be considered in deciding whether abortion and contraception are akin to murder.)

This approach also provides a solution to the problem of temporal asymmetry, pointed out by Lucretius. He observed that no one finds it disturbing to contemplate the eternity preceding his own birth, and he took this to show that it must be irrational to fear death, since death is simply the mirror image of the prior abyss. That is not true, however, and the difference between the two explains why it is reasonable to regard them differently. It is true that both the time before a man's birth and the time after his death are times when he does not exist. But the time after his death is time of which his death deprives him. It is time in which, had he not died then, he would be alive. Therefore any death entails the loss of *some* life that its victim would have led had he not died at that or any earlier point. We know perfectly well what it would be for him to have had it instead of losing it, and there is no difficulty in identifying the loser.

But we cannot say that the time prior to a man's birth is time in which he would have lived had he been born not then but earlier. For aside from the brief margin permitted by premature labor, he *could* not have been born earlier: anyone born substantially earlier than he was would have been someone else. Therefore the time prior to his birth is not time in which his subsequent birth prevents him from living. His birth, when it occurs, does not entail the loss to him of any life whatever.

The direction of time is crucial in assigning possibilities to people or other individuals. Distinct possible lives of a single person can diverge from a common beginning, but they cannot converge to a common conclusion from diverse beginnings. (The latter would represent not a set of different possible lives of one individual, but a set of distinct possible individuals, whose lives have identical conclusions.) Given an identifiable individual, countless possibilities for his continued existence are imaginable, and we can clearly conceive of what it would be for him to go on existing indefinitely. However inevitable it is that this will not come about, its possibility is still that of the continuation of a good for him, if life is the good we take it to be.

We are left, therefore, with the question whether the nonrealization of this possibility is in every case a misfortune, or whether it depends on what can naturally be hoped for. This seems to me the

most serious difficulty with the view that death is always an evil. Even
if we can dispose of the objections against admitting misfortune that is
not experienced, or cannot be assigned to a definite time in the person's life, we still have to set some limits on *how* possible a possibility
must be for its nonrealization to be a misfortune (or good fortune,
should the possibility be a bad one). The death of Keats at 24 is
generally regarded as tragic; that of Tolstoy at 82 is not. Although they
will both be dead for ever, Keats' death deprived him of many years of
life which were allowed to Tolstoy; so in a clear sense Keats' loss was
greater (though not in the sense standardly employed in mathematical
comparison between infinite quantities). However, this does not prove
that Tolstoy's loss was insignificant. Perhaps we record an objection
only to evils which are gratuitously added to the inevitable; the fact
that it is worse to die at 24 than at 82 does not imply that it is not a
terrible thing to die at 82, or even at 806. The question is whether we
can regard as a misfortune any limitation, like mortality, that is normal to the species. Blindness or near-blindness is not a misfortune for
a mole, nor would it be for a man, if that were the natural condition of
the human race.

The trouble is that life familiarizes us with the goods of which
death deprives us. We are already able to appreciate them, as a mole is
not able to appreciate vision. If we put aside doubts about their status
as goods and grant that their quantity is in part a function of their
duration, the question remains whether death, no matter when it
occurs, can be said to deprive its victim of what is in the relevant
sense a possible continuation of life.

The situation is an ambiguous one. Observed from without,
human beings obviously have a natural lifespan and cannot live much
longer than a hundred years. A man's sense of his own experience, on
the other hand, does not embody this idea of a natural limit. His
existence defines for him an essentially open-ended possible future,
containing the usual mixture of goods and evils that he has found so
tolerable in the past. Having been gratuitously introduced to the
world by a collection of natural, historical, and social accidents, he
finds himself the subject of a *life,* with an indeterminate and not
essentially limited future. Viewed in this way, death, no matter how

inevitable, is an abrupt cancellation of indefinitely extensive possible goods. Normality seems to have nothing to do with it, for the fact that we will all inevitably die in a few score years cannot by itself imply that it would not be good to live longer. Suppose that we were all inevitably going to die in agony—physical agony lasting six months. Would inevitability make that prospect any less unpleasant? And why should it be different for a deprivation? If the normal lifespan were a thousand years, death at 80 would be a tragedy. As things are, it may just be a more widespread tragedy. If there is no limit to the amount of life that it would be good to have, then it may be that a bad end is in store for us all.

C. P. CAVAFY (1863–1933)

THE HORSES OF ACHILLES

When they saw Patroklos dead
—so brave and strong, so young—
the horses of Achilles began to weep;
their immortal nature was upset deeply
by this work of death they had to look at.
They reared their heads, tossed their long manes,
beat the ground with their hooves, and mourned
Patroklos, seeing him lifeless, destroyed,
now mere flesh only, his spirit gone,
defenseless, without breath,
turned back from life to the great Nothingness.

Zeus saw the tears of those immortal horses and felt sorry.
"At the wedding of Peleus," he said,
"I should not have acted so thoughtlessly.
Better if we hadn't given you as a gift,
my unhappy horses. What business did you have down there,

among pathetic human beings, the toys of fate.
You are free of death, you will not get old,
yet ephemeral disasters torment you.
Men have caught you up in their misery."
But it was for the eternal disaster of death
that those two gallant horses shed their tears.

Translated by Edmund Keeley and Philip Sherrard.

❧

"I have journeyed back in thought . . . only to discover
that the prison of time is spherical and without exits."

VLADIMIR NABOKOV

SPEAK, MEMORY

*"In [a] . . . sense, both memory and imagination are a negation of time,"
Vladimir Nabokov (1899–1977) told an interviewer shortly after the publication of his revised autobiography,* Speak, Memory, *in 1966. For most
writers we have encountered, death is lamentable for putting an end to our
time on earth, but time remains a segment of eternity of whose indefinite
prolongation we may reasonably dream. Nabokov offers a less familiar,
and perhaps more mischievous, view, in which time-boundedness and the
whole category of the temporal constitute the real sorrow of mortal existence, the thing we strive by all means (even, conceivably, suicide) to flee
from. Against the often repeated argument that we should not mind death
any more than we mind the oblivion that preceded birth, Nabokov—with
the devilish consistency that gives brilliance to his novels—offers the idea
of "chronophobia," an indignation evenly spent on prenatal nonexistence
and postmortem. To his reflections on these themes we have joined a short
passage from a later part of the book in which Nabokov contemplates
the curious transformation of the departed as they return to us in our
dreams.*

The cradle rocks above an abyss, and common sense tells us that our existence is but a brief crack of light between two eternities of darkness. Although the two are identical twins, man, as a rule, views the prenatal abyss with more calm than the one he is heading for (at some forty-five hundred heartbeats an hour). I know, however, of a young chronophobiac who experienced something like panic when looking for the first time at homemade movies that had been taken a few weeks before his birth. He saw a world that was practically unchanged—the same house, the same people—and then realized that he did not exist there at all and that nobody mourned his absence. He caught a glimpse of his mother waving from an upstairs window, and that unfamiliar gesture disturbed him, as if it were some mysterious farewell. But what particularly frightened him was the sight of a brand-new baby carriage standing there on the porch, with the smug, encroaching air of a coffin; even that was empty, as if, in the reverse course of events, his very bones had disintegrated.

Such fancies are not foreign to young lives. Or, to put it otherwise, first and last things often tend to have an adolescent note—unless, possibly, they are directed by some venerable and rigid religion. Nature expects a full-grown man to accept the two black voids, fore and aft, as stolidly as he accepts the extraordinary visions in between. Imagination, the supreme delight of the immortal and the immature, should be limited. In order to enjoy life, we should not enjoy it too much.

I rebel against this state of affairs. I feel the urge to take my rebellion outside and picket nature. Over and over again, my mind has made colossal efforts to distinguish the faintest of personal glimmers in the impersonal darkness on both sides of my life. That this darkness is caused merely by the walls of time separating me and my bruised fists from the free world of timelessness is a belief I gladly share with the most gaudily painted savage. I have journeyed back in thought—with thought hopelessly tapering off as I went—to remote regions where I groped for some secret outlet only to discover that the prison of time is spherical and without exits. Short of suicide, I have tried everything. I have doffed my identity in order to pass for a conventional spook and steal into realms that existed before I was conceived. I have mentally endured the degrading company of Victorian lady novelists and retired colonels who remembered having, in former lives, been slave messengers on a Roman road or sages under the willows of Lhasa. I have ransacked my oldest dreams for keys and clues—and let me say at once that I reject completely the vulgar, shabby, fundamentally medieval world of Freud, with its crankish quest for sexual symbols (something like searching for Baconian acrostics in Shakespeare's works) and its bitter little embryos spying, from their natural nooks, upon the love life of their parents.

Initially, I was unaware that time, so boundless at first blush, was a prison. In probing my childhood (which is the next best to probing one's eternity) I see the awakening of consciousness as a series of spaced flashes, with the intervals between them gradually diminishing until bright blocks of perception are formed, affording memory a slippery hold. I had learned numbers and speech more or less simultaneously at a very early date, but the inner knowledge that I was I and that my parents were my parents seems to have been established only later, when it was directly associated with my discovering their age in relation to mine. Judging by the strong sunlight that, when I think of that revelation, immediately invades my memory with lobed sun flecks through overlapping patterns of greenery, the occasion may have been my mother's birthday, in late summer, in the country, and I had asked questions and had assessed the answers I received. All this is as it should be according to the theory of recapitulation; the beginning of reflexive consciousness in the brain of our remotest ancestor must surely have coincided with the dawning of the sense of time.

. . .

Whenever in my dreams I see the dead, they always appear silent, bothered, strangely depressed, quite unlike their dear, bright selves. I am aware of them, without any astonishment, in surroundings they never visited during their earthly existence, in the house of some friend of mine they never knew. They sit apart, frowning at the floor, as if death were a dark taint, a shameful family secret. It is certainly not then—not in dreams—but when one is wide awake, at moments of robust joy and achievement, on the highest terrace of consciousness, that mortality has a chance to peer beyond its own limits, from the mast, from the past and its castle tower. And although nothing much can be seen through the mist, there is somehow the blissful feeling that one is looking in the right direction.

BEING BRAVE
AND
BEING SCARED

Weep not, child,
Weep not, my darling,
With these kisses let me remove your tears,
The ravening clouds shall not be victorious . . .
They shall not long possess the sky, they devour
the stars only in apparition. . . .

WALT WHITMAN
"On the Beach at Night"

PHILIP LARKIN (1922–85)

AUBADE

I work all day, and get half-drunk at night.
Waking at four to soundless dark, I stare.
In time the curtain-edges will grow light.
Till then I see what's really always there:
Unresting death, a whole day nearer now.
Making all thought impossible but how
And where and when I shall myself die.
Arid interrogation: yet the dread
Of dying, and being dead,
Flashes afresh to hold and horrify.

The mind blanks at the glare. Not in remorse
—The good not done, the love not given, time
Torn off unused—nor wretchedly because
An only life can take so long to climb
Clear of its wrong beginnings, and may never;
But at the total emptiness for ever,
The sure extinction that we travel to

And shall be lost in always. Not to be here,
Not to be anywhere,
And soon; nothing more terrible, nothing more true.

This is a special way of being afraid
No trick dispels. Religion used to try,
That vast moth-eaten musical brocade
Created to pretend we never die,
And specious stuff that says *No rational being*
Can fear a thing it will not feel, not seeing
That this is what we fear—no sight, no sound,
No touch or taste or smell, nothing to think with,
Nothing to love or link with,
The anaesthetic from which none come round.

And so it stays just on the edge of vision,
A small unfocused blur, a standing chill
That slows each impulse down to indecision.
Most things may never happen: this one will,
And realisation of it rages out
In furnace-fear when we are caught without
People or drink. Courage is no good:
It means not scaring others. Being brave
Lets no one off the grave.
Death is no different whined at than withstood.

Slowly light strengthens, and the room takes shape.
It stands plain as a wardrobe, what we know,
Have always known, know that we can't escape,
Yet can't accept. One side will have to go.
Meanwhile telephones crouch, getting ready to ring
In locked-up offices, and all the uncaring
Intricate rented world begins to rouse.
The sky is white as clay, with no sun.
Work has to be done.
Postmen like doctors go from house to house.

𝕤

"I have learned how to navigate
this foreshortened life of mine. . . ."

PAUL ZWEIG

DEPARTURES

The poet and critic Paul Zweig (1935–84) was much occupied with the "journey of our life" (as Dante calls it) and studied it in others, in The Adventurer (1974), and in himself, in Three Journeys: An Automythology (1976). In 1978, when he was forty-three, Zweig was diagnosed with a lymphoma that was to prove only transiently treatable and remitting. In the six uncertain years that followed, he was fiercely productive, writing a critical biography of Walt Whitman, his third book of poetry, Eternity's Woods, and Departures (1986), the log he kept of his life's hard passage during these years. It was still in rough draft, much of it in longhand, when Zweig died.

Of that final period Morris Dickstein has written, "His mind never became the stricken reflex of his illness. Without trying to do any more than get along or get his work done, he became something of a hero to many of us, a model of how to look death in the face with fear and hope but without panic or illusion. . . ."

In a late poem entitled "The River," Zweig writes about his daughter Genevieve, who will grow up without him. She was nine when he died.

When my daughter was an hour old, flailing
In the aseptic glow of the hospital cradle,
Her eyes squeezed shut, already bruised by light,
She made thin, rasping sounds,
As if some creature were trapped behind her gums.
Genevieve, one day
You will remember someone: a glimpse,
A voice, telling what I never told
—What the living never say—
Because the words ran backward in my breath.

I've never been much good at transitions. Over the years, I have gone as if expelled, dragged or broken from one life to another, never quite willing or knowing. It has been all zigzags, changes that sprang from nowhere and became irreversible, as if I had been shunted onto another plane of life, never choosing and never prepared. What I wanted was a limited existence: an enchanted ordinariness as an engineer, living in a tract house in Queens, or as an elementary school teacher in Brooklyn, living in a tenement, with a shopping street downstairs and the smell of food in the hallway. A life close to the center, undeviating and unproblematical; a sort of immortality. But then would come the dark shove, the loose wire in my genes, and I would start on some baffling new course: a marriage, a religious conversion, an obsession that filled my life with strangeness. Like the honeybee whose eccentric flight, full of swings and surprises, results from some twist in the bee's genetic grid, I too have apparently been programmed for fuzzy swoops and teeterings beyond reason.

Therefore I was prepared, if that is the word, when several years ago another sort of shove—even darker, more arbitrary—sent me reeling. Again I found myself in a new life, but one that would never become stale or overly familiar to me; that would always be new, always just discovered. This unexplored, unchosen life was the life of the dying—the life of all life, perhaps, but starker and more intense in my case. It is, most likely, my final incarnation, and I will never become tired of it, never leave it by the pratfall of a gene or the shove of an instinct.

I entered this life on a muggy May afternoon when a doctor, feeling my neck with a hard probing touch that I have gotten to know well, discovered a small, mobile lump at the base of my neck. Within an hour, I was getting my chest and belly X-rayed. The doctor was clipped and urgent. Although X-rays showed nothing, there would have to be a biopsy. The lump, buried in the soft tissue of my neck, was oblong and somewhat flaccid. A few days later, the surgeon— again the firm probing with both hands at the base of my neck— seemed undecided. The lump was so sleepy and obscure; but what the hell, let's do it. I remember the sizzling of the electric knife; the odor of burnt blood; the pushes and clips of the tools in the freshly opened slit. I lay there as if clubbed, not thinking, not thinking. Then the doctor lifted out the rubbery clot, dropped it into a container, and went down the hall to get a quick reading by the pathologist. The tissue is sliced and quick-frozen, and then given a preliminary look which must be confirmed later when the tissue has been appropriately dyed to emphasize the structure of the cells. He was back in a few minutes, looking old and heavy.

"There's something there," he said. "We'll have to wait for the slide to be sure."

Those were the words that swung me into my new life. I had walked into the outpatient operating room of the hospital young and immortal; death had been a neurotic tune I wrote about in poems. Now suddenly it was a heaviness that dragged my legs down, a mind that wanted to dissolve back into its spoonfuls of cells, and forget, forget. The slit in my neck was the latch, and now my mortality was seeping out, a thin, freezing gas that filled the operating room. I shivered amid the cutting tools and the bottles of disinfectant, and the doctor talking to me carefully, urgently. I heard what he said, watched his lips, but his words slid off my panic, powerless to reach me in my new life.

"Don't think of this as cancer," he said. "That's a terrifying word. You have a lymphoma. That's a kind of cancer, but it can be treated, kept under control; maybe cured. You're not dying. People do well with a lymphoma."

"Do well" is an oncologist's term that I have heard often since then. You're doing well. He did well. It's a term that must be listened to from the perspective of this new life. Its specific meaning is not "He's well now" but "He's well for the moment"; dying has stopped for a while; he will probably live for a long time. An oncologist's "long time" measures time in the new life. It may mean a few years, which is not bad, although possibly not comforting to a forty-seven-year-old man who still daydreams, at odd moments, of a long life.

For weeks after that my body was inspected for information I never knew it contained. My urine and blood were analyzed; my bone marrow was biopsied. There were sonograms, nuclear scans and grams, X-rays. Incisions were made on the upper part of my feet, through which purple dye was injected into my lymph system. I spent a week in the hospital for some of these tests. I talked to hematologists, surgeons, oncologists, and just plain doctors. I talked to find out. I talked in the hope of hearing some word, some unintended phrase, maybe, that would release me, even for an hour, from the anxiety that spun itself into every corner of my body, deadening my face, giving a buzzing, flattened rhythm to all my thoughts. I felt like someone who had been thrown against an electric fence. Time had been cut off from before my face. The world was unchanged. The streets were full of cars and pedestrians; the sun still caught in the windows of buildings. The radio reported worldwide events. Everything was the same, but time had been removed. And without time, everything was unreal, but I was horribly real, oversized, bursting as a body bursts in a vacuum.

Listening to my doctor was delicate. I took in every shrug, every rise and fall of his voice. I weighed his words on a fine scale, to detect hope or despair. Then I called up another doctor, to hear how the words sounded in his voice. I triangulated and compared, all to find something that would shut off the terror for a while. It was as if there were a key buried in my psyche, and I had to feel around for it, probing in thick, dark waters, and then, not knowing what I'd found, finding it, then losing it again.

While my doctor gathered information, I spent my days walking. I preferred busy shopping streets: the lights and the shop windows, the double-parked cars, the people hurrying into and out of stores. There was energy, there was a present. My feelings would relax a little. I would become a temporary pedestrian, and forget my rarefied life where there was no time.

For months before all this started, my marriage had been in the process of breaking up. Already my wife was honing herself for her own version of a new life. Living with me was like being an old woman, used up, and yet she had hardly lived. It wasn't fair. For her, my lymphoma was the click of a jailer's cell closing upon her life. She boiled with guilty anger, and within a few days could hardly bear the sight of me. So I took long walks, to have something to do that kept me out of the house. Or I went to the playground with my three-year-old daughter and played in the sandbox, trying to imitate my daughter's innocence of time. In a peculiar way, my daughter and I were equals; neither of us had any time, and the irony was terrible, for I had lost mine and she hadn't acquired hers yet. Therefore we had each other. We had the work of filling a tomato-juice can with sand, had the slide polished by thousands of happy behinds. We had the soughing of the spring trees on Riverside Drive, the glow of new leaves, and the twisted, scaly trunks; the portable radios, large as suitcases, throbbing heavily as they went by; and the splintered benches, the yelps of the children, the mothers talking in their not-quite-designer jeans. My life had become a strategy for eluding terror.

It took a few weeks for the test results to be assembled. Then my doctor gave me a course in cell biology as applied to a subclass of malignancy known as lymphoma, a cancer of the lymph system. There were various kinds of lymphoma, all more or less related, more or less combined in any single illness. A given biopsy slide was likely to show several of them, with a predominance of one or another. That is why lymphomas shift and change, speed up or slow down, mysteriously go into hiding, or explode in almost sudden death. They are related also to leukemia. All in all, it is a crowded picture, full of surprises, a little like life itself, but heated up and ominous. All of this was my doctor's way of telling me that he didn't know what was going to happen to me. My particular lymphoma was actually almost benign. Its cells were "well differentiated," their histology was "good." Words like "good" made my heart leap. Anything "good" was probably on my side. There began to be some time before me. Words like "years" were pronounced. There were other words too, but I heard them selectively. Well-differentiated lymphocytic lymphomas developed slowly, but they also tended to resist treatment. They were too benign to behave like cancer cells when they were treated with chemotherapy. Therefore, they came back. And one day, one year, the doctor could run out of treatments, and the sleepy, almost inadvertent disease would expand, like an elephant rolling over you, as if by accident, not knowing you were there, and almost saying, I'm sorry.

At the time I didn't hear all this. I wanted to be cured of terror even more than of the lymphoma, which I'd never seen or touched, and now accepted as an interpretation of pages full of computer letters, graphs and a little box with glass slides in it, not as a physical fact which made my flesh more perishable.

In the end, my doctor chose a middle course. The tests had all been negative. The nodes scattered about in my lymphatic system were too small to register, even on the most sensitive tests; but that didn't mean they weren't there. The pattern of a lymphocytic lymphoma is to be scattered, not localized. A bone-marrow biopsy had disclosed a somewhat high level of lymphocytes that the pathologist called "compatible" with a lymphoma. "Compatible" is one of those cautious words doctors use to say they don't know. It meant that the lymphocytes were probably, but not definitely, connected to the lymphoma; on the other hand, they also could be normal for me. My doctor's decision was to treat with radiation, as a precautionary measure, the spot on my neck where the biopsy had been done, and not to treat the systemic disease, which was still more or less a fiction—an assemblage of data—even to him.

It was July by now, a hot, humid month. The leaves on the trees were heavy, almost flaccid. The radiologist's office was near Central Park. I went every morning at nine o'clock, and was marked with a purple paintbrush, to provide an accurate target for the machine. For twenty days, I received eight minutes and forty-seven seconds of radiation each day on my left shoulder and neck, including a small part of my jaw. The machine resembled a bulky mechanical eye that peered stolidly at the same spot on my body day after day, as if to be sure that it didn't miss anything. The radiologist's office was a warren of tiny dressing rooms, and larger rooms containing complicated machines: sonographs, gamma scanners, X-rays, hard-radiation machines. Eventually each of those machines had its turn with me, but now it was the silent, shadowfilled, almost empty room every morning, and the square, slightly battered bulk of the eye; eight minutes and forty-seven seconds of nothing, no touch, no sound. I lay on my back or stomach according to a schedule, and meditated, breathing evenly in and out. I felt solemn, detached, and then, as weeks passed, a little scared as my skin reddened, my saliva glands on that side of my mouth dried up, and the hair on my neck and jaw fell out.

Every morning, when my treatment was over, I walked to the boathouse in Central Park, and had breakfast on the terrace overlooking the lake. The Central Park South skyline was reflected in the littered heavy shine of the water; the trees tossed their willow limbs in the gusts of breeze. There were always a few regulars at the café, with their shirts off, sunning themselves or doing exercises. The boathouse became my sanctuary. From its dazzled peacefulness, I could contemplate the ruins of my marriage. I could read and write, feeling myself sink into my new life, which now had some time. The terror of the previous weeks was gone. My doctor had dispelled it with his manic, speedy talk, his words like "good" histology, and his feeling that there was "time" to use chemotherapy "if" it became necessary. The implication was that there would be a next year and, surely, other years; that my "good" lymphoma might stay asleep "for a long time." The lymphoma was simply a darker, more underscored form of life, full of life's uncertainties but not a sentence, not a doom.

I didn't exactly relax. I lived in a heavy air, I swam in muted fright; and I came "home" to the boathouse every morning, to feel the hot stillness of summer, to read my books, and to escape my wife's irritation, which increased every day. . . . I had become an emissary of mortality, a messenger from further along, outside the flimsy shelter of endlessness that we spin around us when we're lucky: a portable home, a little immortality, and then suddenly it collapses.

After sitting at the boathouse all morning, I walked home through the Ramble, my shoulder and neck in a state of angry sunburn. Sunlight filtered through the trees. Isolated men sat on benches with an air of melancholy expectation. There were brooks and bridges. It was a little world, strewn with crumpled bags and beer cans, the litter of a night's sexual encounters. The men on the benches resembled night birds who had forgotten to go home. I too was a passing solitude. Time had flowed back around me. Again, I was inside of life. I was freestanding, not thrust against a blankness.

Several times that month, my wife tried to leave me. Each time, my paper-thin peacefulness collapsed, and I became frantic, wild. The breakup of my marriage held an unreasoning terror for me. Perhaps I took it as a foreshadowing, a defeat that bespoke the unsayable defeat I tried to turn my mind from.

Our marriage had long since become Strindberg's dance of death, and we danced it like puppets; but now it was breaking up, for real death had come upon the scene and driven its neurotic imitators from the field.

When I was a boy, I used to wonder what would keep me from sinking to the level of a bum on the street. Every tramp, every stinking hulk of a drunk, was a possible destiny. Later, I saw that it wasn't so easy to sink. You had to dive, you had to work your way down. Society buoyed you up to your level; family and friends, the structure of needs driven into your flesh and psyche, do not let themselves be easily betrayed. I hadn't thought of this other stripping down, the blow of destiny that thrust from within you and then, like a bolt falling from a cloud, from without you too. I was caught in this pincers now: stripped of time, stripped even of a home; afraid that the anguish breaking around my daughter would maim her in some way. For years I had been afraid that if my marriage broke up, I would lose my daughter. It had become an obsession; it summed up all the mysterious harm I felt my wife could do to me. . . .

A month later, the marriage was over. I had come alone to the house we owned in southern France. My wife had refused to come with me, and stayed in Paris with friends. I breathed the aromatic August air like a spiritual substance. The house is a low stone building, with a roof of rough red tiles, on a hilltop far from any road. The fields of barley and alfalfa had been harvested, and a swath of yellow stubble surrounded the house. Petunias splashed brightly in a stone basin. A little way down the hill, a walnut tree dangled its smoky limbs. I sat in front of the house and gazed at the hill crest across the valley or watched the sun ignite at dusk in plumes of red mist and cloud. The days creaked with cicadas. The nights were blocks of blankness, almost a burial, except for a veil of light spilling across the sky, the Milky Way, and the bright nailheads of the largest stars. Every day I jogged down the dirt road into the valley, and walked back. Gradually, I increased the distance. It was a return among the living, a return to youth. Timidly, almost furtively—like Adam hiding his nakedness in the garden—I built the endlessness back around me. My saliva glands began to function again; the red square on my neck healed. One side of my jaw was still baby-smooth; I didn't have to shave it. It was my stigmata. But eventually that too became normal.

As days passed, it seemed that the house itself was healing me: its honey-colored stone walls and red, granular tiles; its days full of wind and somersaulting clouds. I thought of my grandparents' farm. The farm had been a model for my childhood love of empty places: the prairies, deserts and forests I read about in my favorite books; any place where the claustrophobia of emotions was dissolved, where sheer emptiness made man small, as if my genes had conjured up primeval savannas as my true home. Now I had my own house in the woods; my own romantic emptiness that overlay the earlier memories and merged with them.

One day I telephoned my wife from a neighbor's house. No, she didn't want to come down; she also didn't want to live with me anymore. It took only a few words to establish this. The phone cracked against my ear in the long gaps between the few things we had to say to each other. Suddenly there was more room than I knew what to do with. As I climbed the steep path through the woods and crossed the harvested field to the house, I could hear the brittle stubble crunch under my feet. This was ground level: no family, a flimsy life. I hadn't become a derelict, but I had hit bottom in my own way.

I am sitting at my window, looking out over the Hudson. It is a scuffed blue-gray this morning, with patches of ripples and smoke melting into each other. The Palisades directly across from me are still speckled with points of light. At river level, the abandoned factories emerge faintly from the darkness as a slightly powdered gray. The river too is dark, almost an empty trough between its banks, which here are half a mile apart.

Now it is almost full daylight. I can see seagulls wheeling close to the near shore. From this height, they don't seem to be over the river, but on it, sliding and scooting on the surface like water flies.

The far end of my living room slants to the northwest. When the sun comes up eastward over the city—the slits of the streets and the dusty black squares of the rooftops, and beyond them, visible only if I lean my head out the window, the heavy metal arches of the Triborough Bridge—there is a fringing light along the window which lasts for only a few minutes. The imperfections in the glass are heightened, a milkiness veils the sleeve of emptiness: the river; the park on this side with its leafless knobs of trees, and its baseball fields which resemble large brown vulvas; the cliff on the other side, topped by the pale rectangles of condominiums; and closing it off to the north, like a musical instrument poised to produce a humming note, the George Washington Bridge.

When I lean up close to the window, I can see a few people down below waiting for the bus. On the square of pavement, between the soggy winter turf and the benches, they resemble a scattering of grains. There is a clarity in the scene, something unspoken. The sky is blue-white. Beyond the Palisades, the New Jersey hills form parallel pleats, broken here and there by the sharp outlines of factories, gas tanks and distant neighborhoods which I will never visit, and whose names I will never know.

My living room with its five windows resembles a cage suspended from the sky, looking out on space, on the low hum of the city. Below me, the bus opens its doors and inhales the scattered grains. This morning life is distant, a brightness rimming the city.

On several occasions I have thought of jumping—half flying—from my twenty-fourth-story window; not a thought really, a fleeting image of an action. Nothing I would do, but even the image of it has given my life a new vulnerability.

I've seen every kind of storm up here. The splats of thunder; the lightning crinkling in wide swaths over the Palisades; enormous thuds of wind, snaking the water in the toilet bowl and drowning out the radio. Clouds sagged over the bridge; whitenesses of water skidded across the river, dashing up onto the highway, where cars crawled by with their headlights on, even in daylight. And the snowstorms in winter, wiping out space, crawling into my mind: a kind of death, a kind of giving up.

It is afternoon now. Reflected light from the river wavers over my wall like a watermark. There is a peculiar solitude, a nothing spinning out spokes of attention. Soon the light will turn angry, and then begin to dim, contract to a purple disc sliding behind a cluster of high-rise buildings across the river. So much space, such a contraction of time, like a balloon shielding me from what I want to avoid, but which is closer to me than thought.

During these past few months, the lymphoma has wrapped its sluggish coils around me once again. In everything I do, there is an intensity, the tunnel vision of a man making an effort. Days pass when I don't even see the river, and then, suddenly, I am buoyed by a mysterious current, something unreasonable, something like hope, rising like heat from a sidewalk grating. I have learned how to navigate this foreshortened life of mine; to ruse with panic, duck under terror. My will has become a well-exercised muscle.

In November, I made one of my bimonthly visits to the doctor. It is a dimly lighted office piled with coats. People sit demurely and read magazines, or doze. There is not much talking. All of us are self-contained and casual as we wait for our blood test—the prick in the flesh of the fingertip, the small bead of blood, the glass siphon turning pink as the blood climbs inside it, the click of the counter whirring to its level. Then we are shepherded into small, bright consultation rooms with Daumier lithographs on the wall, and shelves full of barbarously named compounds which will weaken us and make us sick, loosen our hair, disrupt the lining of our stomach, thin out our bone marrow, cause a flulike aching of the muscles, but will do even more damage to those inconspicuous additions to our bodies, the nodes, tumors and lymphocytes that gather within us to disrupt our organisms.

A year before, I had undergone a course of chemotherapy. Every few weeks, several large hypodermics of pink or transparent liquid had been injected into a vein on the inside of my elbow. There had been a cool rush in my arm and tongue; a lightheadedness; then I had gone into the bathroom and smoked a joint of marijuana to keep down the nausea. The result was a cool floating feeling, as I put my coat on and waited for a cab, then walked carefully to the elevator in my building, not jiggling or shaking. I felt breakable, as if the injection had turned me into glass. All day I would sit in my reading chair and listen to music or read a novel. This was not a day for thinking, not a day to measure my adequacy to the larger questions of life. Gradually I would get tired and nauseous. By the next morning, I would be sick and try to sleep it off. Then, hour by hour, the ashen feeling in my face would lessen, the wobbly numbness in my legs would vanish. The morning after that, I would go out running, as if I were acting out a private joke: the joke of health and youth, the joke of endlessness.

As months passed, the nodes in various parts of my body shrank, and my blood count went down. My hair fell out, although I didn't become bald, only scalpy. I was hopeful and buoyant, proud that the chemotherapy didn't bother me too much. In the middle of it, I went to my house in France, and spent three weeks there. I felt that I was staring down death, although by then I already suspected that the treatment wasn't fully working. My hard little seeds had shrunk but not vanished. By this time, I knew enough about my illness to understand that those seeds would grow again, at a rate only they would determine. I knew that my doctor, for all his hard medical knowledge, observed my blood counts and my nodes as a witness to a mystery, ready to be surprised by variables that no instrument could measure. There were lymphomas that simmered for twenty years, others that "went sour" right away. The clock ticked, but no one could hear it. It was a subcase of the clock of life itself. In the four years since my lymphoma was diagnosed, my radiologist had died of a heart attack and the surgeon who had performed the lymphangiogram had drowned in a boating accident on Long Island Sound. Like me, they were young men. The fates had spun a short skein for them. And for me? Who can say? The bell curve does not favor me, but a bell curve is not destiny. Each year laboratories churn out results that may be altering the curve: new drugs, new regimens, entire new methods. Am I hopeful? Not exactly. I am trying to live until tomorrow, and then tomorrow.

Those three weeks at the house were a miracle. The winter trees resembled gray, upswept brushes; the fire grumbled all day in the fireplace. For four years I had been bending myself to a shorter arc of life. I wanted elbow room; I wanted an enlarged present, and I had managed by discipline and willpower, by selfishness, to thicken the everyday, attenuate the far-off. Normally we live in a double sphere of consciousness: a near shell reverberating with needs and hopes, full of urgency, heavy with the flesh of our lives; and a far, attenuated hood of thoughts and projects which spin us years into the future, where we pretend that there is time. The near shell is tribal and blood-real; the far, attenuated shell is glorious, flimsy; it is man's experiment with immortality, without which books would not be written and buildings would not be erected to last centuries. It is the lie of endlessness, the lie we spin out of ourselves like the "filament, filament" of the "patient spider" in Walt Whitman's poem, to give us time.

For three weeks at the house, I lived a purely tribal life. The days were empty and cold. I read long books by the fire, and felt thoughtless and happy as I jogged down the muddy road into the valley, past my neighbor's tobacco-drying shed, past the low, mossy roofs of the village, and then, laboriously, rasping and out of breath, up a long stony incline through the woods to my house. I felt that death could not harm me. I was neither young nor old. I was simply a man living alone in a stone house, surrounded by books, baking in the glowing heat of oak logs in the fireplace, feeling the sharp chill of black nights when I went outside to pee on the gravel, and heard the splatter of my urine mingling with the wind, and the reverberating hoot of an owl in the nearby woods.

Soon after that, my doctor decided to stop the chemotherapy. The most potent drug in the combination, Adriamycin, could damage my heart if more than a certain quantity was used over my lifetime. He had used about half of that, and wanted to save Adriamycin—a new kind of antibiotic which had been one of the important discoveries for cancer treatment in the 1970s—for another round of chemotherapy, "if" needed. A sonogram revealed a shadow persisting in my abdomen. No, I wasn't cured. The lymphoma had been ground down and compressed, but not extirpated. I was released into uncertainty. My outer shell of time had been broken; I would never give my thoughts to it again without an undercurrent of disbelief. Only tribal time was real to me, and tribal time was a kind of eternity. The gray smoky water of the river outside my window; the boys playing baseball on the large brown vulva that is the playing field in the park, my daughter's bony ballerina's grace, were real. Unreal were pension plans, and the conquering of cancer by the year 2000; unreal was my daughter as a young woman, a future I sometimes saw tentatively in her face. My daughter fluttered between the two times. Loving her drove holes in my body of time, and let in distance; distance that was denied me, distance I strove for and wished for without hoping, because hope devalued my one secure possession: the roomy present, which I savored best in the solitude that was the legacy of my childhood. My grandparents' farm, my house in France, my window overlooking the river.

Then, in November, came the visit to my doctor, to be palpated, X-rayed, to have my blood tested. These visits were never routine. I knew that when my doctor spoke, I would listen as to no one I had ever listened to in my life. He would push down at the base of my neck, probe under my arms and in my groin. He would feel at the margin of my rib cage on the right side and below my rib cage on the left side, for my liver and spleen. My doctor is a small, balding, energetic man. Over the years, we have gotten to know each other well. I've heard his jokes, listened to his fervent Zionism, his humorous indignation at divorce lawyers, and other favorite topics. There is a manic optimism about him, a speedy, sometimes angry intolerance. He doesn't like to answer questions, but he answers them, and I ask them. Too many of them. It is our joke. Even when I'm not sure if I want to know, I ask, and then sometimes I feel I know too much. I know how fundamentally helpless my doctor feels under his energetic manner. I know that all the clinical tests and the statistics still leave him face to face with luck every time he examines a patient in his confidence-giving little rooms. It boils down, finally, to intuition, and to ignorance. "I don't know" is the answer to many of my questions. I don't know how long you will live, if you will go into remission, if your disease will "go sour"; there are no signs, there is no text. I don't know how effective the latest combination of drugs will be; I don't know if the side effects in your case will be mild or severe; if, as a result of the treatment, you will get hepatitis, shingles or pneumonia. To him as to me, my body reveals itself sporadically, at its own pace. From it he can derive sheets full of data on the level of trace minerals in a burnt sample of my hair; on my T cell, B cell and lymphocyte counts, my red blood cells, my platelets, my sodium or glucose levels, my cholesterol. He can read my heartbeat on a graph, and my internal organs on an X-ray; test my urine; get the opinion of a pathologist on my bone marrow; perform biopsies. But finally he must say, "I don't know." And I've got to accept that my life is indeterminate; that my questions can receive only conditional answers; that no one can have the knowledge or the authority to make me safe again.

My doctor came into the consultation room holding my folder, thick with four and a half years' worth of data, including my latest platelet and white blood cell counts. He was subdued, almost casual, but he got to the point immediately without any jokes.

"I'm going to take a bone-marrow biopsy. We haven't done one in several years, and it's time to have a look. Your white count has been drifting up. I also can feel your spleen for the first time. It could be that something's up. The lymphoma may be changing over."

"Changing over" was an oncologist's phrase for something bad, that was clear. "A lymphoma can start spilling lymphocytes into the blood," he explained, "and that may be happening here. But let's not jump to conclusions. I could be overreacting to a few numbers. Let's talk it over when we get some more data."

He brought in an apparatus equipped with a short hollow needle, anesthetized a patch of my hip, and drilled out a core sample of marrow. Despite the anesthetic, a deep, creaky pain radiated from the spot.

I felt heavy-headed and chilled as I sat on the examining table. Suddenly, all my philosophy had vanished. Again, time had been flung up close to me. I was not in remission and never had been. For months, under cover of my apparent good health, the disease had been heating up. My spleen had become a "bag full of lymphocytes," to use my doctor's phrase. When I got home, I felt under my arms, around my ribs, in my groin. There were small, inconspicuous lumps that probably hadn't been there before. I was sprouting, I was in flower. Almost immediately I began my panicky phone calls; to my doctor, first of all, in the hope that what he said would be less frightening than my imagination. This time, the truth itself was frightening. A lymphoma that "changes over" can "go sour" very quickly, or it can simmer gently. In the first case, I could be sick very soon, and he seemed almost surprised that I wasn't feeling the effects already. On the other hand, he said, that could be a good sign. I called the head of immunological oncology at the Sidney Farber Cancer Center in Boston, where I knew work was being done on a new approach to cancer treatment using something called monoclonal antibodies. I called a friend who knew doctors at Stanford who were also working with monoclonal antibodies. I called the National Cancer Institute in Washington, and spoke for an hour with a technician, who gave me all sorts of imprecise and reassuring information. I was plunged in a paradox. These monoclonal antibodies represented a radical new approach, and much of the research was being done on lymphoma. The whole field of cancer research was in an excitable state. Several lymphomas and leukemias had been traced to a virus. A type of cancer-stimulating gene, called an oncogene, had been discovered. Recombinant DNA was beginning to produce quantities of pure interferon that could represent a new form of treatment. The hope existed that malignancies could one day be turned off by genetic manipulation. Cheerful substances like vitamin A might have a normalizing effect on cancer cells. It was exciting, full of horizon. But my interest was peculiarly narrow and avid. I wanted to be saved, I wanted it now. But now there was nothing. My doctor, hardheaded, even conservative, under his manic ebullience, didn't get excited about anything that he couldn't use on the demure, patient people who sat in his waiting room. He was a pragmatist, the test was clinical usefulness.

Suddenly the wall had been shoved up close to me, and I felt bruised, as if I had been beaten with fists. Was it possible that my time was to be measured in months now, instead of years? I ran every day under the leafless November trees along Riverside Drive. The raw, moist air rasped in my lungs. The sunlight was thin, almost metallic. It was an absurd act, an act of faith, I suppose; or maybe an admission that I possessed no better kind of day than the ones I was living: teaching class, writing a book, caring for my daughter on the days that she was with me. For almost two years, I had been living with a woman, and from the start chemotherapy had been our companion, a third person that never left us alone. But now time had been brutally torn from me. I had been thrust far into the new life, where my friend couldn't follow me, where nobody could follow me. At times, while I waited for my doctor to assemble his information, it seemed to me that my fright was a way of drowning my aloneness. I had become a member of a heavy tribe, those who walked minute by minute into a blankness that ate the near distance, like the winter fog one year in Venice, unfurling in thick billows, until I walked in a blur of weight which made every step seem heavier, more obsessed. Now, too, space had clamped shut on me, except for sudden vanishing when the river, opening beyond the window, gave me room.

A week later, my doctor was ready to talk. My lymphoma had probably "changed over" to something called a lymphosarcoma-cell leukemia. If so, this was a relatively infrequent occurrence, and he was not willing to predict what would happen next.

On the other hand, looking over the flow chart of my visits to him during the past four years, he had noticed a slow upward drift of my white blood cell count all along. He had reread the original pathologist's report on my first bone-marrow biopsy, remarking a high level of lymphocytes, and remembered that a hematologist, at the time, had guessed that my lymphoma could well be accompanied by one of its near cousins, a chronic lymphocytic leukemia. By now I understood that these daunting terms—lymphoma, lymphosarcoma-cell leukemia, chronic lymphocytic leukemia—were not as definitive as they sounded. They were nets cast into a turmoil, freeze-frames of a complex flow. The conditions they referred to tended to blur into each other, and become each other. The immunological oncologists used other nomenclatures entirely, and the whole classificatory system for lymphomas was put in doubt by some scientists.

Medicine was still related to voodoo and witchcraft by one tenuous, life-giving link: it boiled down, finally, to educated guesses, habit, long practice and clinical intuition. My doctor's knowledge, extensive and up-to-date as it was, provided him not with recipes but with a kind of yoga. In a given case, he absorbed the sheets of test results, the feel of the patient's body, the years of working through similar cases, exploring life at its extremity, life at its breaking point; and then he decided, the way a baseball player swings at a fast ball. It was disturbingly close to guesswork. In my case, it meant that what I wanted to know—live or die, now or later?—would emerge over time, as the blood tests accumulated, and my state of health spoke for itself.

I lived in a suspended breath. I waited—what else could I do?—and yet I could not bear to wait. I ran harder every day, and tugged at the exercise machines in the health club. My friend Vikki and I flew up to Boston, and I had bagfuls of blood extracted by the immunologists there. I saw another oncologist, who seemed grim about my prospects, frightening me to a new pitch of tension. I called my lawyer to get my will in order. I called my ex-wife, pleading with her to take good care of our daughter. I felt an incongruous need to finish the book I was working on. Did the world need another book? I knew that wasn't the question. I felt that writing was my best self. It was, internalized, the view from my window, or my stone house on a hilltop in southwestern France. It was the cohered tensions of living made deliberate and clear. Writing, I touched the roots of my life, as I did when Vikki and I made love, or when I spent an afternoon with my daughter. But writing was stronger, more sustaining than these. Every day, I spilled words onto my yellow pad, crossed out, inverted sentences, inserted new paragraphs on the back of the page. I raced my fountain pen from line to line, in erratic humps and jags. And this crabbed hieroglyphic, curling from top to bottom of the page, was my mind climbing quietly and privately to a plane of spirit that balanced above my sick body. There my limitations were acceptable; they were the language spoken by my pen, which drank at a deep source.

I saw that a writer's immortality exists in the moment of conception, in which language has seized hold of him, and not in the posterity which few of us believe in, in these days of nuclear shadow. A work is not a life, but writing is living, and now especially I wanted to live with all my might. I wanted to fight off the shrinking effect of fear. Therefore, I wrote my book, while I waited for the blood tests to speak. And gradually they spoke, in a temporary, self-revising idiom.

"At least your count isn't shooting through the roof," my doctor said, "and that's good."

With chemotherapy the count began to come down, my nodes and spleen began to shrink again. I could see, as at the end of an alley, a brightness: the crisscrossing of passers-by, the honking and snoozing of cars; it was the bland ribbon of time that runs on, runs on.

Oh, yes, it is a flimsy ordinariness, an eroded shell. It is Vikki and her children, my daughter and me, at the Botanic Gardens, surprised by the pastel blossoms of the cherry trees like bursts of softness, in the chilly breeze of early April. It is cutting up parsnip roots, carrots and broccoli for a stew; feeding the children, and then sitting in the high shadowy living room of Vikki's apartment late at night, reading or talking. It is the old dream of an enchanted ordinariness come true in snippets and jigsaw-puzzle fragments that don't last, but lasting isn't what's important now, as long as the puzzle is real. And then, every few weeks, it is the remembering again that I'm the loose piece, the medical case with the catheter in my arm, and the large hypodermics of clear fluid; the two days of homeopathic misery; the predictable weathering of the predictable storm, a man holding on; running under trees ready to thicken into spring; looking from my window, as now, on the rim of darkness over the Palisades, and the white street lamps of the road slanting to river level; the beige necklace of lights outlining the George Washington Bridge; the river, become a nothing of black and depth, almost unreal, like a fault line burst asunder into the earth's interior.

JOHN KEATS (1795-1821)

SONNET

When I have fears that I may cease to be
Before my pen has gleaned my teeming brain,
Before high-piled books in charact'ry,
Hold like rich garners the full-ripened grain;
When I behold, upon the night's starred face,
Huge cloudy symbols of a high romance,
And think that I may never live to trace
Their shadows with the magic hand of chance;
And when I feel, fair creature of an hour,
That I shall never look upon thee more,
Never have relish in the faery power
Of unreflecting love!—Then on the shore
Of the wide world I stand alone, and think
'Til Love and Fame to nothingness do sink.

". . . I consider it detestable for any person
to be robbed of his death."

MARGUERITE YOURCENAR

WITH OPEN EYES

*The esteemed French writer Marguerite Yourcenar (1903–87) lived for
over forty years in the United States, in relative isolation on an island
off the coast of Maine. During her last summer, she wrote: "I began to
discern the profile of my death." She precisely arranged the details of her
memorial service, and among the readings she selected were the Sermon on
the Mount (Matthew 5); the First Epistle of Paul to the Corinthi-
ans, chapter 13; Saint Francis's Canticle of Living Creatures; the Four
Buddhist Vows; and a poem by the nineteenth-century Japanese nun
Rye-Nen.*

 *The interview from which the following passages were excerpted was
conducted over the course of several years—when Yourcenar was in
her seventies—by the literary critic Matthieu Galey. Yourcenar's rigorous
and unconventional religiosity is a repeated theme in the interview. Here
she is describing her sense that as an author, she is "an instrument
through which currents, vibrations, have passed." She continues, "That is
true of all my books and I would even say of all my life. Perhaps of all
life."*

Y: . . . in thinking of my friends, those still living as well as those who are dead, I frequently find myself repeating the fine words that I was once told were uttered by the eighteenth century's "unknown philosopher, Saint-Martin. . . ." They are beings through whom God loved me. Everything began before us, in other words, and we feel humble and amazed when we serve as instruments in a greater scheme.

G: Don't such sentiments lead to a passive attitude toward life?

Y: Not at all. One must toil and struggle to the bitter end, one must swim in the river that both lifts us up and carries us away, knowing in advance that the only way out is to drown in the vastness of the open sea. But the question is, *Who* drowns? We must accept all the evils, cares, and afflictions that beset us and others, as we must accept our own death and the deaths of others, as a *natural* part of life, as, say, Montaigne would have done—Montaigne, the man who of all Western thinkers comes closest to the Taoist philosophers and whom only superficial readers take to be an antimystic. Death, the supreme form of life—on this point my thinking is exactly contrary to that of Julius Caesar, whose wish (more or less fulfilled) was to die as quickly as possible. For my part, I would like to die fully conscious that I am dying, of an illness whose progress would be slow enough to allow death to insinuate itself into my body and fully unfold.

G: Why?

Y: So as not to miss the ultimate experience, the passage. Hadrian speaks of dying with his eyes open. It was in this spirit, moreover, that I had Zeno experience his death.

G: You would like to emulate Proust, then, who changed his description of Bergotte's death by modeling it after his own.

Y: I understand quite well why he attempted what he did. To use his own demise in this way is a novelist's form of heroism. For me, however, it would be more a matter of not missing out on an essential experience, and it is because I am determined to have this experience that I consider it detestable for any person to be robbed of his death. In the United States medical people are surprisingly honest, whereas in France doctors and especially families frequently do their utmost to keep things back from the patient. This is an attitude of which I disapprove. By the same token, I love and respect people who prepare for death.

G: That means living in constant intimacy with one's demise.

Y: Which is a very good thing indeed. We should think of death as a friend, even if we feel a certain instinctive repugnance to do so. It is true that animals don't think about death. Or do they? It is quite obvious that some animals do anticipate that they are going to die.

G: Yet we are inevitably ill prepared for this passage.

Y: So ill prepared that we end up sniveling wretches or cringing cowards, though these are no doubt mere physical reactions, like seasickness. The acceptance that matters will have occurred at an earlier stage.

And then, who knows? Perhaps we will be taken in hand by certain memories, as if by angels. Tibetan mystics tell us that the dying are supported by the presence of whatever it was they believed in: Siva or Buddha for some, Christ or Muhammed for others. Convinced skeptics and people without imagination will doubtless see nothing, like the fourth officer of Marlborough, who brought nothing. A friend of mine who was resuscitated after nearly drowning told me that the widespread belief that one sees one's whole life flash by in an instant is true. If so, it must be disagreeable at times. Greater selectivity is called for. But what would I like to see again?

Perhaps the hyacinths of Mont-Noir or the violets of Connecticut in springtime; the oranges my father cleverly hung from the branches in our garden in the Midi; a cemetery in Switzerland crushed by the weight of its roses; another buried in snow in the midst of white birches; and still other cemeteries whose names and locations escape me, but these, after all, are not the things that matter. The dunes of Flanders and of the Virginia sea islands, with the sound of the ocean that has persisted since the beginning of time; the modest little Swiss music box that plays pianissimo an arietta of Haydn, which I started playing at Grace's bedside one hour before her death, when she ceased to respond to word or touch. Or again, the huge icicles that form on the rocks here on Mount Desert Island, icicles which, come April, form channels for the melting snows that flow with a geyser's roar. Cape Sounion at sunset. Olympia at noon. Peasants on a road in Delphi, offering to give their mule's bells to a stranger. The mass of the Resurrection in a Euboean village, following a nocturnal mountain crossing on foot. A morning arrival in Segesta, on horseback, via trails that in those days were deserted and rocky and smelled of thyme. A walk at Versailles one sunless afternoon, or a day at Corbridge in Northumberland when, having fallen asleep in the middle of an archeological dig overgrown with grass, I passively allowed the rain to penetrate my bones, as it penetrated the bones of the dead Romans. Some cats I picked up with the help of André Embiricos in an Anatolian village. The "angels game" in the snow. A mad toboggan ride down a Tyrolian hillside under stars full of omens. Or again, from more recent times and still hardly distilled enough to qualify as memories, the green sea of the tropics, stained here and there by oil. A triangular flight of wild swans en route to the Arctic. Easter's rising sun (which didn't know that it was the sun of Easter), viewed this year from a rocky spur of Mount Desert, high above a half-frozen lake hatched with fissures by the approach of spring.

I toss out these images at random with no intention of making them into symbols. And I should probably add the faces of a few loved ones, living and dead, along with other faces, drawn from history or my imagination.

Or perhaps none of these things, but only the great blue-white void which, in Mishima's last novel completed only hours before his death, is contemplated by the octogenarian Honda—a perspicacious judge who is also a voyeur (in the worst sense of the word)—at the end of his life. What he sees is a flamboyant emptiness like that of the summer sky, which devours all things and reduces the rest to a train of shadows.

> ". . . I am dying as fast as my enemies . . . could wish,
> and as easily and cheerfully as my best friends
> could desire."

ADAM SMITH

ON THE DEATH
OF DAVID HUME

*The Scottish moralist and political economist Adam Smith (1723–90) be-
came a friend of David Hume (1711–76) more than twenty years before
the great philosopher's death. He is one of many sources for the view that
Hume was not only a philosophic technician of great prowess but a true
"philosopher" in the popular sense, a model of equanimity and elevation.
And Smith is hardly alone among contemporary witnesses to Hume's sto-
icism and genuine tranquillity during his last illness. Another of Hume's
friends, James Boswell, reported to Dr. Samuel Johnson (who professed a
fierce "horror of the last") that he "had reason to believe that the thought of
annihilation gave Hume no pain." Johnson, who had never met Hume,
replied impatiently, "It was not so, Sir. He had a vanity in being thought
easy." But Johnson was apparently alone in doubting the genuineness of
Hume's composure.*

*Smith's description of Hume's last days was given in a letter to
William Strahan, a friend of both men.*

Kirkaldy, Fifeshire, 9 Nov. 1776

Dear Sir,

It is with a real, though a very melancholy pleasure, that I sit down to give you some account of the behaviour of our late excellent friend, Mr. Hume, during his last illness.

Though, in his own judgement, his disease was mortal and incurable, yet he allowed himself to be prevailed upon, by the entreaty of his friends, to try what might be the effects of a long journey. A few days before he set out, he wrote that account of his own life, which, together with his other papers, he has left to your care. My account, therefore, shall begin where his ends.

He set out for London towards the end of April, and at Morpeth met with Mr. John Home and myself, who had both come down from London on purpose to see him, expecting to have found him at Edinburgh. Mr. Home returned with him, and attended him during the whole of his stay in England, with that care and attention which might be expected from a temper so perfectly friendly and affectionate.

. . .

His disease seemed to yield to exercise and change of air, and when he arrived in London, he was apparently in much better health than when he left Edinburgh. He was advised to go to Bath to drink the waters, which appeared for some time to have so good an effect upon him, that even he himself began to entertain, what he was not apt to do, a better opinion of his own health. His symptoms, however, soon returned with their usual violence, and from that moment he gave up all thoughts of recovery, but submitted with the utmost cheerfulness, and the most perfect complacency and resignation. Upon his return to Edinburgh, though he found himself much weaker, yet his cheerfulness never abated, and he continued to divert himself, as usual, with correcting his own works for a new edition, with reading books of amusement, with the conversation of his friends; and, sometimes in the evening, with a party at his favourite game of whist. His cheerfulness was so great, and his conversation and amusements run so much in their usual strain, that, notwithstanding all bad symptoms, many people could not believe he was dying. "I shall tell your friend, Colonel Edmondstone," said Doctor Dundas to him one day, "that I left you much better, and in a fair way of recovery." "Doctor," said he, "as I believe you would not chuse to tell any thing but the truth, you had better tell him, that I am dying as fast as my enemies, if I have any, could wish, and as easily and cheerfully as my best friends could desire."

Mr. Hume's magnanimity and firmness were such, that his most affectionate friends knew, that they hazarded nothing in talking or writing to him as to a dying man, and that so far from being hurt by this frankness, he was rather pleased and flattered by it.

"Well," said I, "if it must be so, you have at least the satisfaction of leaving all your friends, your brother's family in particular, in great prosperity." He said that he felt that satisfaction so sensibly, that when he was reading a few days before, Lucian's Dialogues of the Dead, among all the excuses which are alleged to Charon for not entering readily into his boat, he could not find one that fitted him; he had no house to finish, he had no daughter to provide for, he had no enemies upon whom he wished to revenge himself. "I could not well imagine," said he, "what excuse I could make to Charon in order to obtain a little delay. I have done every thing of consequence which I ever meant to do, and I could at no time expect to leave my relations and friends in a better situation than that in which I am now likely to leave them; I, therefore, have all reason to die contented." He then diverted himself with inventing several jocular excuses, which he supposed he might make to Charon, and with imagining the very surly answers which it might suit the character of Charon to return to them. "Upon further consideration," said he, "I thought I might say to him, 'Good Charon, I have been correcting my works for a new edition. Allow me a little time, that I may see how the Public receives the alterations.' But Charon would answer, 'When you have seen the effect of these, you will be for making other alterations. There will be no end of such excuses; so, honest friend, please step into the boat.' But I might still urge, 'Have a little patience, good Charon, I have been endeavouring to open the eyes of the Public. If I live a few years longer, I may have

the satisfaction of seeing the downfall of some of the prevailing systems of superstition.' But Charon would then lose all temper and
decency. 'You loitering rogue, that will not happen these many hundred years. Do you fancy I will grant you a lease for so long a term?
Get into the boat this instant, you lazy loitering rogue.' "

But, though Mr. Hume always talked of his approaching dissolution with great cheerfulness, he never affected to make any parade of
his magnanimity. He never mentioned the subject but when the conversation naturally led to it, and never dwelt longer upon it than the
course of the conversation happened to require: it was a subject indeed which occurred pretty frequently, in consequence of the inqui-
ries which his friends, who came to see him, naturally made concerning the state of his health. The conversation which I mentioned above,
and which passed on Thursday the 8th of August, was the last, except
one, that I ever had with him. He had now become so very weak, that
the company of his most intimate friends fatigued him; for his cheerfulness was still so great, his complaisance and social disposition were
still so entire, that when any friend was with him, he could not help
talking more, and with greater exertion, than suited the weakness of
his body. At his own desire, therefore, I agreed to leave Edinburgh,
where I was staying partly upon his account, and returned to my
mother's house here, at Kirkaldy, upon condition that he would send
for me whenever he wished to see me. . . .

. . .

I received . . . a letter from Mr. Hume himself, of which the following is an extract.

Edinburgh, 23d August, 1776.

My Dearest Friend,

I am obliged to make use of my nephew's hand in writing to
you, as I do not rise today . . . I go very fast to decline, and
last night had a small fever, which I hoped might put a quicker
period to this tedious illness, but unluckily it has, in a great

measure, gone off. I cannot submit to your coming over here on my account, as it is possible for me to see you so small a part of the day, but Doctor Black can better inform you concerning the degree of strength which may from time to time remain with me. Adieu, &c.

Three days after I received the following letter from Doctor Black.

Edinburgh, Monday, 26th August, 1776.

Dear Sir,

Yesterday about four o'clock afternoon, Mr. Hume expired. The near approach of his death became evident in the night between Thursday and Friday, when his disease became excessive, and soon weakened him so much, that he could no longer rise out of his bed. He continued to the last perfectly sensible, and free from much pain or feelings of distress. He never dropped the smallest expression of impatience; but when he had occasion to speak to the people about him, always did it with affection and tenderness. I thought it improper to write to bring you over, especially as I heard that he had dictated a letter to you desiring you not to come. When he became very weak, it cost him an effort to speak, and he died in such a happy composure of mind, that nothing could exceed it.

Thus died our most excellent, and never to be forgotten friend; concerning whose philosophical opinions men will, no doubt, judge variously, every one approving or condemning them, according as they happen to coincide or disagree with his own; but concerning whose conduct there can scarce be a difference of opinion! His temper, indeed, seemed to be more happily balanced, if I may be allowed such an expression, than that perhaps of any other man I have ever known. Even in the lowest state of his fortune, his great and necessary frugality never hindered him from exercising, upon proper occasions, acts both of charity and generosity. It was a frugality founded, not upon avarice, but upon the love of independency. The extreme gentleness of his nature never weakened either the firmness of his mind, or the steadiness of his resolutions. His constant pleasantry was the genuine effusion of good-nature and good-humour, tempered with delicacy and modesty, and without even the slightest tincture of malignity, so frequently the disagreeable source of what is called wit in other men. It never was the meaning of his raillery to mortify; and therefore, far from offending, it seldom failed to please and delight, even those who were the objects of it. To his friends, who were frequently the objects of it, there was not perhaps any one of all his great and amiable qualities, which contributed more to endear his conversation. And that gaiety of temper, so agreeable in society, but which is so often accompanied with frivolous and superficial qualities, was in him certainly attended with the most severe application, the most extensive learning, the greatest depth of thought, and a capacity in every respect the most comprehensive. I have always considered him, both in his lifetime and since his death, as approaching as nearly to the idea of a perfectly wise and virtuous man, as perhaps the nature of human frailty will permit.

> I ever am, dear Sir,
> Most affectionately your's,
> *Adam Smith.*

"People walk along the streets the day
after our deaths just as they did before. . . ."

WILLIAM HAZLITT

ON THE FEAR OF DEATH

*It is said that William Hazlitt (1778–1830) began the essay from which the
following passages are taken in the anguished aftermath of his father's
death. ". . . I saw death shake him by the palsied hand, and stare him in
the face," Hazlitt confided in an early version of these reflections. A latter-
day Montaigne ready to address every subject from fine art to pugilism,
Hazlitt wrote a lucid, kinetic prose whose shifts of mood dramatize the
suddenness of thought and its ability to be vigorously at odds with itself. As
a drama critic, Hazlitt greatly advanced what we should now call the
psychological approach to Shakespeare and other playwrights. Correspond-
ingly, his conception of mind and feeling is inherently dramatic: these are
not merely motives to action, but forms of action in their own right. In the
passages that follow, Hazlitt characteristically locates both the fear of
death—or, rather, the fears, for he distinguishes several kinds—and their
remedy in the tumult of active life, which simultaneously engages our passions and "teaches us the precarious tenure on which we hold our present
being." The theatrical metaphor is implicit throughout: life has a beginning,
so it must have a middle and end; we are all hams where life is concerned,*

unwilling to yield the stage to others; but we must do so at last, and then it is better to quit the theater entirely than to fall in among the snoozing audience.

And our little life is rounded with a sleep."

Perhaps the best cure for the fear of death is to reflect that life has a beginning as well as an end. There was a time when we were not: this gives us no concern—why then should it trouble us that a time will come when we shall cease to be? I have no wish to have been alive a hundred years ago, or in the reign of Queen Anne: why should I regret and lay it so much to heart that I shall not be alive a hundred years hence, in the reign of I cannot tell whom?

. . .

There is nothing in the recollection that at a certain time we were not come into the world, that "the gorge rises at"—why should we revolt at the idea that we must one day go out of it? To die is only to be as we were before we were born; yet no one feels any remorse, or regret, or repugnance, in contemplating this last idea. It is rather a relief and disburthening of the mind: it seems to have been holiday-time with us then: we were not called to appear upon the stage of life, to wear robes or tatters, to laugh or cry, be hooted or applauded; we had lain *perdus* all this while, snug, out of harm's way; and had slept out our thousands of centuries without wanting to be waked up; at peace and free from care, in a long nonage, in a sleep deeper and calmer than that of infancy, wrapped in the softest and finest dust. And the worst that we dread is, after a short, fretful, feverish being, after vain hopes, and idle fears, to sink to final repose again, and forget the troubled dream of life! . . . Ye armed men, knights templars, that sleep in the store aisles of that old Temple church, where all is silent above, and where a deeper silence reigns below (not broken by the pealing organ), are ye not contented where ye lie? Or would you come out of your long homes to go to the Holy War? Or do ye complain that pain no longer visits you, that sickness has done its worst, that you have paid the last debt to nature, that you hear no more of the thickening phalanx of the foe, or your lady's waning love; and that while this ball of earth rolls its eternal round, no sound shall ever pierce through to disturb your lasting repose, fixed as the marble over your tombs, breathless as the grave that holds you! And thou, oh thou, to whom my heart turns, and will turn while it has feeling left, who didst love in vain, and whose first was thy last sigh, wilt not thou too rest in peace (or wilt thou cry to me complaining from thy clay-cold bed) when that sad heart is no longer sad, and that sorrow is dead which thou wert only called into the world to feel!

.   .   .

The love of life . . . is an habitual attachment, not an abstract principle. Simply to *be* does not "content man's natural desire": we long to be in a certain time, place, and circumstance. We would much rather be now, "on this bank and shoal of time," than have our choice of any future period, than take a slice of fifty or sixty years out of the Millennium, for instance. This shows that our attachment is not confined either to *being* or to *well-being;* but that we have an inveterate prejudice in favour of our immediate existence, such as it is. The mountaineer will not leave his rock, nor the savage his hut; neither are we willing to give up our present mode of life, with all its advantages and disadvantages, for any other that could be substituted for it. No man would, I think, exchange his existence with any other man, however fortunate. We had as lief *not be,* as *not be ourselves.* There are some persons of that reach of soul that they would like to live two hundred and fifty years hence, to see to what height of empire America will have grown up in that period, or whether the English constitution will last so long. These are points beyond me. But I confess I should like to live to see the downfall of the Bourbons. That is a vital question with me; and I shall like it the better, the sooner it happens!

No young man ever thinks he shall die. He may believe that others will, or assent to the doctrine that "all men are mortal" as an abstract proposition, but he is far enough from bringing it home to himself individually. Youth, buoyant activity, and animal spirits, hold absolute antipathy with old age as well as with death; nor have we, in the hey-day of life, any more than in the thoughtlessness of childhood, the remotest conception how

> This sensible warm motion can become
> A kneaded clod—

nor how sanguine, florid health and vigour, shall "turn to withered, weak, and grey." Or if in a moment of idle speculation we indulge in this notion of the close of life as a theory, it is amazing at what a distance it seems; what a long, leisurely interval there is between; what a contrast its slow and solemn approach affords to our present gay dreams of existence! We eye the farthest verge of the horizon, and think what a way we shall have to look back upon, ere we arrive at our journey's end; and without our in the least suspecting it, the mists are at our feet, and the shadows of age encompass us. The two divisions of our lives have melted into each other: the extreme points close and meet with none of that romantic interval stretching out between them, that we had reckoned upon; and for the rich, melancholy, solemn hues of age "the sear, the yellow leaf," the deepening shadows of an autumnal evening, we only feel a dank, cold mist, encircling all objects, after the spirit of youth is fled. There is no inducement to look forward; and what is worse, little interest in looking back to what has become so trite and common. The pleasures of our existence have worn themselves out, are "gone into the wastes of time," or have turned their indifferent side to us: the pains by their repeated blows have worn us out, and have left us neither spirit nor inclination to encounter them again in retrospect. We do not want to rip up old grievances, nor to renew our youth like the phoenix nor to live our lives twice over. Once is enough. As the tree falls, so let it lie. Shut up the book and close the account once for all!

. . .

It is not wonderful that the contemplation and fear of death become more familiar to us as we approach nearer to it: that life seems to ebb with the decay of blood and youthful spirits; and that as we find every thing about us subject to chance and change, as our strength and beauty die, as our hopes and passions, our friends and our affections leave us, we begin by degrees to feel ourselves mortal!

I have never seen death but once, and that was in an infant. It is years ago. The look was calm and placid, and the face was fair and firm. It was as if a waxen image had been laid out in the coffin, and strewed with innocent flowers. It was not like death, but more like an image of life! No breath moved the lips, no pulse stirred, no sight or sound would enter those eyes or ears more. While I looked at it, I saw no pain was there; it seemed to smile at the short pang of life which was over: but I could not bear the coffin-lid to be closed—it seemed to stifle me; and still as the nettles wave in a corner of the churchyard over his little grave, the welcome breeze helps to refresh me, and ease the tightness at my breast!

An ivory or marble image, like Chantry's monument of the two children, is contemplated with pure delight. Why do we not grieve and fret that the marble is not alive, or fancy that it has a shortness of breath? It never was alive; and it is the difficulty of making the transition from life to death, the struggle between the two in our imagination, that confounds their properties painfully together, and makes us conceive that the infant that is but just dead, still wants to breathe, to enjoy, and look about it, and is prevented by the icy hand of death, locking up its faculties and benumbing its senses; so that, if it could, it would complain of its own hard state. Perhaps religious considerations reconcile the mind to this change sooner than any others, by representing the spirit as fled to another sphere, and leaving the body behind it. So in reflecting on death generally, we mix up the idea of life with it, and thus make it the ghastly monster it is. We think how we should feel, not how the dead feel.

. . .

There is usually one pang added voluntarily and unnecessarily to the fear of death, by our affecting to compassionate the loss which others will have in us. If that were all, we might reasonably set our minds at rest. The pathetic exhortation on country tombstones, "Grieve not for me, my wife and children dear," &c. is for the most part speedily followed to the letter. We do not leave so great a void in society as we are inclined to imagine, partly to magnify our own importance, and partly to console ourselves by sympathy. Even in the same family the gap is not so great; the wound closes up sooner than we should expect. Nay, *our room* is not unfrequently thought better than *our company*. People walk along the streets the day after our deaths just as they did before, and the crowd is not diminished. While we were living, the world seemed in a manner to exist only for us, for our delight and amusement, because it contributed to them. But our hearts cease to beat, and it goes on as usual, and thinks no more about us than it did in our life-time. The million are devoid of sentiment, and care as little for you or me as if we belonged to the moon. We live the week over in the Sunday's paper, or are decently interred in some obituary at the month's end! It is not surprising that we are forgotten so soon after we quit this Mortal stage: we are scarcely noticed, while we are on it. It is not merely that our names are not known in China—they have hardly been heard of in the next street. We are hand and glove with the universe, and think the obligation is mutual. This is an evident fallacy. If this, however, does not trouble us now, it will not hereafter. A handful of dust can have no quarrel to pick with its neighbours, or complaint to make against Providence, and might well exclaim, if it had but an understanding and a tongue, "Go thy ways, old world, swing round in blue ether, voluble to every age, you and I shall no more jostle!"

It is amazing how soon the rich and titled, and even some of those who have wielded great political power, are forgotten.

A little rule, a little sway,
Is all the great and mighty have
Betwixt the cradle and the grave—

and, after its short date, they hardly leave a name behind them. "A great man's memory may, at the common rate, survive him half a year." His heirs and successors take his titles, his power, and his wealth—all that made him considerable or courted by others; and he has left nothing else behind him either to delight or benefit the world. Posterity are not by any means so disinterested as they are supposed to be. They give their gratitude and admiration only in return for benefits conferred. They cherish the memory of those to whom they are indebted for instruction and delight; and they cherish it just in proportion to the instruction and delight they are conscious they receive. The sentiment of admiration springs immediately from this ground; and cannot be otherwise than well founded.

The effeminate clinging to life as such, as a general or abstract idea, is the effect of a highly civilised and artificial state of society. Men formerly plunged into all the vicissitudes and dangers of war, or staked their all upon a single die, or some one passion, which if they could not have gratified, life became a burthen to them—now our strongest passion is to think, our chief amusement is to read new novels, and this we may do at our leisure, in plays, new poems, perfect security, *ad infinitum.* If we look into the old histories and romances, before the *belles-lettres* neutralised human affairs and reduced passion to a state of mental equivocation, we find the heroes and heroines not setting their lives "at a pin's fee," but rather courting opportunities of throwing them away in very wantonness of spirit. They raise their fondness for some favourite pursuit to its height, to a pitch of madness, and think no price too dear to pay for its full gratification. Everything else is dross. They go to death as to a bridal bed, and sacrifice themselves or others without remorse at the shrine of love, of honour, of religion, or any other prevailing feeling. . . .

A life of action and danger moderates the dread of death. It not only gives us fortitude to bear pain, but teaches us at every step the precarious tenure on which we hold our present being. Sedentary and studious men are the most apprehensive on this score. Dr. Johnson was an instance in point. A few years seemed to him soon over, compared with those sweeping contemplations on time and infinity with which he had been used to pose himself. In the *still-life* of a man of letters, there was no obvious reason for a change. He might sit in an arm-chair and pour out cups of tea to all eternity. Would it had been possible for him to do so! The most rational cure after all for the inordinate fear of death is to set a just value on life. If we merely wish to continue on the scene to indulge our headstrong humours and tormenting passions, we had better begone at once: and if we only cherish a fondness for existence according to the good we derive from it, the pang we feel at parting with it will not be very severe!

JOHN ASHBERY

FEAR OF DEATH

What is it now with me
And is it as I have become?
Is there no state free from the boundary lines
Of before and after. The window is open today

And the air pours in with piano notes
In its skirts, as though to say, "Look, John,
I've brought these and these"—that is,
A few Beethovens, some Brahmses,

A few choice Poulenc notes. . . . Yes,
It is being free again, the air, it has to keep coming back
Because that's all it's good for.
I want to stay with it out of fear

That keeps me from walking up certain steps,
Knocking at certain doors, fear of growing old

Alone, and of finding no one at the evening end
Of the path except another myself

Nodding a curt greeting: "Well, you've been awhile
But now we're back together, which is what counts."
Air in my path, you could shorten this,
But the breeze has dropped and silence is the last word.

❧

> "A man may very well love beef, or hunting, or a woman;
> but surely, surely, not a Permanent Possibility
> of Sensation!"

ROBERT LOUIS STEVENSON

AES TRIPLEX

Robert Louis Stevenson (1850–94) never enjoyed good health. As a child he was beset by bronchitis and digestive problems, and throughout his short life his "consumption" kept death always before him. Stevenson died, however, not of tuberculosis, but of a stroke, in Samoa, where he had taken up residence in 1889. To his widow, Fanny Stevenson, Henry James wrote:

> *What can I say to you that will not seem cruelly irrelevant or vain? . . . You are such a visible picture of desolation that I need remind myself, that courage, and patience, and fortitude are also abundantly with you. . . . To have lived in the light of that splendid life, that beautiful, bountiful being—only to see it, from one moment to the other converted into a fable as strange and romantic as one of his own, a thing that has been and has ended, is an anguish into which no one can enter with you fully and of which no one can drain the cup for you. He lighted up one whole side of the globe, and was in himself a whole province of one's imagination. . . .*

In the essay excerpted here, written when he was twenty-eight, Ste-
venson celebrates a peculiar courage he observes in our habitual oblivi-
ousness to death—and our haphazard tendency to defy it, despite our
abstract terror of the fact. His title, "Aes Triplex," means "triple brass,"
and is taken from an ode of Horace: "Oak and triple brass surrounded the
breast of the man who first sailed a fragile boat on the wild sea." Here
Stevenson applies the phrase to Samuel Johnson ("our respected lexicogra-
pher"), whose buoyancy and intrepidity were undiminished by his renowned
terror of the end.

We have all heard of cities in South America built upon the side of
fiery mountains, and how, even in this tremendous neighborhood, the
inhabitants are not a jot more impressed by the solemnity of mortal
conditions than if they were delving gardens in the greenest corner of
England. There are serenades and suppers and much gallantry among
the myrtles overhead; and meanwhile the foundation shudders underfoot, the bowels of the mountain growl, and at any moment living
ruin may leap sky-high into the moonlight, and tumble man and his
merry-making in the dust. In the eyes of very young people, and very
dull old ones, there is something indescribably reckless and desperate
in such a picture. It seems not credible that respectable married people, with umbrellas, should find appetite for a bit of supper within
quite a long distance of a fiery mountain; ordinary life begins to smell
of high-handed debauch when it is carried on so close to a catastrophe; and even cheese and salad, it seems, could hardly be relished in
such circumstances without something like a defiance of the Creator.
It should be a place for nobody but hermits dwelling in prayer and
maceration, or mere born-devils drowning care in a perpetual carouse.

. . .

Indeed, it is a memorable subject for consideration with what unconcern and gaiety mankind pricks on along the Valley of the Shadow of
Death. The whole way is one wilderness of snares, and the end of it,

for those who fear the last pinch, is irrevocable ruin. And yet we go
spinning through it all, like a party for the Derby. Perhaps the reader
remembers one of the humorous devices of the deified Caligula: how
he encouraged a vast concourse of holiday-makers on to his bridge
over Baiae bay; and when they were in the height of their enjoyment,
turned loose the Praetorian guards among the company, and had
them tossed into the sea. This is no bad miniature of the dealings of
nature with the transitory race of man. Only, what a checkered picnic
we have of it, even while it lasts! and into what great waters, not to be
crossed by any swimmer, God's pale Praetorian throws us over in the
end!

We live the time that a match flickers; we pop the cork of a
ginger-beer bottle, and the earthquake swallows us on the instant. Is it
not odd, is it not incongruous, is it not, in the highest sense of human
speech, incredible, that we should think so highly of the ginger beer,
and regard so little the devouring earthquake? The love of Life and the
fear of Death are two famous phrases that grow harder to understand
the more we think about them. It is a well-known fact that an im-
mense proportion of boat accidents would never happen if people
held the sheet in their hands instead of making it fast; and yet, unless
it be some martinet of a professional mariner or some landsman with
shattered nerves, every one of God's creatures makes it fast. A strange
instance of man's unconcern and brazen boldness in the face of death!

We confound ourselves with metaphysical phrases, which we
import into daily talk with noble inappropriateness. We have no idea
of what death is, apart from its circumstances and some of its consequences to others; and although we have some experience of living,
there is not a man on earth who has flown so high into abstraction as
to have any practical guess at the meaning of the word *life*. All literature, from Job and Omar Khayyam to Thomas Carlyle and Walt Whitman, is but an attempt to look upon the human state with such
largeness of view as shall enable us to rise from the consideration of
living to the Definition of Life. And our sages give us about the best
satisfaction in their power when they say that it is a vapor, or a show,
or made of the same stuff with dreams. Philosophy, in its more rigid
sense, has been at the same work for ages; and after a myriad bald

heads have wagged over the problem, and piles of words have been heaped one upon another into dry and cloudy volumes without end, philosophy has the honor of laying before us, with modest pride, her contribution toward the subject: that life is a Permanent Possibility of Sensation. Truly a fine result! A man may very well love beef, or hunting, or a woman; but surely, surely, not a Permanent Possibility of Sensation! He may be afraid of a precipice, or a dentist, or a large enemy with a club, or even an undertaker's man; but not certainly of abstract death. We may trick with the word life in its dozen senses until we are weary of tricking; we may argue in terms of all the philosophies on earth, but one fact remains true throughout—that we do not love life, in the sense that we are generally preoccupied about its conservation—that we do not, properly speaking, love life at all, but living. Into the views of the least careful there will enter some degree of providence; no man's eyes are fixed entirely on the passing hour, but although we have some anticipation of good health, good weather, wine, active employment, love, and self-approval, the sum of these anticipations does not amount to anything like a general view of life's possibilities and issues; nor are those who cherish them most vividly, at all the most scrupulous of their personal safety. To be deeply interested in the accidents of our existence, to enjoy keenly the mixed texture of human experience, rather leads a man to disregard precautions, and risk his neck against a straw. For surely the love of living is stronger in an Alpine climber roping over a peril, or a hunter riding merrily at a stiff fence, than in a creature who lives upon a diet and walks a measured distance in the interests of his constitution.

There is a great deal of very vile nonsense talked upon both sides of the matter: tearing divines reducing life to the dimensions of a mere funeral procession, so short as to be hardly decent; and melancholy unbelievers yearning for the tomb as if it were a world too far away. Both sides must feel a little ashamed of their performances now and again when they draw in their chairs to dinner. Indeed, a good meal and a bottle of wine is an answer to most standard works upon the question. When a man's heart warms to his viands, he forgets a great deal of sophistry, and soars into a rosy zone of contemplation. Death may be knocking at the door, like the Commander's statue; we have something else in hand, thank God, and let him knock. Passing bells are ringing all the world over. All the world over, and every hour, some one is parting company with all his aches and ecstasies. For us also the trap is laid. But we are so fond of life that we have no leisure to entertain the terror of death. It is a honeymoon with us all through, and none of the longest. Small blame to us if we give our whole hearts to this glowing bride of ours, to the appetites, to honor, to the hungry curiosity of the mind, to the pleasure of the eyes in nature, and the pride of our own nimble bodies.

We all of us appreciate the sensations; but as for caring about the Permanence of the Possibility, a man's head is generally very bald, and his senses very dull, before he comes to that. Whether we regard life as a lane leading to a dead wall—a mere bag's end as the French say—or whether we think of it as a vestibule or gymnasium, where we wait our turn and prepare our faculties for some more noble destiny; whether we thunder in a pulpit, or pule in little atheistic poetry-books, about its vanity and brevity, whether we look justly for years of health and vigor, or are about to mount into a Bath chair, as a step toward the hearse; in each and any of these views and situations there is but one conclusion possible: that a man should stop his ears against paralyzing terror, and run the race that is set before him with a single mind. No one surely could have recoiled with more heartache and terror from the thought of death than our respected lexicographer; and yet we know how little it affected his conduct, how wisely and boldly he walked, and in what a fresh and lively vein he spoke of life. Already an old man, he ventured on his Highland tour; and his heart, bound with triple brass, did not recoil before twenty-seven individual cups of tea. As courage and intelligence are the two qualities best worth a good man's cultivation, so it is the first part of intelligence to recognize our precarious estate in life, and the first part of courage to be not at all abashed before the fact. A frank and somewhat headlong carriage, not looking too anxiously before, not dallying in maudlin regret over the past, stamps the man who is well armored for this world. . . .

TIME TO BE OLD

———

Man cannot purge his body of its theme
As can the silkworm on a running thread
Spin a shroud to re-consider in.

DJUNA BARNES
"Rite of Spring"

A. R. AMMONS

from **GARBAGE**

sometimes old people snap back into life
for a streak and start making plans, ridiculous, you know,

when they will suddenly think of death again
and they will see their coffins plunge upward

like whales out of the refused depths of their
minds and the change will feel so shockingly

different—from the warm movement of a possibility
to a cold acknowledgment—they will seem not

to understand for a minute: at other times
with the expiration of plans and friends and

dreams and with the assaults on all sides of
relapses and pains, they will feel a

smallish ambition to creep into their boxes
at last and lid the light out and be gone,

nevermore, nevermore to see again,
let alone see trouble come on anyone again: oh, yes, there

are these moods and transitions, these bolt
recollections and these foolish temptations and

stratagems to distract them from the
course: this is why they and we must keep our

minds on the god-solid, not on the vain silks
and sweets of human dissipation, no, sirree:

unless of course god is immanent in which case
he may be to some slight extent part of the

sweets, god being in that case nothing more than or
as much as energy at large, a hair of it caught

in candy: I just want you to know I'm perfectly
serious much of the time: when I kid around

I'm trying to get in position to be serious: my
daffydillies are efforts to excuse the

presumption of assumption, direct address, my
self-presentation: I'm trying to mean what I

mean to mean something: best for that is a kind
of matter-of-fact explicitness about the facts:

best of all, facts of action: actions, actions, actions
human or atomic: these actions cut

curves out in space, spiral up or in, turn and
turn back, stall, whirl: these are the motions

we learn from, these are the central figures,
this is the dance, here attitude and character,

precision and floundering lay out for us to see
their several examples, comically wasteful, as

with clowns or young squirrels playful at dusk:
here is the real morality, the economy of

action and reaction, of driving ahead, of going
slow, of walking the line, the tightrope, here

the narratives of motion that tell the story
the stories figure into facticity: let's

study the motions, are they slovenly, choppy,
attenuating, high, meandering, wasteful: we

need nothing more, except the spelling out of
these for those inattentive or too busily lost

in the daily elaborations to prize the essential:
(1) don't complain—ills are sufficiently

clear without reiterated description: (2) count
your blessings, spelling them over and over into

sharp contemplation: (3) do what you can—
take action: (4) move on, keep the mind

allied with the figurations of ongoing: when
I was a kid I always, it seemed, had a point

I couldn't say or that no one could accept—
I always sounded unconvincing; I lost the

arguments: people became impatient and stuck
to their own beliefs; my explanations struck

them as strange, unlikely: when I learned
about poetry, I must have recognized a means

to command silence in them, the means so to
combine thinking and feeling, imagination and

movement as to spell them out of speech:
people would buy the enchantment and get the

point reason couldn't, the point delivered below
the level of argument, straight into the fat

of feeling: so I'm asking you to help me, now:
yield to this possibility: I'm going to try to

say everything all over again: I've discovered
at sixty-three that the other thing I wished of

poetry, that it prevent death, has kept me a
little strange, that I have not got my feet out

of the embranglements of misapplication and out
into a clear space to go; that I have to start

again from a realization of failure: in fact,
having learned about commanding silence and

having, mostly by accident, commanded it a few
times, I've become afraid of convincingness,

what harm it can do if there is too much of
it along with whatever good, so I am now a

little uncertain on purpose: I recognize cases
in other words from time to time that I'd rather

see go through than my own: they seem wiser
cases: they come from people who seem better

wrapped around their spines: when their mouths
are open, their vertebrae form a sounding

foundation for their words: I have never,
frankly, grown up, not if growing up means I

wouldn't trade in what I have today for something
I might get tomorrow: I'm a trader: I'm still

looking for the buy to go all the way with:
I've become convinced that I don't have

anything particularly to convince anybody of: my
rhetoric goes on, though, with a terrible

machine-like insistence whether potholes
appear in the streets or not, or knots in my

line, or furriers in my traps: the trap shut
displeases no prey: pray you, go ahead around

me; I'm letting go a few springs and bolts from
my current mechanism: I'm getting down: I'm

not recommending more altitude than wings, not
anymore, not lately: no, no: not on your life.

❦

". . . nothing left but You, a remnant, a tradition, belated fag-end of a foolish dream. . . ."

SAMUEL CLEMENS
(MARK TWAIN)

ON OLD AGE

A lavish seventieth-birthday party was given in honor of Samuel Clemens (1835–1910) at Delmonico's in New York for 172 guests. He closed his birthday speech with the reflection that at this age, one no longer needs to make excuses for declining invitations:

> *The previous engagement plea, which in forty years has cost you so many twinges, you can lay aside for ever. . . . you need only reply, "Your invitation honors me, and pleases me because you still keep me in your remembrance, but I am seventy; seventy, and would nestle in the chimney corner, and smoke my pipe, and read my book, and take my rest, wishing you well in all affection, and that when you in your turn shall arrive at pier No. 70 you may step aboard your waiting ship with a reconciled spirit, and lay your course toward the sinking sun with a contented heart."*

The piece that follows, written shortly after the birthday speech, reflects a different and perhaps a darker mood about aging. In 1904, a year earlier, Clemens had lost his wife, Livy, and his sister, Pamela. He was troubled by gout, dyspepsia, and bronchitis.

I think it likely that people who have not been here will be interested to know what it is like. I arrived on the thirtieth of November, fresh from care-free and frivolous 69, and was disappointed.

There is nothing novel about it, nothing striking, nothing to thrill you and make your eye glitter and your tongue cry out, "Oh, but it is wonderful, perfectly wonderful!" Yes, it is disappointing. You say, "Is *this* it?—*this*? after all this talk and fuss of a thousand generations of travelers who have crossed this frontier and looked about them and told what they saw and felt? why, it looks just like 69."

And that is true. Also it is natural; for you have not come by the fast express, you have been lagging and dragging across the world's continents behind oxen; when that is your pace one country melts into the next one so gradually that you are not able to notice the change: 70 looks like 69; 69 looked like 68; 68 looked like 67—and so on, back, and back, to the beginning. If you climb to a summit and look back—ah, then you see!

Down that far-reaching perspective you can make out each country and climate that you crossed, all the way up from the hot equator to the ice-summit where you are perched. You can make out where Infancy merged into Boyhood; Boyhood into down-lipped Youth; Youth into indefinite Young-Manhood; indefinite Young-Manhood into definite Manhood; definite Manhood with aggressive ambitions into sobered and heedful Husbandhood and Fatherhood; these into troubled and foreboding Age, with graying hair; this into Old Age, white-headed, the temple empty, the idols broken, the worshippers in their graves, nothing left but You, a remnant, a tradition, belated fag-end of a foolish dream, a dream that was so ingeniously dreamed that it seemed real all the time; nothing left but You, centre of a snowy desolation, perched on the ice-summit, gazing out over the stages of that long *trek* and asking Yourself "would you do it again if you had the chance?"

"When all is said and done, there's nothing, nothing but
decay and the sweetish smell of eternity."

LUIS BUÑUEL

SWAN SONG

*In these pithy reflections, Spanish filmmaker Luis Buñuel (1900–83) toys
with various approaches to his death—and afterward. An atheist oriented
by Catholic doctrine and iconography, Buñuel showed a career-long preoccupation with the "exterminating angel." Buñuel's younger sister, Conchita,
describes an early episode of playful blasphemy, familiar from the auteur's
films:*

> *The great adventure of our childhood . . . occurred during a sum-
> mer in Calanda when Luis must have been in his early teens. We
> decided to sneak away to the neighboring town with some cousins our
> age, but without our parents' permission. Heaven only knows why,
> but we all got dressed as if we were going to a fancy party. When we
> got to Foz . . . we made the rounds of all our tenant farmers. At
> every house, they fed us sweet wine and cookies, and by the time
> we'd seen them all, we were so euphoric that we decided to explore
> the local cemetery. I remember Luis stretching out on the autopsy
> table and demanding that someone take out his entrails. I also re-*

member one of us sticking her head through a hole in a tomb and becoming so firmly wedged in that Luis had to tear away the plaster with his nails to get her out. . . .

After our innocent, albeit blasphemous, invasion, we started back through the sun-blasted mountains. . . . When we began to get hungry, [Luis] heroically offered himself for consumption.

The passages that follow are entitled "Swan Song," and they are taken from Buñuel's memoir My Last Sigh *(1983), which he wrote with the help of Jean-Claude Carrière. With equal delight and horror, he purveys this world and the next, imagining, in passing, a kind of secular heaven of returning from the grave every ten years or so to read the newspapers.*

According to the latest reports, we now have enough nuclear bombs not only to destroy all life on the planet but also to blow the planet itself, empty and cold, out of its orbit altogether and into the immensity of the cosmic void. I find that possibility magnificent, and in fact I'm tempted to shout bravo, because from now on there can be no doubt that science is our enemy. She flatters our desires for omnipotence, desires that lead inevitably to our destruction. A recent poll announced that out of 700,000 "highly qualified" scientists now working throughout the world, 520,000 of them are busy trying to streamline the means of our self-destruction, while only 180,000 are studying ways of keeping us alive.

. . .

Imaginatively speaking, all forms of life are equally valuable—even the fly, which seems to me as enigmatic and as admirable as the fairy. But now that I'm alone and old, I foresee only catastrophe and chaos. I know that old people always say that the sun was warmer when they were young, and I also realize how commonplace it is to announce the end of the world at the end of each millennium. Nonetheless, I still think the entire century is moving toward some cataclysmic moment. Evil seems victorious at last; the forces of destruction have carried the day; the human mind hasn't made any progress whatsoever toward clarity. Perhaps it's even regressed. We live in an age of frailty, fear, and morbidity. Where will the kindness and intelligence come from that can save us? Even chance seems impotent.

I was born at the dawn of the century, and my lifetime often seems to me like an instant. Events in my childhood sometimes seem so recent that I have to make an effort to remember that they happened fifty or sixty years ago. And yet at other times life seems to me very long. The child, or the young man, who did this or that doesn't seem to have anything to do with me anymore.

In 1975, when I was in New York with Silberman, we went to an Italian restaurant I'd been fond of thirty-five years before. The owner had died, but his wife recognized me, and I suddenly felt as if I'd eaten there just a few days before. Time is so changeable that there's just not much point in repeating how much the world has changed. Until I turned seventy-five, I found old age rather agreeable. It was a tremendous relief to be rid at last of nagging desires; I no longer wanted anything—no more houses by the sea or fancy cars or works of art. "Down with *l'amour fou!*" I'd say to myself. "Long live friendship!" Whenever I saw an old man in the street or in the lobby of a hotel, I'd turn to whoever was with me and say: "Have you seen Buñuel lately? It's incredible. Even last year, he was so strong—and now, what terrible deterioration!" I enjoyed playing at early senility, I loved reading Simone de Beauvoir's *La Vieillesse,* I no longer showed myself in bathing suits at public swimming pools, and I traveled less and less. But my life remained active and well balanced; I made my last movie at seventy-seven.

During the last five years, however, true old age has begun. Whole series of petty annoyances attack me; I've begun to complain about my legs, my eyes, my head, my lapses of memory, my weak coordination. In 1979 I spent three days in the hospital plugged into an IV; at the end of the third day, I tore out the tubes, got out of bed, and went home. But in 1980 I was back in again for a prostate operation, and in 1981 it was the gall bladder. The enemy is everywhere, and I'm painfully conscious of my decrepitude.

The diagnosis couldn't be simpler: I'm an old man, and that's all

there is to it. I'm only happy at home following my daily routine:
wake up, have a cup of coffee, exercise for half an hour, wash, have a
second cup of coffee, eat something, walk around the block, wait until
noon. My eyes are weak, and I need a magnifying glass and a special
light in order to read. My deafness keeps me from listening to music,
so I wait, I think, I remember, filled with a desperate impatience and
constantly looking at my watch.

Noon's the sacred moment of the aperitif, which I drink very
slowly in my study. After lunch, I doze in my chair until mid-after-
noon and then, from three to five, I read a bit and look at my watch,
waiting for six o'clock and my predinner aperitif. Sometimes I cheat,
but only by fifteen minutes or so. Sometimes, too, friends come by to
chat. Dinner's at seven, with my wife, and then I go to bed.

It's been four years now since I've been to the movies, because
of my eyesight, my hearing, and my horror of traffic and crowds. I
never watch television. Sometimes an entire week goes by without a
visitor, and I feel abandoned. Then someone shows up unexpectedly,
someone I haven't seen for a long time, and then the following day
several friends arrive at the same time. There's Alcoriza, my collaborator, or Juan Ibañez, a superb director who drinks cognac all day long,
or Father Julian, a modern Dominican, an excellent painter and en-
graver and the maker of two unusual films. He and I often talk about
faith and the existence of God, but since he's forever coming up
against the stone wall of my atheism, he only says to me:

"Before I knew you, Luis, my faith wavered sometimes, but now
that we've started these conversations, it's become invincible!"

. . .

. . . For a long time now, I've written the names of friends who've
died in a special notebook I call *The Book of the Dead*. I leaf through it
from time to time and see hundreds of names, one beside the other, in
alphabetical order. There are red crosses next to the surrealists, whose
most fatal year was 1977–78 when Man Ray, Calder, Max Ernst, and
Prévert all died within a few months of one another. Some of my
friends are upset about this book—dreading, no doubt, the day they

will be in it. I try to tell them that it helps me remember certain people who'd otherwise cease to exist. . . .

The thought of death has been familiar to me for a long time. From the time that skeletons were carried through the streets of Calanda during the Holy Week procession, death has been an integral part of my life. I've never wished to forget or deny it, but there's not much to say about it when you're an atheist. When all is said and done, there's nothing, nothing but decay and the sweetish smell of eternity. (Perhaps I'll be cremated so I can skip all that.) Yet I can't help wondering how death will come, when it does. Sometimes, just to amuse myself, I conjure up old images of hell. Of course, in these modern times, the flames and the pitchforks have disappeared, and hell is now only a simple absence of divine light. I see myself floating in a boundless darkness, my body still intact for the final resurrection; but suddenly another body bumps into mine. It's a Thai who died two thousand years ago falling out of a coconut tree. He floats off into the infernal obscurity and millions of years go by, until I feel another body. This time, it's one of Napoleon's camp followers. And so it goes, over and over again, as I let myself be swept along for a moment in the harrowing shadows of this post-modern hell.

Sometimes I think, the quicker, the better—like the death of my friend Max Aub, who died all of a sudden during a card game. But most of the time I prefer a slower death, one that's expected, that will let me revisit my life for a last goodbye. Whenever I leave a place now, a place where I've lived and worked, which has become a part of me—like Paris, Madrid, Toledo, El Paular, San José Purua—I stop for a moment to say adieu. "Adieu, San José," I say aloud. "I've had so many happy moments here, and without you my life would have been so different. Now I'm going away and I'll never see you again, but you'll go on without me." I say goodbye to everything—to the mountains, the streams, the trees, even the frogs. And, of course, irony would have it that I often return to a place I've already bid goodbye, but it doesn't matter. When I leave, I just say goodbye once again.

I'd like to die knowing that this time I'm not going to come back. When people ask me why I don't travel more, I tell them: Because I'm afraid of death. Of course, they all hasten to assure me that there's no more chance of my dying abroad than at home, so I explain that it's not a fear of death in general. Dying itself doesn't matter to me, but not while I'm on the road. I don't want to die in a hotel room with my bags open and papers lying all over the place.

On the other hand, an even more horrible death is one that's kept at bay by the miracles of modern medicine, a death that never ends. In the name of Hippocrates, doctors have invented the most exquisite form of torture ever known to man: survival. Sometimes I even pitied Franco, kept alive artificially for months at the cost of incredible suffering. And for what? Some doctors do help us to die, but most are only moneymakers who live by the canons of an impersonal technology. If they would only let us die when the moment comes, and help us to go more easily! Respect for human life becomes absurd when it leads to unlimited suffering, not only for the one who's dying but for those he leaves behind.

As I drift toward my last sigh I often imagine a final joke. I convoke around my deathbed my friends who are confirmed atheists, as I am. Then a priest, whom I have summoned, arrives; and to the horror of my friends I make my confession, ask for absolution for my sins, and receive extreme unction. After which I turn over on my side and expire.

But will I have the strength to joke at that moment?

Only one regret. I hate to leave while there's so much going on. It's like quitting in the middle of a serial. I doubt there was so much curiosity about the world after death in the past, since in those days the world didn't change quite so rapidly or so much. Frankly, despite my horror of the press, I'd love to rise from the grave every ten years or so and go buy a few newspapers. Ghostly pale, sliding silently along the walls, my papers under my arm, I'd return to the cemetery and read about all the disasters in the world before falling back to sleep, safe and secure in my tomb.

Translated by Abigail Israel.

KINGSLEY AMIS (1922–95)

LOVELY

Look thy last on all things lovely
    Every hour, an old shag said,
Meaning they turn lovelier if thou
    Thinkst about soon being dead.

Do they? When that "soon" means business
    They might lose their eye-appeal,
Go a bit like things unlovely,
    Get upstaged by how you feel.

The best time to see things lovely
    Is in youth's primordial bliss,
Which is also when you rather
    Go for old shags talking piss.

PHILIP LARKIN (1922–85)

THE OLD FOOLS

What do they think has happened, the old fools,
To make them like this? Do they somehow suppose
It's more grown-up when your mouth hangs open and drools,
And you keep on pissing yourself, and can't remember
Who called this morning? Or that, if they only chose,
They could alter things back to when they danced all night,
Or went to their wedding, or sloped arms some September?
Or do they fancy there's really been no change,
And they've always behaved as if they were crippled or tight,
Or sat through days of thin continuous dreaming
Watching light move? If they don't (and they can't), it's strange:
                Why aren't they screaming?

At death, you break up: the bits that were you
Start speeding away from each other for ever
With no one to see. It's only oblivion, true:
We had it before, but then it was going to end,

And was all the time merging with a unique endeavour
To bring to bloom the million-petalled flower
Of being here. Next time you can't pretend
There'll be anything else. And these are the first signs:
Not knowing how, not hearing who, the power
Of choosing gone. Their looks show that they're for it:
Ash hair, toad hands, prune face dried into lines—
                How can they ignore it?

Perhaps being old is having lighted rooms
Inside your head, and people in them, acting.
People you know, yet can't quite name; each looms
Like a deep loss restored, from known doors turning,
Setting down a lamp, smiling from a stair, extracting
A known book from the shelves; or sometimes only
The rooms themselves, chairs and a fire burning,
The blown bush at the window, or the sun's
Faint friendliness on the wall some lonely
Rain-ceased midsummer evening. That is where they live:
Not here and now, but where all happened once.
                This is why they give

An air of baffled absence, trying to be there
Yet being here. For the rooms grow farther, leaving
Incompetent cold, the constant wear and tear
Of taken breath, and them crouching below
Extinction's alp, the old fools, never perceiving
How near it is. This must be what keeps them quiet:
The peak that stays in view wherever we go
For them is rising ground. Can they never tell
What is dragging them back, and how it will end? Not at night?
Not when the strangers come? Never, throughout
The whole hideous inverted childhood? Well,
                We shall find out.

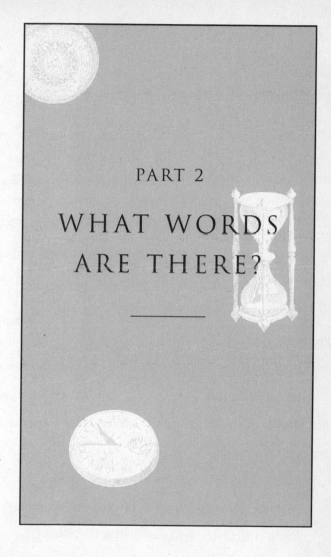

PART 2

WHAT WORDS
ARE THERE?

In death's proximity, words take on new obligations; we grow cautious in their use and hesitate in case a clumsy word should discompose the stricken. We become conscious of their inadequacy and yet at the same time of their authority. All too aware that there's nothing anyone can say, we try and try to find some words of comfort—and sometimes we succeed.

Precision counts for more in death's precincts than anywhere. What violence a wrong turn of phrase can do when a eulogist, priest or rabbi, fumbles in his effort to capture a precious and singular trait. The dead are too vulnerable to misrepresentation, suddenly unable to enact their uniqueness by themselves. There is an urgency to capture with utter accuracy the tiniest and most evocative of mannerisms, markers of their singularity, words to forestall the absence, to secure the memories—and to share them. Our ability to describe—in words and images—is no small part of our sacred charge to remember.

The pain of loss seeks its own syntax too. Without expression, the suffering mounts; "Give sorrow words: the grief that does not speak / Whispers the oe'r fraught heart, and bids it break," Shakespeare writes. If sometimes with words we stir the pain, getting it right, saying it in a way that makes it seem to us to have been said, can break the rhythm of suffering and gather us back to ourselves, if only for a moment.

———————

LEFT BEHIND

_____

The breaking of so great a thing should make
A greater crack. The round world
Should have shook lions into civil streets,
And citizens to their dens.

WILLIAM SHAKESPEARE
Antony and Cleopatra

※

"In themselves, the things mean nothing . . . And yet
they say something to us . . . emblems of the
solitude in which a man comes to make decisions
about himself: whether to color his hair, whether to
wear this or that shirt. . . ."

PAUL AUSTER

PORTRAIT OF AN INVISIBLE MAN

Paul Auster wrote this "Portrait" in 1979, following the death of his father.
Auster writes of this distant and elusive man, "He ate, he went to work, he
had friends, he played tennis, and yet for all that he was not there. In the
deepest, most unalterable sense, he was an invisible man. Invisible to oth-
ers, and most likely invisible to himself as well. If, while he was alive, I
kept looking for him, kept trying to find the father who was not there, now
that he is dead I still feel as though I must go on looking for him. Death
has not changed anything." In 1970, Auster had learned a dark family
secret that seemed, if not to reveal his father to him, at least to account for
his remoteness. The story unfolds for him through yellowed newspaper
accounts of the 1919 murder by Sam Auster's mother of his father, of her
confession and eventual acquittal.

In the following excerpts, Auster describes sifting through his father's
unyielding possessions, as he slowly empties the house in which his father
had lived alone for the prior fifteen years. "Portrait of an Invisible Man"
appeared as the first part of Auster's book The Invention of Solitude *in*
1982.

There is nothing more terrible, I learned, than having to face the objects of a dead man. Things are inert: they have meaning only in function of the life that makes use of them. When that life ends, the things change, even though they remain the same. They are there and yet not there: tangible ghosts, condemned to survive in a world they no longer belong to. What is one to think, for example, of a closetful of clothes waiting silently to be worn again by a man who will not be coming back to open the door? Or the stray packets of condoms strewn among brimming drawers of underwear and socks? Or an electric razor sitting in the bathroom, still clogged with the whisker dust of the last shave? Or a dozen empty tubes of hair coloring hidden away in a leather travelling case?—suddenly revealing things one has no desire to see, no desire to know. There is a poignancy to it, and also a kind of horror. In themselves, the things mean nothing, like the cooking utensils of some vanished civilization. And yet they say something to us, standing there not as objects but as remnants of thought, of consciousness, emblems of the solitude in which a man comes to make decisions about himself: whether to color his hair, whether to wear this or that shirt, whether to live, whether to die. And the futility of it all once there is death.

Each time I opened a drawer or poked my head into a closet, I felt like an intruder, a burglar ransacking the secret places of a man's mind. I kept expecting my father to walk in, to stare at me in disbelief, and ask me what the hell I thought I was doing. It didn't seem fair that he couldn't protest. I had no right to invade his privacy.

A hastily scrawled telephone number on the back of a business card that read: H. Limeburg—Garbage Cans of All Descriptions. Photographs of my parents' honeymoon in Niagara Falls, 1946: my mother sitting nervously on top of a bull for one of those funny shots that are never funny, and a sudden sense of how unreal the world has always been, even in its prehistory. A drawer full of hammers, nails, and more than twenty screwdrivers. A filing cabinet stuffed with cancelled checks from 1953 and the cards I received for my sixth birthday. And then, buried at the bottom of a drawer in the bathroom: the monogrammed toothbrush that had once belonged to my mother and which had not been touched or looked at for more than fifteen years.

The list is inexhaustible.

. . .

The house began to resemble the set for a trite comedy of manners. Relatives swooped in, asking for this piece of furniture or that piece of dinnerware, trying on my father's suits, overturning boxes, chattering away like geese. Auctioneers came to examine the merchandise ("Nothing upholstered, it's not worth a nickel"), turned up their noses, and walked out. Garbage men clumped in with heavy boots and hauled off mountains of trash. The water man read the water meter, the gas man read the gas meter, the oil man read the oil gauge. (One of them, I forget which, who had been given a lot of trouble by my father over the years, said to me with savage complicity, "I don't like to say this"—meaning he did—"but your father was an obnoxious bastard.") The real estate agent came to buy some furniture for the new owners and wound up taking a mirror for herself. A woman who ran a curio shop bought my mother's old hats. A junkman came with a team of assistants (four black men named Luther, Ulysses, Tommy Pride, and Joe Sapp) and carted away everything from a set of barbells to a broken toaster. By the time it was over, nothing was left. Not even a postcard. Not even a thought.

If there was a single worst moment for me during those days, it came when I walked across the front lawn in the pouring rain to dump an armful of my father's ties into the back of a Good Will Mission truck. There must have been more than a hundred ties, and many of them I remembered from my childhood: the patterns, the colors, the shapes that had been embedded in my earliest consciousness, as clearly as my father's face had been. To see myself throwing them away like so much junk was intolerable to me, and it was then, at the precise instant I tossed them into the truck, that I came closest to tears. More than seeing the coffin itself being lowered into the ground, the act of throwing away these ties seemed to embody for me the idea of burial. I finally understood that my father was dead.

In his bedroom closet I had found several hundred photographs—stashed away in faded manila envelopes, affixed to the black pages of warped albums, scattered loosely in drawers. From the way they had been stored I gathered he never looked at them, had even forgotten they were there. One very big album, bound in expensive leather with a gold-stamped title on the cover—This is Our Life: The Austers—was totally blank inside. Someone, probably my mother, had once gone to the trouble of ordering this album, but no one had ever bothered to fill it.

Back home, I pored over these pictures with a fascination bordering on mania. I found them irresistible, precious, the equivalent of holy relics. It seemed that they could tell me things I had never known before, reveal some previously hidden truth, and I studied each one intensely, absorbing the least detail, the most insignificant shadow, until all the images had become a part of me. I wanted nothing to be lost. . . .

Discovering these photographs was important to me because they seemed to reaffirm my father's physical presence in the world, to give me the illusion that he was still there. The fact that many of these pictures were ones I had never seen before, especially the ones of his youth, gave me the odd sensation that I was meeting him for the first time, that a part of him was only just beginning to exist. I had lost my father. But at the same time, I had also found him. As long as I kept these pictures before my eyes, as long as I continued to study them with my complete attention, it was as though he were still alive, even in death. Or if not alive, at least not dead. Or rather, somehow suspended, locked in a universe that had nothing to do with death, in which death could never make an entrance.

. . .

From the house: a watch, a few sweaters, a jacket, an alarm clock, six tennis rackets, and an old rusted Buick that barely runs. A set of dishes, a coffee table, three or four lamps. A barroom statue of Johnnie Walker for Daniel. The blank photograph album, This Is Our Life: The Austers.

At first I thought it would be a comfort to hold on to these things, that they would remind me of my father and make me think of him as I went about my life. But objects, it seems, are no more than objects. I am used to them now, I have begun to think of them as my own. I read time by his watch, I wear his sweaters, I drive around in his car. But all this is no more than an illusion of intimacy. I have already appropriated these things. My father has vanished from them, has become invisible again. And sooner or later they will break down, fall apart, and have to be thrown away. I doubt that it will even seem to matter.

DONALD JUSTICE

SONNET TO MY FATHER

Father, since always now the death to come
Looks naked out from your eyes into mine,
Almost it seems the death to come is mine
And that I also shall be overcome,
Father, and call for breath when you succumb,
And struggle for your hand as you for mine
In hope of comfort that shall not be mine
Till for the last of me the angel come.
But, father, though with you in part I die
And glimpse beforehand that eternal place
Where we forget the pain that brought us there,
Father, and though you go before me there
And leave this likeness only in your place,
Yet while I live, you do not wholly die.

". . . she had, for the first time that day,
forgotten that he was dead."

COLETTE

HE DIED IN HIS
SEVENTY-FOURTH YEAR . . .

A year before she died, the mother of the celebrated French writer Colette
(1873–1954) wrote this letter to Colette's husband:

Sir,

You ask me to come and spend a week with you, which means I
would be near my daughter, whom I adore. You who live with her
know how rarely I see her, how much her presence delights me, and I
am touched that you should ask me to come and see her. All the
same I'm not going to accept your kind invitation, for the time being
at any rate. The reason is that my pink cactus is probably going to
flower. . . . I'm told that in our climate it flowers only once every
four years. Now, I am already a very old woman, and if I went away
when my pink cactus is about to flower, I am certain I shouldn't see
it flower again.

So I beg you, sir, to accept my sincere thanks and my regrets,
together with my kind regards.

Beneath this letter, Colette wrote, ". . . Whenever I feel myself inferior to everything about me, threatened by my own mediocrity, frightened by the discovery that a muscle is losing its strength, a desire its power, I can still hold up my head and say to myself: 'I am the daughter of the woman who wrote that letter . . . a woman who herself never ceased to flower, untiringly, over three quarters of a century.' "

Of her father, a handsome ex-officer and aspiring writer, Colette wrote, "He was not only misunderstood but unappreciated. . . . And now the thought of my father tortures me, because I know that he possessed a virtue more precious than any facile charms: that of knowing full well why he was sad, and never revealing it."

The two excerpts which follow, from La Maison de Claudine *(1923) and* Sido *(1929), describe the aftermath of her father's death in 1904. The legacies of both parents are revealed in these passages.*

He died in his seventy-fourth year, holding the hands of his beloved and fixing on her weeping eyes a gaze that gradually lost its colour, turned milky blue, and faded like a sky veiled in mist. He was given the handsomest of village funerals, a coffin of yellow wood covered only by an old tunic riddled with wounds—the tunic he had worn as a captain in the First Zouaves—and my mother accompanied him steadily to the grave's edge, very small and resolute beneath her widow's veil, and murmuring under her breath words of love that only he must hear.

We brought her back to the house, and there she promptly lost her temper with her new mourning, the cumbersome crepe that caught on the keys of doors and presses, the cashmere dress that stifled her. She sat resting in the drawing room, near the big green chair in which my father would never sit again and which the dog had already joyfully invaded. She was dry-eyed, flushed and feverish and kept on repeating:

"Oh, how hot it is! Heavens! The heat of this black stuff! Don't you think I might change now, into my blue sateen?"

"Well . . ."

"Why not? Because of my mourning? But I simply loathe black!"

For one thing, it's melancholy. Why should I present a sad and un-pleasant sight to everyone I meet? What connection is there between this cashmere and crepe and my feelings? Don't let me ever see you in mourning for me! You know well enough that I only like you to wear pink, and some shades of blue."

She got up hastily, took several steps towards an empty room, and stopped abruptly:

"Ah! . . . Of course . . ."

She came back and sat down again, admitting with a simple and humble gesture that she had, for the first time that day, forgotten that he was dead.

"Shall I get you something to drink, mother? Wouldn't you like to go to bed?"

"Of course not. Why should I? I'm not ill!"

She sat there and began to learn patience, staring at the floor, where a dusty track from the door of the sitting room to the door of the empty bedroom had been marked by rough, heavy shoes.

A kitten came in, circumspect and trustful, a common and irre-sistible little kitten four or five months old. He was acting a dignified part for his own edification, pacing grandly, his tail, erect as a candle, in imitation of lordly males. But a sudden and unexpected somersault landed him head over heels at our feet, where he took fright at his own temerity, rolled himself into a ball, stood up on his hind legs, danced sideways, arched his back, and then spun around like a top.

"Look at him, oh, do look at him, Minet-Chéri! Goodness! Isn't he funny!"

And she laughed, sitting there in her mourning, laughed her shrill, young girl's laugh, clapping her hands with delight at the kit-ten. Then, of a sudden, searing memory stemmed that brilliant cas-cade and dried the tears of laughter in my mother's eyes. Yet she offered no excuse for having laughed, either on that day or on the days that followed; for though she had lost the man she passionately loved, in her kindness for us she remained among us just as she always had been, accepting her sorrow as she would have accepted the advent of a long and dreary season, but welcoming from every source the fleeting benediction of joy. So she lived on, swept by shadow and sunshine, bowed by bodily torments, resigned, unpredictable and generous, rich in children, flowers, and animals like a fruitful domain.

. . .

I can still see, on one of the highest shelves of the library, a row of volumes bound in boards, with black linen spines. The firmness of the boards, so smoothly covered in marbled paper, bore witness to my father's manual dexterity. But the titles, handwritten in Gothic lettering, never tempted me, more especially since the black-rimmed labels bore no author's name. I quote from memory: *My Campaigns, The Lessons of '70, The Geodesy of Geodesies, Elegant Algebra, Marshal MacMahon seen by a Fellow Soldier, From Village to Parliament, Zouave Songs* (in verse) . . . I forget the rest.

When my father died, the library became a bedroom and the books left their shelves.

"Just come and see," my elder brother called one day. In his silent way, he was moving the books himself, sorting and opening them in search of a smell of damp-stained paper, of that embalmed mildew from which a vanished childhood rises up, or the pressed petal of a tulip still marbled like a tree agate.

"Just come and see."

The dozen volumes bound in boards revealed to us their secret, a secret so long disdained by us, accessible though it was. Two hundred, three hundred, one hundred and fifty pages to a volume; beautiful, cream-laid paper, or thick "foolscap" carefully trimmed, hundreds and hundreds of blank pages. Imaginary works, the mirage of a writer's career.

There were so many of these virgin pages, spared through timidity or listlessness, that we never saw the end of them. My brother wrote his prescriptions on them, my mother covered her pots of jam with them, her granddaughters tore out the leaves for scribbling, but we never exhausted those cream-laid notebooks, his invisible "works." All the same, my mother exerted herself to that end with a sort of fever of destruction: "You don't mean to say there are still some left? I must have some for cutlet frills. I must have some to line my little drawers with. . . ." And this, not in mockery, but out of piercing regret and the painful desire to blot out this proof of incapacity.

At the time when I was beginning to write, I too drew on this spiritual legacy. Was that where I got my extravagant taste for writing on smooth sheets of fine paper, without the least regard for economy? I dared to cover with my large round handwriting the invisible cursive script, perceptible to only one person in the world, like a shining tracery which carried to a triumphant conclusion the single page lovingly completed and signed, the page that bore the dedication:

> TO MY DEAR SOUL,
> HER FAITHFUL HUSBAND
> JULES-JOSEPH COLETTE

Translated by Una Vicenzo Troubridge
and Enid McLeod.

ALVIN FEINMAN

TRUE NIGHT

So it is midnight, and all
The angels of ordinary day gone,
The abiding absence between day and day
Come like true and only rain
Comes instant, eternal, again:

As though an air had opened without sound
In which all things are sanctified,
In which they are at prayer—
The drunken man in his stupor,
The madman's lucid shrinking circle;

As though all things shone perfectly,
Perfected in self-discrepancy:
The widow wedded to her grief,
The hangman haloed in remorse—
I should not rearrange a leaf,

No more than wish to lighten stones
Or still the sea where it still roars—
Here every grief requires its grief,
Here every longing thing is lit
Like darkness at an altar.

As long as truest night is long,
Let no discordant wing
Corrupt these sorrows into song.

"I see him in the Star, and meet his
sweet velocity in everything that flies."

EMILY DICKINSON

POEMS AND A LETTER

*Emily Dickinson (1830–86) is the preeminent American poet of death. She
treats of it in hundreds of poems, testing conceptions that range from conventional (by nineteenth-century New England standards) to audacious and
irreverent. Yet even in the former cases, the reader cannot fail to recognize
the troubled depths of the poet's mind, its sense of the scandal brewing in
acquired ideas. For Dickinson, death is a personal force, an intimate
agency, sometimes cruel, sometimes courtly, but in any case fervent and
near. Certain of Dickinson's poems of death are among the most frequently
anthologized; here we offer several less often seen.*

*We also offer a letter of lamentation and condolence, written by
Dickinson to the child's mother at the death of her beloved nephew Gilbert,
her brother Austin and her friend Susan Gilbert's son, who was stricken
with typhoid fever when he was ten. A year or so earlier, when he was
recovering from an attack of croup, his aunt wrote teasingly though ten-
derly to him, "Poor Little Gentleman, and so revered—." Her letter to
Susan makes obvious his place in her life and the scale of her reverence.*

*Her grief remained a shadow over Dickinson's last years. Typhoid was a
quick death sentence then. Gilbert's illness lasted only a few days.*

1.
'Twas just this time, last year, I died.
I know I heard the Corn,
When I was carried by the Farm—
It had the Tassels on—

I thought how yellow it would look—
When Richard went to mill—
And then, I wanted to get out,
But something held my will.

I thought just how Red—Apples wedged
The Stubble's joints between—
And Carts went stooping round the fields
To take the Pumpkins in—

I wondered which would miss me, least,
And when Thanksgiving, came,
If Father'd multiply the plates—
To make an even Sum—

And would it blur the Christmas glee
My Stocking hang too high
For any Santa Claus to reach
The Altitude of me—
But this sort, grieved myself,
And so, I thought the other way,
How just this time, some perfect year—
Themself, should come to me—

(1862)

2.
We talked as Girls do—
Fond, and late—
We speculated fair, on every subject, but the Grave—
Of our's, none affair—

We handled Destinies, as cool—
As we—Disposers—be—
And God, a Quiet Party
To our Authority—

But fondest, dwelt upon Ourself
As we eventual—be—
When Girls to Women, softly raised
We—occupy—Degree—

We parted with a contract
To cherish, and to write
But Heaven made both, impossible
Before another night.

                              (1862)

3.
Those who have been in the Grave the longest—
Those who begin Today—
Equally perish from our Practise—
Death is the other way—

Foot of the Bold did least attempt it—
It—is the White Exploit—
Once to achieve, annuls the power
Once to communicate—

                              (1864)

4.
Death is a Dialogue between
The Spirit and the Dust.
"Dissolve" says Death—The Spirit "Sir
I have another Trust"—

Death doubts it—Argues from the Ground
The Spirit turns away
Just laying off for evidence
An Overcoat of Clay.

                                        (1864)

5.
Death is the supple Suitor
That wins at last—
It is a stealthy Wooing
Conducted first
By pallid innuendoes
And dim approach
But brave at last with bugle
And a bisected Coach
It bears away in triumph
To Troth unknown
And Kinsmen as divulgeless
As throngs of Down—
                                        (1878)

6.
Death is like the insect
Menacing the tree,
Competent to kill it,
But decoyed may be.

Bait it with the balsam,
Seek it with the saw,

Baffle, if it cost you
Everything you are.

Then, if it have burrowed
Out of reach of skill
Wring the tree and leave it,
'Tis the vermin's will.

> *(no date)*

A LETTER TO SUSAN GILBERT DICKINSON
(EARLY OCTOBER 1883)

Dear Sue

The Vision of Immortal Life has been fulfilled—

How simply at the last the Fathom comes! The Passenger and not the
Sea, we find surprises us—

Gilbert rejoiced in Secrets—

His Life was panting with them—With what menace of Light he cried
"Dont tell, Aunt Emily"! Now my ascended Playmate must instruct
me. Show us, prattling Preceptor, but the way to thee!

He knew no niggard moment—His Life was full of Boon—The Play-
things of the Dervish were not so wild as his—

No crescent was this Creature—He traveled from the Full—

Such soar, but never set—

I see him in the Star, and meet his sweet velocity in everything that
flies—His Life was like the Bugle, which winds itself away, his Elegy
an echo—his Requiem ecstasy—

Dawn and Meridian in one.

Wherefore would he wait, wronged only of Night, which he left for
us—

Without a speculation, our little Ajax spans the whole—

Pass to thy Rendezvous of Light,
Pangless except for us—
Who slowly ford the Mystery
Which thou hast leaped across!

Emily.

SHARON OLDS

THE DEATH
OF MARILYN MONROE

The ambulance men touched her cold
body, lifted it, heavy as iron,
onto the stretcher, tried to close the
mouth, closed the eyes, tied the
arms to the sides, moved a caught
strand of hair, as if it mattered,
saw the shape of her breasts, flattened by
gravity, under the sheet,
carried her, as if it were she,
down the steps.

These men were never the same. They went out
afterwards, as they always did,
for a drink or two, but they could not meet
each other's eyes.

    Their lives took
a turn—one had nightmares, strange
pains, impotence, depression. One did not
like his work, his wife looked
different, his kids. Even death
seemed different to him—a place where she
would be waiting,

and one found himself standing at night
in the doorway to a room of sleep, listening to a
woman breathing, just an ordinary
woman
breathing.

ONE FIGHT MORE

. . . are not the thoughts of the dying often turned towards the practical, painful, obscure, visceral aspect, towards that "seamy side" of death which is, as it happens, the side that death actually presents to them and forces them to feel, and which far more closely resembles a crushing burden, a difficulty in breathing, a destroying thirst, than the abstract idea to which we are accustomed to give the name Death?

MARCEL PROUST
Swann's Way

❧

"... 'tis in the power of every hand to destroy us, and
wee are beholding unto every one wee meete hee
doth not kill us."

SIR THOMAS BROWNE

RELIGIO MEDICI

*Sir Thomas Browne (1605–82) was a physician and "virtuoso"—as collec-
tors of scientific and antiquarian curiosities were called in his day. (Among
his innumerable holdings, Browne boasted a complete array of bird's eggs,
carefully sorted by species.) Scientists and medical men were widely suspected then of taking their religion lightly, but for Browne the accumulated
arcana of his several fields of study contributed to a thoroughly reverent
understanding of nature and man, a decipherment of what he called the
"hieroglyph," the holy alphabet, of the cosmos. His profession in particular
offered him a long lesson in the fragility of life—a condition which, far from
being lamentable, was for Browne lovely evidence of a working miracle. His
Religio Medici (A Doctor's Religion), from which the following passage is
drawn, offers a reconciliation of empiricist preoccupations and Christian
faith. Browne's manner is less argumentative than contemplative, however.
His principal figure of thought is the New Testament's powerful paradox of
death as the beginning of authentic life: ". . . man seemes," he writes in
metaphors of medicine and chemistry, "but a digestion, or a preparative
way unto that last and glorious Elixar which lies imprisoned in the chaines*

*of flesh. . . ." His prose, with its baroque rhythms and circumlocutions,
seems the verbal counterpart of tomb sculpture: grave yet dramatic, kept
from ponderousness by continual changes of angle and sudden, intimate
foreshortenings. It seeks to be definitive but is unwilling to rest.*

. . . surely there is no torture to the racke of a disease, nor any
Poynyards in death it selfe like those in the way or prologue unto it.
Emor nolo, sed me esse mortuum nihil curo, I would not die, but care not
to be dead. Were I of *Cesars* Religion I should be of his desires, and
wish rather to goe off at one blow, then to be sawed in peeces by the
grating torture of a disease. Men that looke no further than their
outsides thinke health an appertinance unto life, and quarrell with
their constitutions for being sick; I that have examined the parts of
man, and know upon what tender filaments that Fabrick hangs, doe
wonder that we are not alwayes so; and considering the thousand
dores that lead to death doe thanke my God that we can die but once.
'Tis not onely the mischiefe of diseases, and the villanie of poysons
that make an end of us; we vainly accuse the fury of Gunnes, and the
new inventions of death; 'tis in the power of every hand to destroy us,
and wee are beholding unto every one wee meete hee doth not kill us.
There is therefore but one comfort left, that though it be in the power
of the weakest arme to take away life, it is not in the strongest to
deprive us of death: God would not exempt himselfe from that; the
misery of immortality in the flesh he undertooke not, that was in it
immortall. Certainly there is no happinesse within this circle of flesh,
nor is it in the Opticks of these eyes to behold felicity; the first day of
our Jubilee is death; the devill hath therefore fail'd of his desires; wee
are happier with death than we should have beene without it: there is
no misery but in himselfe where there is no end of misery; and so
indeed in his owne sense, the Stoick is in the right: Hee forgets that
hee can die who complaines of misery, wee are in the power of no
calamitie, while death is in our owne.

JAMES MERRILL (1926-95)

AN UPWARD LOOK

O heart green acre   sown with salt
by the departing   occupier

lay down your gallant   spears of wheat
Salt of the earth   each stellar pinch

flung in blind   defiance backwards
now takes its toll   Up from his quieted

quarry the lover   colder and wiser
hauling himself   finds the world turning

toys triumphs   toxins into
this vast facility   the living come
dearest to die in   How did it happen

In bright alternation   minutely mirrored
within the thinking   of each and every

mortal creature   halves of a clue
approach the earthlights   Morning star

evening star   salt of the sky
First the grave   dissolving into dawn

then the crucial   recrystallizing
from inmost depths   of clear dark blue

❧

> "Her death brings to light her unique quality . . . you
> feel that she should have had more room in
> your life—all the room, if need be."

SIMONE de BEAUVOIR

A VERY EASY DEATH

In her account of her mother's final illness, A Very Easy Death *(1964),
Simone de Beauvoir (1908–86) helped establish the genre of the memoir of
loss. Maman, hospitalized for a broken leg, began to suffer from an intesti-
nal obstruction, soon diagnosed as cancer. Stunned by the news of the
cancer, Simone and her sister, Poupette, consented to drastic surgery, knowing that without it their mother would be dead within days, and fearing that
her death would be an appalling one. The operation won them a month's
reprieve. The once routine practice of deceiving the patient about the nature
and seriousness of her condition is recorded here with little commentary.
Maman is not told about the cancer, or even about the surgery she will
undergo ("They will say they are going to X-Ray her again"). Death is in the
room but is never openly acknowledged between the daughters and their
mother. The following selections, in diary-like form, are extracted from de
Beauvoir's larger narrative. The surgeon is referred to as N.*

Maman had just been taken up to her room, N told us. He was
triumphant: she had been half-dead that morning and yet she had

withstood a long and serious operation excellently. Thanks to the very latest methods of anaesthesia her heart, lungs, the whole organism had continued to function normally. There was no sort of doubt that he entirely washed his hands of the consequences of that feat. My sister had said to the surgeon, "Operate on Maman. But if it is cancer, promise me that you will not let her suffer." He had promised. What was his word worth?

. . . my despair escaped from my control: someone other than myself was weeping in me. I talked to Sartre about my mother's mouth as I had seen it that morning and about everything I had interpreted in it—greediness refused, an almost servile humility, hope, distress, loneliness—the loneliness of her death and of her life—that did not want to admit its existence. And he told me that my own mouth was not obeying me any more: I had put Maman's mouth on my own face and in spite of myself, I copied its movements. Her whole person, her whole being, was concentrated there, and compassion wrung my heart.

. . .

. . . My sister told me that according to the doctors a respite of some weeks or even of some months was not impossible. She had said to Professor B, "But what shall we say to Maman when the disease starts again, in another place?" "Don't worry about that. We shall find something to say. We always do. And the patient always believes it."

In the afternoon Maman had her eyes open: she spoke so that one could hardly make out what she said, but sensibly. "Well," I said to her, "so you break your leg and they go and operate on you for appendicitis!"

She raised one finger and, with a certain pride, whispered, "Not appendicitis. Pe-ri-ton-it-is." She added, "What luck . . . be here."

"You are glad that I am here?"

"No. Me." Peritonitis: and her being in this clinic had saved her! The betrayal was beginning. "Glad not to have that tube. So glad!"

———————

What touched our hearts that day was the way she noticed the slight-est agreeable sensation: it was as though, at the age of seventy-eight, she were waking afresh to the miracle of living. While the nurse was settling her pillows the metal of a tube touched her thigh—"It's cool! How pleasant!" She breathed in the smell of eau de Cologne and talcum powder—"how good it smells." She had the bunches of flow-ers and the plants arranged on her wheeled table. "The little red roses come from Meyrignac. At Meyrignac there are roses still." She asked us to raise the curtain that was covering the window and she looked at the golden leaves of the trees. "How lovely. I shouldn't see that from my flat!" She smiled. And both of us, my sister and I, had the same thought: it was that same smile that had dazzled us when we were little children, the radiant smile of a young woman. Where had it been between then and now?

. . .

. . . when I reached home, all the sadness and horror of these last days dropped upon me with all its weight. And I too had a cancer eating into me—remorse. . . . Often, hearing of sick people under-going a long martyrdom, I had felt indignant at the apathy of their relatives. "For my part, I should kill him." At the first trial I had given in: beaten by the ethics of society, I had abjured my own. "No," Sartre said to me. "You were beaten by technique: and that was fatal." Indeed it was. One is caught up in the wheels and dragged along, powerless in the face of specialists' diagnoses, their forecasts, their decisions.

. . .

. . . would I have dared say to N, "Let her go"? That was what I was suggesting when I begged, "Do not torment her," and he had snubbed me with all the arrogance of a man who is certain of his duty. They would have said to me, "You may be depriving her of several years of life." And I was forced to yield. These arguments did not bring me peace. The future horrified me. When I was fifteen my uncle Maurice died of cancer of the stomach. I was told that for days on end he shrieked, "Finish me off. Give me my revolver. Have pity on me."

Would Dr. P keep his promise: "She shall not suffer"? A race had begun between death and torture. I asked myself how one manages to go on living when someone you love has called out to you, "Have pity on me," in vain.

And even if death were to win, all this odious deception! Maman thought that we were with her, next to her; but we were already placing ourselves on the far side of her history. An evil all-knowing spirit, I could see behind the scenes, while she was struggling, far, far away in human loneliness. Her desperate eagerness to get well, her patience, her courage—it was all deceived.

. . .

. . . On Thursday morning, when the maid brought my sister's breakfast, Maman was scarcely out of her coma, but she whispered, "Conf . . . conf . . ."

"Confessor?"

"No. *Confiture.*" She was remembering that my sister liked jam for breakfast.

. . .

On Saturday she had begun a novel by Simenon and had beaten Poupette at crosswords—there was a pile of squares that she cut out of the papers on her table. On Sunday she had had mashed potatoes for lunch which had not gone down properly (in fact it was the beginning of the metastases that played havoc with her) and she had a long waking nightmare. "I was in a blue sheet, over a hole; your sister was holding the sheet and I begged her, 'Don't let me fall into the hole . . .' 'I am holding you; you will not fall,' said Poupette."

Poupette had spent the night sitting up in an armchair and Maman, who was usually anxious about Poupette's sleep, said, "Stay awake; don't let me go. If I go to sleep, wake me up; don't let me go while I am sleeping." At one moment, my sister told me, Maman closed her eyes, exhausted. Her hands clawed the sheets and she articulated, "Live! Live!"

The day of Tuesday passed off well. In the night Maman had horrible dreams. "They put me in a box," she said to my sister. "I am here, but I am in the box. I am myself, and yet it is not me any longer. Men carry the box away!" She struggled. "Don't let them carry me away!"

For a long while Poupette kept her hand on Maman's forehead. "I promise. They shall not put you in the box."

She asked for an extra dose of Equanil. Saved from her visions at last, Maman questioned her. "But what does it all mean, this box, and these men?"

"They are memories of your operation: male nurses carried you on a stretcher."

Maman went to sleep. But in the morning there was all the sadness of a defenseless animal in her eyes.

"So I am getting worse, since you are both here," she murmured.

"We are always here."

"Not both at the same time."

Once again I pretended to be cross. "I'm staying because you are low in your spirits. But if it only worries you, I'll go away."

"No, no," she said, in a downcast voice.

My unfair harshness wrung my heart. At the time the truth was crushing her and when she needed to escape from it by talking, we were condemning her to silence; we forced her to say nothing about her anxieties and to suppress her doubts: as it had so often happened in her life, she felt both guilty and misunderstood. But we had no choice: hope was her most urgent need. . . .

. . . On Monday morning her wasted face terrified me; it was terribly obvious, the work of those mysterious colonies between her skin and her bones that were devouring her cells. . . .

. . . Tranquilized by Equanil and morphia, she was aware of her sickness, but she accepted it patiently. "One day when I thought I was better already your sister said something that has been very useful to me: she said that I should be unwell again. So I know that it's normal."

I had grown very fond of this dying woman. As we talked in the half-darkness I assuaged an old unhappiness; I was renewing the dialogue that had been broken off during my adolescence and that our differences and our likenesses had never allowed us to take up again. And the early tenderness that I had thought dead for ever came to life again, since it had become possible for it to slip into simple words and actions.

How desolate I was, that Wednesday evening, in the cab that was taking me away! I knew this journey through the fashionable quarters by heart: Lancôme, Houbigant, Hermès, Lanvin. Often a red light stopped me in front of Cardin's: I saw ridiculously elegant hats, waistcoats, scarves, slippers, shoes. Farther on there were beautiful downy dressing-gowns, softly coloured: I thought, "I will buy her one to take the place of the red peignoir." Scents, furs, lingerie, jewels: the sumptuous arrogance of a world in which death had no place: but it was there, lurking behind this facade, in the grey secrecy of nursing-homes, hospitals, sick-rooms. And for me that was now the only truth.

She went to sleep. As she opened her eyes she said to me, "When I see a big white wristband I know I am going to wake up. When I go to sleep, I go to sleep in petticoats." What memories, what phantasms were invading her? Her life had always been turned towards the outward world and I found it very moving to see her suddenly lost within herself. She no longer liked to be distracted. That day a friend, Mademoiselle Vauthier, told her an anecdote about a charwoman, with too much liveliness altogether. I quickly got rid of her, for Maman was closing her eyes. When I came back she said, "You ought not to tell sick people stories of that kind; it does not interest them."

At one o'clock Maman stirred again. In a roguish voice she whispered the words of an old refrain that Papa used to sing, *"You are going away and you will leave us."* "No, no," said Poupette, "I shan't leave you," and Maman gave a little knowing smile. She found it harder and harder to breathe. After another injection she murmured in a rather thick voice, "We must . . . keep . . . back . . . desh."

"We must keep back the desk?"

"No," said Maman. "Death." Stressing the word *death* very strongly. She added, "I don't want to die."

"But you are better now!"

After that she wandered a little. "I should have liked to have the time to bring out my book . . . She must be allowed to nurse whoever she likes."

My sister dressed herself: Maman had almost lost consciousness. Suddenly she cried, "I can't breathe!" Her mouth opened, her eyes stared wide, huge in that wasted, ravaged face: with a spasm she entered into coma.

"Go and telephone," said Mademoiselle Cournot.

Poupette rang me up: I did not answer. The operator went on ringing for half an hour before I woke. Meanwhile Poupette went back to Maman: already she was no longer there—her heart was beating and she breathed, sitting there with glassy eyes that saw nothing. And then it was over. "The doctors said she would go out like a candle: it wasn't like that, it wasn't like that at all," said my sister, sobbing.

"But, Madame," replied the nurse, "I assure you it was a very easy death."

And is one to be sorry that the doctors brought her back to life and operated, or not? She, who did not want to lose a single day, "won" thirty: they brought her joys; but they also brought her anxiety and suffering. Since she did escape from the martyrdom that I sometimes thought was hanging over her, I cannot decide for her. For my sister, losing Maman the very day she saw her again would have been a shock from which she would scarcely have recovered. And as for me? Those four weeks have left me pictures, nightmares, sadnesses that I should never have known if Maman had died that Wednesday morning. But I cannot measure the disturbance that I should have felt since my sorrow broke out in a way that I had not foreseen. We did derive an undoubted good from this respite: it saved us, or almost saved us, from remorse. When someone you love dies you pay for the sin of outliving her with a thousand piercing regrets. Her death brings to light her unique quality; she grows as vast as the world that her absence annihilates for her and whose whole existence was caused by her being there; you feel that she should have had more room in your life—all the room, if need be. . . . But since you never do all you might for anyone—not even within the arguable limits that you have set yourself—you have plenty of room left for self-reproach. With regard to Maman we were above all guilty, these last years, of carelessness, omission and abstention. We felt that we atoned for this by the days that we gave up to her, by the peace that our being there gave her, and by the victories gained over fear and pain. Without our obstinate watchfulness she would have suffered far more.

Translated by Patrick O'Brien.

❧

"Even when a woman kills herself like a man, she
nevertheless dies in her bed, like a woman."

NICOLE LORAUX

A WOMAN'S SUICIDE
FOR A MAN'S DEATH

*Life knows two formidable limits, that of death and that of sex. In some
ways, the strength of the latter exceeds that of the former. Or has done in
the mythologies of most cultures. Sex can impose its meaning even upon
death, so that the common fate of the sexes is inflected by gender into
disparate mortalities. As the French classicist Nicole Loraux demonstrates
in these passages from her book* Tragic Ways of Killing a Woman, *gender
was anciently imagined to be a destiny that did not concede its place to
death.*

"For a woman it is already a distressing evil to remain at home,
abandoned, without a husband. And when suddenly one messenger
arrives, and then another, always bringing worse news, and all pro-
claiming disaster for the house . . . ! If this man had received as
many wounds . . . as were reported to his home through various
channels, his body would now have more cuts . . . than a net has

meshes . . . Those were the cruel rumors which made me more than once hang my neck in a noose, from which I was wrenched only by force" (Aeschylus, *Agamemnon* 861–876).

Beyond the lie that the queen handles with consummate skill, there is a truth, or at least an apparent truth, proper to tragedy, which is expressed in these words of Clytemnestra as she welcomes Agamemnon on his return to his palace. The death of a man inevitably calls for the suicide of a woman, his wife. Why should a woman's death counterbalance a man's? Because of the heroic code of honor that tragedy loves to recall, the death of a man could only be that of a warrior on the field of battle. Thus the children of [the murdered] Agamemnon in *The Libation Bearers* dream for a moment of what might have been their father's glorious death under the walls of Troy; and, on merely being told of her husband's death, his wife, immured in her home, would kill herself with a noose round her neck. It was as part of this tragic pattern that Hecuba [the wife of the Trojan King Priam and mother of Hector and Paris, among others] in *The Trojan Women* (1012–14) was bitterly to rebuke Helen because nobody had ever "surprised her in the act of hanging up a noose or sharpening a dagger as a noble-hearted woman . . . would have done in mourning her first husband."

Of course Clytemnestra did not kill herself, any more than her sister Helen did. Not only was the queen no Penelope (even though in her lying speech she speaks of her eyes burning with tears as she lay sleepless, crying for her absent husband), but she was also no ordinary tragic wife. Clytemnestra did not kill herself, and it was Agamemnon who was to die, ensnared in her veil and his body pierced with wounds. She turned death away from herself and brought it upon the king, just as Medea, instead of killing herself, was to kill Jason indirectly through his children and his newly-wed wife. In Clytemnestra, the mother of Iphigenia and the mistress of Aegisthus triumphed over the king's wife. The murdering queen denied the law of femininity, that in the extreme of misery a knotted rope should provide the way out.

Finding a way out in suicide was a tragic solution, one that was morally disapproved in the normal run of everyday life. But, most important, it was a woman's solution and not, as has sometimes been claimed, a heroic act. That the hero Ajax, both in Sophocles and in the epic tradition, killed himself was one thing; that he killed himself in a virile manner was another, and I shall come back to this. But to infer from this example that in the Greek imagination all suicide was inspired by *andreia* (the Greek word for courage as a male characteristic) is a step we should not take. Heracles in Euripides without doubt conforms much more to the traditional ethic when, from the depths of his disasters, he agrees to go on living. In the case of mere citizens, things are even clearer. Nothing was further from suicide than the [citizen-soldiers'] imperative of a "fine death," which must be accepted and not sought. We know that after the battle of Plataea the Spartan Aristodamus was deprived by his fellow citizens of the posthumous glory of appearing on the roll of valor because he had sought death too openly in action. Whether he were a Spartan or not, a warrior committed suicide only when struck by dishonor, as Othryadas did in book I of Herodotus and Pantites in book VII. Plato in the *Laws* echoes these practices; he is prescribing laws but is loyal to civic conventions when he lays down that the suicide should be formally punished, "for total lack of manliness," by being buried in a solitary and unmarked grave on the edge of the city, in the darkness of anonymity. . . . I would add (and it is relevant) that the Greek language, in the absence of a special word for suicide, describes the act by resorting to the same words as are used for the murder of parents, that ultimate ignominy.

Suicide, then, could be the tragic death chosen under the weight of necessity by those on whom fell "the intolerable pain of a misfortune from which there is no way out." But in tragedy itself it was mainly a woman's death. There was one form of suicide—an already despised form of death—that was more disgraceful and associated more than any other with irremediable dishonor. This was hanging, a hideous death, or more exactly a "formless" death . . . , the extreme of defilement that one inflicted on oneself only in the utmost shame. It also turns out—but is it just chance?—that hanging is a woman's way of death: Jocasta, Phaedra, Leda, Antigone ended in this way, while outside tragedy there were deaths of innumerable young girls who hanged themselves, to give rise to a special cult or to illustrate the mysteries of female physiology.

Hanging was a woman's death. As practiced by women it could lead to endless variations, because women and young girls contrived to substitute for the customary rope those adornments with which they decked themselves and which were also the emblems of their sex, as Antigone strangled herself with her knotted veil. Veils, belts, headbands—all these instruments of seduction were death traps for those who wore them, as *The Suppliant Maidens* [fleeing a sentence of forced marriage to their uncle's sons] explained to King Pelasgus of Argos [with whom they sought refuge]. To borrow Aeschylus' powerful expression, there was here a fine trick . . . by which erotic . . . persuasion became the agent of the most sinister threat.

If we are to believe Euripides, Thanatos (Death) was armed with a sword. This was certainly not pure chance. If death, the same for all, makes no distinction between its victims and cuts the hair of men and women alike, it was for Thanatos, the male incarnation of death, to carry the sword, the emblem of a man's demise.

A man worthy of the name could die only by the sword or the spear of another, on the field of battle. . . .

An astonishing interplay of the seen and the hidden, by which we do not see a woman's death, but do see the dead woman. Then, as though the last ban had been lifted on staring at this mournful scene, the dramatic action could continue—even, as it does in Euripides' *Hippolytus,* center itself on the corpse of the dead woman and her silent presence. Phaedra had disappeared [into suicide], but her corpse was there, released from the fatal noose to be laid out on the ground as was seemly—the corpse which she had wanted to make into evidence against Hippolytus and which, though silent forever, yet bore the message of the absent woman. That was, without the shadow of a doubt, a very feminine way of exploiting one's own death. In the case of Ajax, whose dead body was at least as important a dramatic element as that of Phaedra, things are very different, and what is seen and what is hidden do not bear at all the same relation to one another. As Ajax is the model of the manly suicide, it follows that he has the right to kill himself in front of the spectators; but because his death is only a poor imitation of a warrior's noble death, there is a ban on seeing his body. . . .

. . .

Let us come back to the door of that closed place where a woman takes refuge to die, far out of sight. With its solid bolts that have to be forced back for the dead woman to be reached—or rather the dead body from which the woman has already fled—this room reveals the narrow space that tragedy grants to women for the exercise of their freedom. They are free enough to kill themselves, but they are not free enough to escape from the space to which they belong, and the remote sanctum where they meet their death is equally the symbol of their life—a life that finds its meaning outside the self and is fulfilled only in the institutions of marriage and maternity, which tie women to the world and lives of men. It is by men that women meet their death, and it is for men, usually, that they kill themselves. By a man, for a man: not all texts make the distinction, but Sophocles is particularly careful to mark it—in the *Antigone* where Eurydice [not Orpheus's beloved, but the wife of Creon], dies *for* her sons but *because* of Creon, and in *The Women of Trachis,* where Deianira dies *because* of her son Hyllos but *for* love of her husband Heracles [whose death she has unwittingly caused, thus earning Hyllos's bitter condemnation]. So the death of women confirms or reestablishes their connection with marriage and maternity.

     The place where women kill themselves, to give it its name, is the marriage chamber, the *thalamos.* Deianira plunges into it, as does Jocasta [Oedipus's mother and wife]. Euripides' Alcestis sheds her last tears there before facing Thanatos [as a surrogate for her husband, whose life her willing death prolongs]; and when she leaves the palace to die, it is toward this place that she turns her thoughts and her regrets. As for the funeral pyre of Capaneus [killed for vainglory by Zeus's lightning bolt], onto which Evadne hurls herself to renew her union in the flesh with her husband, it is described [by Aeschylus in *The Seven Against Thebes*] as *thalamai* (funeral chamber), a word that encapsulates the many connections of her death with marriage.

If the *thalamos* is in the depths of the house, there is also within the *thalamos* the bed, scene of the pleasure that the institution of marriage tolerates if it is not excessive and, above all, the place of procreation. No death of a woman takes place without involving the bed. It is there, and there alone, that Deianira and Jocasta are able, before suicide, to affirm their identity to themselves. It is there that Deianira even dies, on that couch that she had too much associated with the pleasures of the *nymphe*. Even when a woman kills herself like a man, she nevertheless dies in her bed, like a woman.

Finally, by fastening the rope to the ceiling of the marriage chamber, Jocasta and Phaedra call attention to the symbolic framework of the house. The rooftree, which the *Odyssey* called *melathron*, Euripides calls *teramna*. By metonymy it can mean the palace considered in its dimension of verticality; but it goes even further. From Sappho's epithalamium ("Come, carpenters, lift up the rooftree [*melathron*], Hymanaeus, for here enters the house a bridegroom the equal of Ares") to Euripides, the roof seems to have been much connected with the husband, whose tall stature it dominates and protects. One might perhaps recall that Clytemnestra, in her irreproachable speech that is also a total lie, called Agamemnon "the column sustaining the high roof" (*Agamemnon* 897–898) Just before a woman leaps into the void, it is the missing presence of the man that she feels for the last time, in every corner of the *thalamos*.

Translated by Anthony Forster.

SONS AND
DAUGHTERS

Speak well of moonlight on a winding stair,
Of light-boned children under great green oaks;
The wonder, yes, but death should not be there.

W. H. AUDEN
"One Circumlocution"

❧

"I have often longed to
see my mother in the doorway."

GRACE PALEY

MOTHER

*In this short reverie on her mother, writer and political activist Grace Paley
evokes the ephemeral quality of recollection—and of life itself, in its baffling
counterpoint with the persistent, tenacious longing for the tangible presence
of a parent.*

One day I was listening to the AM radio. I heard a song: Oh, I Long
to See My Mother in the Doorway. By God! I said, I understand that
song. I have often longed to see my mother in the doorway. As a
matter of fact, she did stand frequently in various doorways looking at
me. She stood one day just so, at the front door, the darkness of the
hallway behind her. It was New Year's Day. She said sadly, If you
come home at 4:00 A.M. when you're seventeen, what time will you
come home when you're twenty? She asked this question without
humor or meanness. She had begun her worried preparations for
death. She would not be present, she thought, when I was twenty. So
she wondered.

Another time she stood in the doorway of my room. I had just issued a political manifesto attacking the family's position on the Soviet Union. She said, Go to sleep for godsakes, you damn fool, you and your Communist ideas. We saw them already, Papa and me, in 1905. We guessed it all.

At the door of the kitchen she said, You never finish your lunch. You run around senselessly. What will become of you?

Then she died.

Naturally for the rest of my life I longed to see her, not only in doorways, in a great number of places—in the dining room with my aunts, at the window looking up and down the block, in the country garden among zinnias and marigolds, in the living room with my father.

They sat in comfortable leather chairs. They were listening to Mozart. They looked at one another amazed. It seemed to them that they'd just come over on the boat. They'd just learned the first English words. It seemed to them that he had just proudly handed in a 100 percent correct exam to the American anatomy professor. It seemed as though she'd just quit the shop for the kitchen.

I wish I could see her in the doorway of the living room.

She stood there a minute. Then she sat beside him. They owned an expensive record player. They were listening to Bach. She said to him, Talk to me a little. We don't talk so much anymore.

I'm tired, he said. Can't you see? I saw maybe thirty people today. All sick, all talk talk talk talk. Listen to the music, he said. I believe you once had perfect pitch. I'm tired, he said.

Then she died.

"... there is also something very gallant about children
at such moments. It has something to do with their
silence and gravity and with the fact that one
cannot help them."

JAMES BALDWIN

NOTES OF A NATIVE SON

In these pages from Notes of a Native Son, *James Baldwin (1924–87)
chronicles the eventful day of his father's funeral. Long unstable, David
Baldwin, Sr., was placed in a mental hospital shortly before he died of
tuberculosis. Baldwin's struggle with this complex man (who was in fact his
stepfather and the father of James's eight younger siblings) continued long
after his death, as James reworked and rediscovered his father's legacy to
him. In* The Devil Finds Work *(1975), written twenty years after* Notes,
*he comments: "... the pride and sorrow and beauty of my father's face:
for that man I called my father really was my father in every sense except
the biological, or literal one. He formed me, and he raised me, and he did
not let me starve: and he gave me something, however harshly, and however little I wanted it, which prepared me for an impending horror which he
could not prevent."*

*Baldwin's first and last books were partly dedicated to him. In this
death, and in the surrounding events, Baldwin describes how he found a
way out of the rage and despair that threatened to engulf him during the
racially explosive years of the Second World War.*

On the 29th of July, in 1943, my father died. On the same day, a few hours later, his last child was born. Over a month before this, while all our energies were concentrated in waiting for these events, there had been, in Detroit, one of the bloodiest race riots of the century. A few hours after my father's funeral, while he lay in state in the undertaker's chapel, a race riot broke out in Harlem. On the morning of the 3rd of August, we drove my father to the graveyard through a wilderness of smashed plate glass.

The day of my father's funeral had also been my nineteenth birthday. As we drove him to the graveyard, the spoils of injustice, anarchy, discontent, and hatred were all around us. It seemed to me that God himself had devised, to mark my father's end, the most sustained and brutally dissonant of codas. And it seemed to me, too, that the violence which rose all about us as my father left the world had been devised as a corrective for the pride of his eldest son. I had declined to believe in that apocalypse which had been central to my father's vision; very well, life seemed to be saying, here is something that will certainly pass for an apocalypse until the real thing comes along. I had inclined to be contemptuous of my father for the conditions of his life, for the conditions of our lives. When his life had ended I began to wonder about that life and also, in a new way, to be apprehensive about my own.

. . .

For my father's funeral I had nothing black to wear and this posed a nagging problem all day long. It was one of those problems, simple, or impossible of solution, to which the mind insanely clings in order to avoid the mind's real trouble. I spent most of that day at the downtown apartment of a girl I knew, celebrating my birthday with whiskey and wondering what to wear that night. When planning a birthday celebration one naturally does not expect that it will be up against competition from a funeral and this girl had anticipated taking me out that night, for a big dinner and a night club afterwards. Sometime during the course of that long day we decided that we would go out anyway, when my father's funeral service was over. I imagine *I* decided it, since, as the funeral hour approached, it became clearer and clearer to me that I would not know what to do with myself when it was over. The girl, stifling her very lively concern as to the possible effects of the whiskey on one of my father's chief mourners, concentrated on being conciliatory and practically helpful. She found a black shirt for me somewhere and ironed it and, dressed in the darkest pants and jacket I owned, and slightly drunk, I made my way to my father's funeral.

The chapel was full, but not packed, and very quiet. There were, mainly, my father's relatives, and his children, and here and there I saw faces I had not seen since childhood, the faces of my father's one-time friends. They were very dark and solemn now, seeming somehow to suggest that they had known all along that something like this would happen. Chief among the mourners was my aunt, who had quarreled with my father all his life; by which I do not mean to suggest that her mourning was insincere or that she had not loved him. I suppose that she was one of the few people in the world who had, and their incessant quarreling proved precisely the strength of the tie that bound them. The only other person in the world, as far as I knew, whose relationship to my father rivaled my aunt's in depth was my mother, who was not there.

It seemed to me, of course, that it was a very long funeral. But it was, if anything, a rather shorter funeral than most, nor, since there were no overwhelming, uncontrollable expressions of grief, could it be called—if I dare to use the word—successful. The minister who preached my father's funeral sermon was one of the few my father had still been seeing as he neared his end. He presented to us in his sermon a man whom none of us had ever seen—a man thoughtful, patient, and forbearing, a Christian inspiration to all who knew him, and a model for his children. And no doubt the children, in their disturbed and guilty state, were almost ready to believe this; he had been remote enough to be anything and, anyway, the shock of the incontrovertible, that it was really our father lying up there in that casket, prepared the mind for anything. His sister moaned and this grief-stricken moaning was taken as corroboration. The other faces held a dark, non-committal thoughtfulness. This was not the man they had known, but they had scarcely expected to be confronted with *him;* this was, in a sense deeper than questions of fact, the man they had not known, and the man they had not known may have been the real one. The real man, whoever he had been, had suffered and now he was dead: this was all that was sure and all that mattered now. Every man in the chapel hoped that when his hour came he, too, would be eulogized, which is to say forgiven, and that all of his lapses, greeds, errors, and strayings from the truth would be invested with coherence and looked upon with charity. This was perhaps the last thing human beings could give each other and it was what they demanded, after all, of the Lord. Only the Lord saw the midnight tears, only He was present when one of His children, moaning and wringing hands, paced up and down the room. When one slapped one's child in anger the recoil in the heart reverberated through heaven and became part of the pain of the universe. And when the children were hungry and sullen and distrustful and one watched them, daily, growing wilder, and further away, and running headlong into danger, it was the Lord who knew what the charged heart endured as the strap was laid to the backside; the Lord alone who knew what one *would* have said if one had had, like the Lord, the gift of the living word. It was the Lord who knew of the impossibility every parent in that room faced: how to prepare the child for the day when the child would be despised and how to *create* in the child—by what means?—a stronger antidote to this poison than one had found for oneself. The avenues, side streets, bars, billiard halls, hospitals, police stations, and even the playgrounds of Harlem—not to mention the houses of correction, the jails, and the morgue—testified to the potency of the poison while remaining silent as to the efficacy of whatever antidote, irresistibly raising the question of whether or not such an antidote existed; raising, which was worse, the question of whether or not an antidote was desirable; perhaps poison should be fought with poison. With these several schisms in the mind and with more terrors in the heart than could be named, it was better not to judge the man who had gone down under an impossible burden. It was better to remember: *Thou knowest this man's fall; but thou knowest not his wrassling.*

While the preacher talked and I watched the children—years of changing their diapers, scrubbing them, slapping them, taking them to school, and scolding them had had the perhaps inevitable result of making me love them, though I am not sure I knew this then—my mind was busily breaking out with a rash of disconnected impressions. Snatches of popular songs, indecent jokes, bits of books I had read, movie sequences, faces, voices, political issues—I thought I was going mad; all these impressions suspended, as it were, in the solution of the faint nausea produced in me by the heat and liquor. For a moment I had the impression that my alcoholic breath, inefficiently disguised with chewing gum, filled the entire chapel. Then someone began singing one of my father's favorite songs and, abruptly, I was with him, sitting on his knee, in the hot, enormous, crowded church which was the first church we attended. It was the Abyssinian Baptist Church on 138th Street. We had not gone there long. With this image, a host of others came. I had forgotten, in the rage of my growing up, how proud my father had been of me when I was little. Apparently, I had had a voice and my father had liked to show me off before the members of the church. I had forgotten what he had looked like when he was pleased but now I remembered that he had always been grinning with pleasure when my solos ended. I even remembered certain expressions on his face when he teased my mother—had he loved her? I would never know. And when had it all begun to change? For now it seemed that he had not always been cruel. I remembered being taken for a haircut and scraping my knee on the footrest of the barber's chair and I remembered my father's face as he soothed my crying and applied the stinging iodine. Then I remembered our fights, fights which had been of the worst possible kind because my technique had been silence.

I remembered the one time in all our life together when we had really spoken to each other.

It was on a Sunday and it must have been shortly before I left home. We were walking, just the two of us, in our usual silence, to or from church. I was in high school and had been doing a lot of writing and I was, at about this time, the editor of the high school magazine. But I had also been a Young Minister and had been preaching from the pulpit. Lately, I had been taking fewer engagements and preached as rarely as possible. It was said in the church, quite truthfully, that I was "cooling off."

My father asked me abruptly, "You'd rather write than preach, wouldn't you?"

I was astonished at his question—because it was a real question. I answered, "Yes."

That was all we said. It was awful to remember that that was all we had *ever* said.

The casket now was opened and the mourners were being led up the aisle to look for the last time on the deceased. The assumption was that the family was too overcome with grief to be allowed to make this journey alone and I watched while my aunt was led to the casket and, muffled in black, and shaking, led back to her seat. I disapproved of forcing the children to look on their dead father, considering that the shock of his death, or, more truthfully, the shock of death as a reality, was already a little more than a child could bear, but my judgment in this matter had been overruled and there they were, bewildered and frightened and very small, being led, one by one, to the casket. But there is also something very gallant about children at such moments. It has something to do with their silence and gravity and with the fact that one cannot help them. Their legs, somehow, seem *exposed,* so that it is at once incredible and terribly clear that their legs are all they have to hold them up.

I had not wanted to go to the casket myself and I certainly had not wished to be led there, but there was no way of avoiding either of these forms. One of the deacons led me up and I looked on my father's face. I cannot say that it looked like him at all. His blackness had been equivocated by powder and there was no suggestion in that casket of what his power had or could have been. He was simply an old man dead, and it was hard to believe that he had ever given anyone either joy or pain. Yet, his life filled that room. Further up the avenue his wife was holding his newborn child. Life and death so close together, and love and hatred, and right and wrong, said something to me which I did not want to hear concerning man, concerning the life of man.

After the funeral, while I was downtown desperately celebrating my birthday, a Negro soldier, in the lobby of the Hotel Braddock, got into a fight with a white policeman over a Negro girl. Negro girls, white policemen, in or out of uniform, and Negro males—in or out of uniform—were part of the furniture of the lobby of the Hotel Braddock and this was certainly not the first time such an incident had occurred. It was destined, however, to receive an unprecedented publicity, for the fight between the policeman and the soldier ended with the shooting of the soldier. Rumor, flowing immediately to the streets outside, stated that the soldier had been shot in the back, an instantaneous and revealing invention, and that the soldier had died protecting a Negro woman. The facts were somewhat different—for example, the soldier had not been shot in the back, and was not dead, and the girl seems to have been as dubious a symbol of womanhood as her white counterpart in Georgia usually is, but no one was interested in the facts. They preferred the invention because this invention expressed and corroborated their hates and fears so perfectly. It is just as well to remember that people are always doing this. Perhaps many of those legends, including Christianity, to which the world clings began their conquest of the world with just some such concerted surrender to distortion. The effect, in Harlem, of this particular legend was like the effect of a lit match in a tin of gasoline. The mob gathered before the doors of the Hotel Braddock simply began to swell and to spread in every direction, and Harlem exploded.

. . .

"But as for me and my house," my father had said, "we will serve the Lord." I wondered, as we drove him to his resting place, what this line had meant for him. I had heard him preach it many times. I had preached it once myself, proudly giving it an interpretation different from my father's. Now the whole thing came back to me, as though my father and I were on our way to Sunday school and I were memo-

rizing the golden text: *And if it seem evil unto you to serve the Lord,
choose you this day whom you will serve; whether the gods which your
fathers served that were on the other side of the flood or the gods of the
Amorites, in whose land ye dwell: but as for me and my house, we will
serve the Lord.* I suspected in these familiar lines a meaning which had
never been there for me before. All of my father's texts and songs,
which I had decided were meaningless, were arranged before me at
his death like empty bottles, waiting to hold the meaning which life
would give them for me. This was his legacy: nothing is ever escaped.
That bleakly memorable morning I hated the unbelievable streets and
the Negroes and whites who had, equally, made them that way. But I
knew that it was folly, as my father would have said, this bitterness
was folly. It was necessary to hold on to the things that mattered. The
dead man mattered, the new life mattered; blackness and whiteness
did not matter; to believe that they did was to acquiesce in one's own
destruction. Hatred, which could destroy so much, never failed to
destroy the man who hated and this was an immutable law.

It began to seem that one would have to hold in the mind
forever two ideas which seemed to be in opposition. The first idea was
acceptance, the acceptance, totally without rancor, of life as it is, and
men as they are: in the light of this idea, it goes without saying that
injustice is a commonplace. But this did not mean that one could be
complacent, for the second idea was of equal power: that one must
never, in one's own life, accept these injustices as commonplace but
must fight them with all one's strength. This fight begins, however, in
the heart and it now had been laid to my charge to keep my own heart
free of hatred and despair. This intimation made my heart heavy and,
now that my father was irrecoverable, I wished that he had been
beside me so that I could have searched his face for the answers which
only the future would give me now.

"Dying is work and he was a worker."

PHILIP ROTH

PATRIMONY

Philip Roth accompanied his eighty-six-year-old, widowed father, Herman, through each stage of his final ordeal, his death from a brain tumor. In the first of two passages from Patrimony: A True Story, *Roth presents his father with a living will, and in the second, Roth is compelled to enforce it. (Philip Roth's hospital stay, mentioned in passing, was for a bypass operation.)*

"What happened to Charlie Raskus?"

"He's dead. He died. Natural causes. He wasn't that old. Even the bastards die," my father said.

"That's about the only good thing you can say for death—it gets the sons of bitches, too."

About ten-thirty, after we'd caught the Mets score on the news and he seemed, at least for the moment, to have been distracted from his gloom, I took the living wills, his and mine, which I'd carried rather officially with me in something I rarely ever use—my ancient briefcase—and drove with them back to New York, thinking maybe it was a mistake to force him to face the most bitter of all possibilities. "Enough," I thought, and went home, where, unable to sleep, I passed the night studying, in Appendix V [of *The Jewish Boxers' Hall of Fame*], the won-and-lost records of some fifty Jewish world champions and contenders, including Jersey's own Abie Bain, who'd won forty-eight—thirty-one by knockout—lost eleven, and, strangely, according to this book, had thirty-one no decisions.

Early the next morning, however, before he'd begun to have a chance to be worn down by worrying, I telephoned my father and launched into my spiel: I told him how my lawyer had suggested that I ought to have a living will, how she had explained its function to me, how I had said it sounded like a good idea and had asked her as she was preparing one for me, to draw up one for him as well. I said, "Let me read you mine. Listen." And of course, his reaction was nothing like what I'd feared it would be.

How could I have forgotten that I was dealing with somebody who'd spent a lifetime talking to people about the thing they least wanted to think about? When I was a small boy and would go with him to his office on a Saturday morning, he used to tell me, "Life insurance is the hardest thing in the world to sell. You know why? Because the only way the customer can win is if he dies." He was an old and knowledgeable expert in these contracts dealing with death, more used to them by far than I was, and as I slowly read him each sentence over the phone, he responded as matter-of-factly as if I were reading the fine-print boilerplate prose off an insurance policy.

" 'Measures of artificial life support in the face of impending death,' " I read, " 'that I specifically refuse are: (a) Electrical or mechanical resuscitation of my heart when it has stopped beating.' "

"Uh-huh," he said.

" '(b) Nasogastric tube feeding'—that's feeding through the nose—'when I am paralyzed or unable to take nourishment by mouth.' "

"Uh-huh, yeah."

" '(c) Mechanical respiration when I am no longer able to sustain my own breathing.' "

"Uh-huh."

I continued on through to where my brother and I were named as the people who should make his medical decisions for him if he became unable to do so. Then I said, "So? How does it strike you?"

"Send it over and I'll sign."

And that was it. Instead of feeling like the insurance man's son, I felt like an insurance man myself. One who'd just sold his first policy to a customer who could win only if he died.

. . .

On the bureau across from the sofa was the enlargement of the fifty-two-year-old snapshot, taken with a box camera at the Jersey shore, that my brother and I also had framed and situated prominently in our houses. We are posing in our bathing suits, one Roth directly behind the other, in the yard outside the Bradley Beach rooming house where our family rented a bedroom and kitchen privileges for a month each summer. This is August of 1937. We are four, nine and thirty-six. The three of us rise upward to form a V, my two tiny sandals its pointed base, and the width of my father's solid shoulders—between which Sandy's pixyish bright face is exactly centered—the letter's two impressive serifs. Yes, V for Victory is written all over that picture: for Victory, for Vacation, for upright, unbent Verticality! There we are, the male line, unimpaired and happy, ascending from nascency to maturity!

To unite into a single image the robust solidity of the man in the picture with that strickenness on the sofa was and was not an impossibility. Trying with all my mental strength to join the two fathers and make them one was a bewildering, even hellish job. And yet I suddenly did feel (or made myself feel) that I could perfectly well remember (or make myself think I remembered) the very moment when that picture had been taken, over half a century before. I could even believe (or make myself believe) that our lives only seemed to have filtered through time, that everything was actually happening simultaneously, that I was as much back in Bradley with him towering over me as here in Elizabeth with him all but broken at my feet.

"What is it?" I asked when I realized that merely from seeing me he was upset enough to cry. "Dad—I'm fine now," I said. "You can tell that. Look at me. Look. Dad, what's the matter?"

"I should have been there," he told me in a breaking voice, the words barely words now because of what the paralysis had made of his mouth. "I should have been there!" he repeated, this time with fury.

He meant by my side at the hospital.

He died three weeks later. During a twelve-hour ordeal that began just before midnight on October 24, 1989, and ended just after noon the next day, he fought for every breath with an awesome eruption, a final display, of his lifelong obstinate tenacity. It was something to see.

Early on the morning of his death, when I arrived at the hospital emergency room to which he had been rushed from his bedroom at home, I was confronted by an attending physician prepared to take extraordinary measures and to put him on a breathing machine. Without it there was no hope, though, needless to say—the doctor added—the machine wasn't going to reverse the progress of the tumor, which appeared to have begun to attack his respiratory function. The doctor also informed me that, by law, once my father had been hooked up to the machine he would not be disconnected, unless he could once again sustain breathing on his own. A decision had to be made immediately and, since my brother was still en route by plane from Chicago, by me alone.

And I who had explained to my father the provisions of the living will and got him to sign it, didn't know what to do. How could I say no to the machine if it meant that he needn't continue to endure this agonizing battle to breathe? How could I take it on myself to decide that my father should be finished with life, life which is ours to know just once? Far from invoking the living will, I was nearly on the verge of ignoring it and saying, "Anything! Anything!"

I asked the doctor to leave me alone with my father, or as alone as he and I could be in the middle of the emergency room bustle. As I sat there and watched him struggle to go on living, I tried to focus on what the tumor had done with him already. This wasn't difficult, given that he looked on that stretcher as though by then he'd been through a hundred rounds with Joe Louis. I thought about the misery that was sure to come, provided he could even be kept alive on a respirator. I saw it all, all, and yet I had to sit there for a very long time before I leaned as close to him as I could get and, with my lips to his sunken, ruined face, found it in me finally to whisper, "Dad, I'm going to have to let you go." He'd been unconscious for several hours and couldn't hear me, but, shocked, amazed, and weeping, I repeated it to him again and then again, until I believed it myself.

After that, all I could do was to follow his stretcher up to the room where they put him and sit by the bedside. Dying is work and he was a worker. Dying is horrible and my father was dying. I held his hand, which at least still felt like his hand: I stroked his forehead, which at least still looked like his forehead; and I said to him all sorts of things that he could no longer register. Luckily, there wasn't anything I told him that morning that he didn't already know.

Later in the day, at the bottom of a bureau drawer in my father's bedroom, my brother came upon a shallow box containing two neatly folded prayer shawls. These he hadn't parted with. These he hadn't ferreted off to the Y locker room or given away to one of his great-nephews. The older tallis I took home with me and we buried him in the other. When the mortician, at the house, asked us to pick out a suit for him, I said to my brother, "A suit? He's not going to the office. No, no suit—it's senseless." He should be buried in a shroud, I said, thinking that was how his parents had been buried and how Jews were buried traditionally. But as I said it I wondered if a shroud was any less senseless: he wasn't Orthodox and his sons weren't religious at all—and if it wasn't perhaps pretentiously literary and a little hysterically sanctimonious as well. I thought how bizarrely out-of-character an urban earthling like my insurance-man father, a sturdy man rooted all his life in everydayness, would look in a shroud even while I understood that that was the idea. But as nobody opposed me and as I hadn't the audacity to say, "Bury him naked," we used the shroud of our ancestors to clothe his corpse.

ANNE SEXTON (1928–74)

THE CHILD-BEARERS

Jean, death comes close to us all,
flapping its awful wings at us
and the gluey wings crawl up our nose.
Our children tremble in their teen-age cribs,
whirling off on a thumb or a motorcycle,
mine pushed into gnawing a stilbestrol cancer
I passed on like hemophilia,
or yours in the seventh grade, with her spleen
smacked in by the balance beam.

And we, mothers, crumpled, and flyspotted
with bringing them this far
can do nothing now but pray.

Let us put your three children
and my two children,
ages ranging from eleven to twenty-one,

and send them in a large air net up to God,
with many stamps, *real* air mail,
and huge signs attached:
SPECIAL HANDLING
DO NOT STAPLE, FOLD OR MUTILATE!
And perhaps He will notice
and pass a psalm over them
for keeping safe for a whole,
for a whole God-damned life-span.

And not even a muddled angel will
peek down at us in our foxhole.
And He will not have time
to send down an eyedropper of prayer for us,
the mothering thing of us,
as we drop into the soup
and drown
in the worry festering inside us,
lest our children go so fast
they go.

꙰

"In the body that I once lived within,
I saw my past and my future."

ELIZABETH ROSEN

MY MOTHER'S DEATH

The bond of daughter to mother may be unique in its a priori intimacy, a sense of identification both deeper and more intricate than the familiar psychology of "role models" can explain. In the following essay, attorney and literary-critic Elizabeth Rosen searchingly recounts her own grateful discovery of the strength of this bond, and her gradual recognition of its presence in surprising regions of her life, during her mother's last illness.

Summer knowledge is not the winter's truth.
DELMORE SCHWARTZ

My mother was diagnosed with cancer a year before she died of it. She spent six months in chemotherapy, and during part of this time she enjoyed the odd medical syndrome known as *la belle indifférence*.

This syndrome is associated with patients who have been diagnosed with a fatal illness. *La belle indifférence* is a mixture of denial and a last gasp embrace of life, and patients with this syndrome experience a giddy lightheartedness despite their prognoses. My mother, like many elderly widows, had become measured in her pleasures—most things cost too much, or were too fattening. After her diagnosis, she changed. When we visited a restaurant, she took childlike delight in the variety of the menu. No more did she demure, or refuse temptation. She even made fast friends with the waiters. Shopping in a department store left her elated. When her hair fell out and she had to wear a wig, she was convinced that store keepers showed her greater deference, men held doors open for her, all because her "hair" would now at last hold a set. Death might have been breathing down her neck, but I could not recall when she had been more garrulous, or more engaged in living.

Eventually, however, she came home to die, and I moved back into my childhood home to take care of her. The summer seemed at times to stop, and often I would look at the expiration date on the milk carton and think, still? it is good even yet? Still time has not moved? Death had moved in, and we felt it lumbering slowly all through the house.

When I was a child, I am told I used to ask in grave tones, "Is today tomorrow?" I was an uninitiate, still learning the secrets of the big hand of the clock. I can remember staring at the second hand of my father's watch, and trying to figure out what ordered all of this. It confused me then, these demarcations we now accept, the rifts we travel past.

Fifteen years ago, my father died, and when he did, I thought no loss could equal his. His once portly and solid frame became hunched and frail, his expansive voice grew weak, his eyes, always so glad to see me, grew distant and unfocused. Against each of these changes, I railed inwardly. But these changes occurred in someone else, a body not my own. As much as I loved him, we were separate. With my mother, there was no such distinction. Her coughs rattled my chest. There was no part of her I did not know.

We had always had the same pear shape—slim at the midriff and waist, and thick in the hips and thighs. All our lives we fought against the same fifteen pounds that would disappear and return. As a grown woman, when I started to see the familiar etching of varicose veins on my legs, I hoped they would not grow as pronounced as hers. But now I see a kind of eschatology of the flesh. That slightly sunken hollow underneath my eyes will some day mirror her cadaverous stare. Now I can see with a physical certainty how my legs, too, may someday be a tangle of femurs without flesh, how my energy may spend itself by inhaling, how speech and thought, action and appetite finally expire. In the body that I once lived within, I saw my past and my future. As her body has gone, so I imagine will my own.

On one summer afternoon, two weeks before she died, when I was alone with her, I had bent down to kiss her, and she whispered, "I will always be holding you, Liz." She fell asleep, and I sat on the living room couch fitfully writing in a journal. I wrote, "How I wish I could hold on to this moment, in my childhood home, Mom asleep in her bed, Robert Frost's poetry in my lap, and I, for a brief moment am master here, in the bosom of this love, in the exquisite sweetness of this hour before the fall, while all that will be lost is still here."

I had never wanted to stop time, and I am not certain that I did then. But I have never felt its talons so deeply, its movement so keenly. I knew that a moment was before me, and in that moment I would be saved from many things and lost to many others. I listened for it, and was grateful every time I did not hear it.

My older sister and I, born of the same genes, reared with the same accidents of history, had completely different reactions to what was before us. I was afraid to leave the house; she was afraid to stay in it. I was afraid I might not be there at the moment all this ended. She was terrified she might be.

It was a death my mother might have chosen. She was in the home she loved, surrounded by the people and things she cared most for. But if my mother were here, she would rebel at these words—she knew she was dying, she was gracious about life, she was gracious to us all, but she was not gracious about her death. As wasted and ill as she was, she did not want to leave—not us, not her backyard or her flats of petunias, or her unopened mail, her scented soaps or her dog-eared books. It was only in death that my mother was not wanting something. Only in death did that engine of want, the thing that kept her alive and so strong, stop.

For a series of weeks and days, she grew incredibly smaller, like those wooden nesting dolls, where each contains one smaller than the one that contained it. The house was filled not with the largeness of death, but the smallness of life. Her breathing was labored, her life, once so encompassing, frail and bird-like. Her pupils had become irradiated and white. She could no longer speak.

I lay down with her. I had a wet washcloth and I mopped her brow. Even now I marvel at what small comfort this was, for her and for me—that I wiped the perspiration from her face as life took her from me. I told her words I then believed—that it was okay for her to leave us, that we were well on our way. That she should go and join my father (so odd, this suggestion, in a family of atheists). My mother would not let go, and I wanted her pain to end. The room seemed in the grip of some great vortex, sucking energy from everything. She reached wordlessly to me, and her arms, so thin, extended and embraced me.

In that instant, I was forgiven—for every door I had slammed, for every foolish remark, for every show of petulance, even for everything I had hated her for, even for that anger—I was forgiven. And I forgave her for every quarrel, ancient and recent, real and imagined. I held her for a long time, and left, of all things, to go to the bathroom.

When I came back, I nestled myself under her arm, and searched her face as if I could retrieve the moments we had just shared. It took me several minutes to realize that the almost imperceptible rise of her chest had stopped. I stayed for a while, staring at her as if she could give me one last look, the last look I could ever receive as someone's child. But all that moved had become solid, all that acted had become still. Even now I find it hard to believe—the mother who had hoisted me on her hip, who had taught me how to use a fork, how to use a tampon, how to bake a strudel, how to spot a cardinal—even now I cannot reconcile this lithe actor with the lifeless, pale body I held.

My mother died on my sister's birthday, but only after, as she had insisted just hours earlier in what were her last words, my sister opened the birthday present she had ordered for her. The hospice nurse who attended her could not account for how she had managed to hang on so many days after she could no longer eat, and could barely swallow. She had asked us if some anniversary or special day was approaching. The happiest day of her life, my mother had always said, was the day my sister was born and she became a mother. And she hung on to life until the anniversary of that day.

My sister's birthday will always be shadowed by this sadness. But for me, it so clearly circumscribes who my mother was. With a grown-up mind, I try to recognize that she was once a girl, once a woman, and only then a mother. But in truth I confess that to me she is always and completely just my mother—the one to run to when no one else was there, the one who knew my body so well that she could pick clothes for me that always fit, the one who worried what I ate, where I went and whether I'd gotten home. When I was in my thirties and she heard I had had a bad day, she would always suggest that she cook me a chicken and drive it to my home. I lived in midtown Manhattan, where cooked chickens were hardly a rarity, and it annoyed me and sometimes amused me, this willingness to soothe via unnecessary (and always food-related) means. But now I canvas the larger world, and realize of course there is no one out there who would want to roast a chicken and drive it thirty miles to my door because I was blue. There is no one to remind me of a distant day in my past, no one to tell me that just as I survived the defection of my best friend I will somehow survive a more recent betrayal. No one to remember the pieces I played on the violin, no one to recount (almost by heart) the first article I ever published, no one to embarrass me with memories of boys I dated. I live in the present now, and the record of my history is reduced to the fallible faculty of my memory.

Not long ago a cousin told me, "Your mother always said you were too sensitive." As she uttered that first phrase, I caught my breath. I treasured those words, hardly a revelation, but they were news from the front, from a now silent source. How well I knew that voice, those complaints, and with what ease I had dismissed them. Now I turn the complaint around like a jewel in the light, seeing its many sides, its refractions, its manifold expression of a self I can no longer see or touch.

Shortly after I learned that my mother's cancer was terminal, I remember having a moment of clarity. I realized the enormity of the change that was to come. For the past two decades of my life, I had always had someone to care for, someone whose needs often overtook my own. My father had had a very long illness. For ten years after that I was involved with a man I loved dearly, but who required much tending and attention. That relationship had ended several months before my mother was pronounced terminal. And now this last responsibility, the care of my mother, would end. After that, I thought, I will be liberated. I will at last live for myself.

This emancipation is not what I expected. This "freedom" that I had imagined with such clarity died with her. I had never realized the sweetness of this bondage. That moment of clarity was only a moment of unknowing. I think on occasion of *la belle indifférence,* and I realize that it is simply an exaggeration of the way we all live. Death is always in our midst, always in our future, and life is possible because we manage to remain indifferent to it.

It is now a year since my mother died, and I still cannot quantify all that I have lost. I am alone and unsponsored, but not free. I am forever caught, and perhaps best, in that moment when I rose to the occasion, when I felt her alive for the last time. I had risen to that occasion, and now I am only a small part of its refuse. There was a summer once where every moment mattered.

Today is not tomorrow. I can tell the difference.

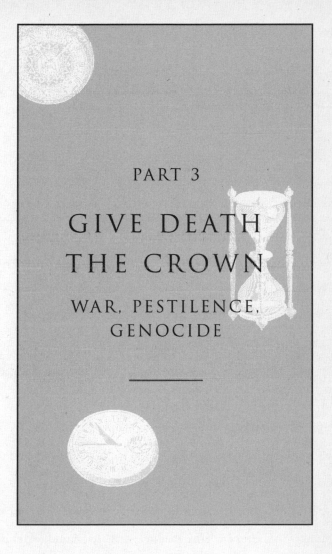

PART 3

GIVE DEATH THE CROWN

WAR, PESTILENCE, GENOCIDE

"As flies to wanton boys, are we to th' gods," says Gloucester in *King Lear,* "they kill us for their sport." When we learn of death in large numbers, we feel a compound horror: at the wretchedness of our nature, which turns out to be more frail than we knew; and at the helpless manifold selves, egos much like our own, filled with affectations and yearnings we know from introspection, reduced by a careless act of God or the willing brutality of men to a statistical lump sum.

Our imaginations are notoriously bad with statistics. We need homely analogies to avert the paradoxical trivialization large numbers induce. More than a third of the population of Europe dead from plague by 1350. Ten million dead in the First World War and twice that number in the flu epidemic that followed. Two hundred thousand dead at Hiroshima, almost as many again at Nagasaki. Six million in the Holocaust. Nineteen million instances of HIV worldwide as of 1995. How are we to envision such quantities? By the football stadiums the casualties of flood or fever might have packed? By the endless parade the victims of this or that genocide might have conducted to celebrate their liberation?

Death by numbers violates our expectation that a person's end, however unwelcome, however ill timed, will be his own, something capable upon reflection of being made commensurate with his life. Even in tranquil and solitary circumstances, this reconciliation is not easy. But mass death threatens to make nonsense of the very idea that life can have completeness, a closure from which some meaning follows. Survivors' tales and historical accounts do weaken that threat: they are gestures of poignant commemoration, bringing the whole populous catastrophe into focus within a part. But in most of them you are likely to detect a lingering despair, a distrust of the sense they are striving for, so volatile, so tentative, so wearisome to persevere in.

———————

IN ITS MIDST

Above all I am not concerned with poetry.
My subject is War, and the pity of War.
The poetry is in the pity.

WILFRED OWEN, 1918

※

"... his prayer for life rejected, he crouches with arms
spread out waiting for the death-stroke."

JASPER GRIFFIN

ON EPIC DEATH

*The glory and wretchedness of martial heroism, and the inseparableness of
the two, are the constant themes of Homer's Iliad, and the Greek poet is
ample and assiduous in his depiction of the ways warriors die the death.
Here the English classical scholar Jasper Griffin offers eloquent inventories
of the arsenal of death in the ancient epic. The very concision of his account
lends a hypnotic, high-speed ferocity to the vivid yet stately slaughter in
Homer.*

When a hero dies, dark night covers him, he is seized by hateful
darkness; he is robbed of his sweet life, his soul rushes forth from his
wound; it goes down to Hades bewailing its fate, leaving behind its
youth and strength. The doom of death covers his eyes and nostrils,
his armour rings upon him, he breathes out his life in the dust, hateful
fate swallows him up, he gluts the god of war with his blood. Stabbed
in the back, he lies in the dust, stretching out his hands to his friends;
wounded in the bladder, he crouches breathing his last, and lies

stretched out on the earth like a worm. With a spear driven through his eye he collapses, arms spread wide, and his killer cuts off and brandishes his head; he lies on his back in the dust, breathing his last, while all his guts pour from his wound to the earth; he dies bellowing with pain, clutching the bloody earth, or biting the cold bronze which has severed his tongue, or wounded between the navel and genitals, "where the wound is most painful for poor mortal men," writhing like a roped bull about the spear. His eyes are knocked out and fall bloody before his feet in the dust; stabbed in the act of begging for his life, his liver slides out and his lap is filled with his blood; the spear is thrust into his mouth, splitting his white bones, and filling his eye sockets with blood which spouts at his mouth and nose; hit in the head, his blood and brains rush from the wound. Wounded in the arm and helpless, he awaits his slayer, seeing death before him; his prayer for life rejected, he crouches with arms spread out waiting for the death-stroke. After death his corpse may be driven over by chariots, his hands and head may be lopped off, all his enemies may surround his corpse and stab it at their leisure, his body may be thrown into the river and gnawed by fishes, or lie un-recognizable in the mêlée. His soul goes down to a dark and comfortless world, to a shadowy and senseless existence, for ever banished from the light and warmth and activity of this life.

☙

"When he remarked to the enemy soldiers . . . that they
would probably shoot him on the following day, they
answered in a horrified chorus, 'God forbid.' "

ALAN MOOREHEAD

GALLIPOLI

*Nothing brings out the absurdity of war more clearly than the anecdote of
truce. In that interlude of agreed-upon recess, it is particularly difficult to
accept the notion that war is a natural disaster, more or less like pestilence
or flood, beyond the wills of human beings despite its genesis in them. The
battle waged in 1915 at Gallipoli in the Dardanelles between Australian,
New Zealand, British, and French forces on the one side, and Turkish forces
on the other, resulted in some of the heaviest casualties of the First World
War and ended only with the evacuation of the devastated allied armies ten
months after it began. In the following passage, from his book-length chronicle of the battle, British historian Alan Moorehead describes a truce called
for the purpose of collecting the dead, a task made urgent by the humid
heat of the region. The negotiations that establish the terms of the truce
could not be more polite. As the hostile troops go about their dejecting work,
their sense of enmity gives way to a curious fellow-feeling which becomes,
by the end of the designated interval, colloquial and almost fond. When
their twenty-four hours are up, they wish one another well, give earnest
assurances of friendship, and return as ordered to war.*

The conference in the narrow cave was a stiff and strained affair, the Turkish Beys in their gold lace, the British generals in their red tabs, each side trying to make it clear that it was not they who were eager for the armistice. But the atmosphere was relieved by one moment of pure farce: an Australian soldier, not knowing or caring about what was going on inside the dugout, put his head round the canvas flap and demanded, "Have any of you bastards got my kettle?"

Herbert meanwhile had been taken into the Turkish lines as a hostage. He was mounted on a horse and blindfolded, and then led round and round in circles to confuse his sense of direction. At one stage the fierce Arab officer cried out to the man who was supposed to be leading the horse, "You old fool. Can't you see he's riding straight over the cliff?" Herbert protested strongly and they went on again. When finally the bandage was taken from his eyes he found himself in a tent in a grove of olives, and the Arab officer said, "This is the beginning of a lifelong friendship." He ordered cheese, tea and coffee to be brought, and offered to eat first to prove that the food was not poisoned. They had an amiable conversation, and in the evening when Kemal and the other Turks came back from Birdwood's head-quarters Herbert was blindfolded again and returned to the British lines.

The terms of the truce had been settled as precisely as possible; it was to take place on May 24 and was to continue for nine hours. Three zones were to be marked out with white flags for the burial of the dead—one Turkish, one British and the third common to both sides. Priests, doctors and soldiers taking part in the burials were to wear white armbands and were not to use field-glasses or enter enemy trenches. All firing was of course to cease along the line, and the soldiers in the opposing trenches were not to put their heads above their parapets during the period of the truce. It was also agreed that all rifles minus their bolts were to be handed back to whichever side they belonged to—but this move was circumvented to some extent by the Australians, who on the previous evening crept out into no man's-land and gathered up as many weapons as they could find.

The morning of May 24 broke wet and cold, and the soldiers were in their greatcoats. Soon after dawn the firing died away, and at six-thirty Herbert set out again with a group of officers for Gaba Tepe beach. Heavy rain was falling. After an hour the Turks arrived—Herbert's acquaintance of two days before and several others, including a certain Arif, the son of Achmet Pasha, who handed Herbert a visiting card inscribed with the words, *Sculpteur et Peintre. Etudiant de Poésie*.

Together the two parties left the beach, and passing through cornfields flecked with poppies walked up to the hills where the battle had taken place. "Then," Herbert says, "the fearful smell of death began as we came upon scattered bodies. We mounted over a plateau and down through gullies filled with thyme, where there lay about 4,000 Turkish dead. It was indescribable. One was grateful for the rain and the grey sky. A Turkish Red Crescent man came and gave me some antiseptic wool with scent on it, and this they renewed frequently. There were two wounded crying in that multitude of silence."

Many of the dead had sunk to the ground in the precise attitude they had adopted at the moment when the bullets stopped their rush, their hands clasping their bayonets, their heads thrust forward or doubled up beneath them. Nothing was missing except the spark of life. They lay in mounds on the wet earth, whole companies of soldiers, like some ghastly tableau made of wax.

Among the living men there was at first some little friction. Everyone was nervous, everyone expected that even in these awful nightmarish surroundings some kind of treachery had been planned by the other side. There were complaints: the Australians were stealing arms: the Turks were coming too close to the Anzac trenches. At Quinn's Post, where the lines were only ten or fifteen yards apart, the tension was almost a palpable thing in the air, an inflammable essence that might explode at any moment. Hands on their triggers the men watched one another across the narrow space, expecting at every minute that someone would make some foolish gesture that would start the fighting again. On the wider stretches of the battlefield, however, Turks and Anzac troops worked together in digging great communal graves, and as the hours went by they began to fraternize, offering cigarettes to one another, talking in broken scraps of English and Arabic, exchanging badges and gadgets from their pockets as souvenirs.

Herbert was kept busy settling points of difference. He allowed the Turks to extract for burial some bodies which had been built into their emplacements, and once he was even permitted to go into the enemy trenches to satisfy himself that the Turks were not using this lull to fortify and advance their positions. He found there a group of soldiers whom he had known previously in Albania. They gathered round him cheering and clapping, and he had to stop them because they were interrupting the burial services which were being conducted round about by the Moslem Imams and the Christian priests. From this time onwards the Turks were constantly coming up to him for orders, and even getting him to sign receipts for money taken from the dead. Intervals of bright sunshine had now followed the rain.

Compton Mackenzie and Major Jack Churchill (the brother of Winston Churchill) had come over from the *Arcadian* for the day, and they stood on a parapet constructed chiefly of dead bodies to watch the scene. "In the foreground," Mackenzie writes, "was a narrow stretch of level scrub along which white flags were stuck at intervals, and a line of sentries, Australians and Turks, faced one another. Staff officers of both sides were standing around in little groups, and there was an atmosphere about the scene of local magnates at the annual sports making suggestions about the start of the obstacle race. . . .

"The impression which that scene from the ridge by Quinn's Post made on my mind has obliterated all the rest of the time at Anzac. I cannot recall a single incident on the way back down the valley. I know only that nothing could cleanse the smell of death from the nostrils for a fortnight afterwards. There was no herb so aromatic but it reeked of carrion, not thyme nor lavender, nor even rosemary."

By three in the afternoon the work was practically done. There were two crises: it was discovered at the last minute that the Turks' watches were eight minutes ahead of the British, and a hurried adjustment had to be made. Then, as the hour for the ending of the truce was approaching, a shot rang out. Standing there in the open with tens of thousands of rifles pointed towards them the burial parties stood in a sudden hush, but nothing followed and they returned to their work again.

At four o'clock the Turks near Quinn's Post came to Herbert for their final orders, since none of their own officers were about. He first sent back the grave-diggers to their own trenches, and at seven minutes past four retired the men who were carrying the white flags. He then walked over to the Turkish trenches to say good-bye. When he remarked to the enemy soldiers there that they would probably shoot him on the following day, they answered in a horrified chorus, "God forbid." Seeing Herbert standing there, groups of Australians came up to the Turks to shake hands and say good-bye. "Good-bye, old chap; good luck." The Turks answered with one of their proverbs: "Smiling may you go and smiling may you come again."

All the remaining men in the open were now sent back to their lines, and Herbert made a last minute inspection along the front, reminding the Turks that firing was not to begin again for a further twenty-five minutes. He was answered with salaams, and he too finally dropped out of sight. At 4:45 P.M. a Turkish sniper fired from somewhere in the hills. Immediately the Australians answered and the roar of high explosive closed over the battlefield again.

✄

"Now there was no throng of women to bemoan one's passing: for many, there was no witness at all."

GIOVANNI BOCCACCIO

THE PLAGUE IN FLORENCE

Plague is a bacterial disease of the Asian black rat which is spread chiefly by fleas—to other rodents and, in the right environments, to man. The black rat lives contentedly at close quarters with human beings (unlike its more familiar gray cousin, which stays on the periphery): it is a great habitué of trading centers and seaports and a ready stowaway aboard ship. Wherever in history humanity is on the move, in war or commerce, the black rat is a fellow traveler. In this way, repeatedly from antiquity through the Middle Ages and well into modern times, regional, endemic forms of plague were transformed into terrible pandemics affecting entire continents.

The first manifestation of the disease is a swollen lymph node in the region of the flea bite—usually in the groin or armpit (since fleas tend to attack the limbs). This swelling is the "bubo," after which the plague is called. Certain outbreaks of bubonic plague were probably made more lethal by an accompanying "pneumonic" variant, a quickly destructive infection spread directly from respiratory tract to respiratory tract. If there is any accuracy in Boccaccio's claim in the following selection that mere conversation with an infected person was enough to communicate the dis-

ease to the well, the presence of pneumonic plague during the pandemic of 1348 is the reason. But the fact is that, until the very close of the nineteenth century, nobody understood either the biology or the epidemiology of plague. (The bacillus is easily destroyed by antibiotics, as a matter of fact, and since their advent in the early forties has been a trivial matter wherever they are available.) Even the culpability of the rat went unobserved. For this reason, most precautions against the disease were misdirected, and many, of course, were merely superstitious and destructive. But flight, for those who could afford it and had someplace to retreat to, did offer a little protection.

The Decameron, the renowned collection of tales by Giovanni Boccaccio (1313–75), purports to be a record of the entertainment a small band of young Florentine aristocrats, taking refuge from the plague in the hills of Fiesole, provide for themselves. An account of the epidemic serves as a prologue to the tales. Boccaccio probably errs on the high side in estimating the death toll, but the plague did destroy at least a third of Europe's population during the pandemic of 1348–49. Despite his imperfect understanding of the nature of the contagion itself, Boccaccio's account of its social effect is authoritative and profound. In his tenacious depiction, the collapse of civic spirit, natural kindness, even personal enterprise—and the crazed, despairing hedonism that flourished in their stead—seem as inescapable a part of the pestilence as the lethal infection itself.

In the year of Our Lord's fruitful incarnation one thousand three hundred and forty-eight, the deadly plague arrived in the famous city of Florence, the most beautiful in Italy. Whether through the mere operation of the stars and planets or as God's just punishment for mankind's sins, the plague had appeared several years before in the east, where it killed countless human beings. It spread rapidly westward and neither knowledge nor foresight could thwart it, although special officers were appointed to rid the city of accumulated filth, and sick travelers were kept away. Bulletins were issued on the subject of hygiene and the religious attempted to propitiate God through processions and other rituals. All the same, by spring-time the plague was showing its devastating, supernatural power.

It manifested itself differently here than it had in the east. There a nose-bleed was an inevitable sign of death. But here the disease began with a swelling in the groin or armpit which could become as big as an apple or an egg. Some swellings were large, some small, but people called them all alike buboes. Soon these buboes multiplied throughout the body. Then the symptoms changed: black or livid spots appeared on the limbs, thighs and trunk . . . and these, like the buboes themselves, were understood to mean certain death.

Doctors had no good advice against the disease, and medicines no effect. Everyone offered remedies—not only learned physicians, but ignorant men and women peddling "alternative cures"—but nothing helped. Perhaps the disease itself resisted all treatment, or, at any rate, concealed its nature from physicians well enough to keep them from devising even preventative measures. In any case, next to nobody recovered: almost everyone died within three days of the appearance of the first signs of the disease, give or take a day, and most people never even raised a fever or showed other symptoms. The virulence of the plague resembled the easy spread of fire to dry matter or to grease: the sick communicated it readily to the well. Conversation was enough to do it, or contact with clothing or with any other object the sick person had touched.

Now I have something very strange to tell. I should hardly have believed it myself, even if the most dependable witness had reported it. But, as a matter of fact, I saw it with my own eyes, and I was not alone. The plague, then, was so fiercely contagious that, besides afflicting human beings, it infected and quickly killed any animal that happened to come into contact with something that had belonged to a human victim. As I say, I observed this effect myself one day when some rags that had clothed a poor man now dead were discarded in the street, where a pair of pigs found them and began to investigate them with their snouts and eventually to chew on them. Soon, spinning and writhing as though they had been poisoned, both pigs fell dead upon the shreds of their unlucky find.

Such sights, and others similar and worse, stirred people's fears and superstitions, which largely encouraged a single desperate policy—that of spurning the sick and everything they owned. In this way everyone imagined his own health might be secured. Some people decided that temperance would keep them immune. They formed little companies and took up residence together in pleasant houses in which no one had yet fallen ill. There they quarantined themselves. They ate moderately but well and drank the best wines, but avoided real indulgence. They had music and other polite entertainment, and they simply forbade all news of the outside world, permitting no one to bring them reports of the plague's ravages.

There were others, though, who came to the contrary conclusion. In their view, the best precaution against disease was high living: drinking and carousing, singing and gourmandizing—laughing in the face of doom. And they did all that they could to carry out this philosophy, roaming day and night from one tavern to another, drunk and riotous. They would freely invade private homes too, if anything enticed them there, since nothing prevented such freedom: considering their lives at an end, people abandoned all solicitude for their own property, as for their own selves, and most houses became common quarters, into which strangers could wander at will and make themselves as at home as any owner. Such was the uncivilized contrivance many used for fleeing from the sick.

Amid all this misery and disease the sacred authority of the law, both divine and human, crumbled and all but collapsed. For judges and clerics, like other men, became sick and died—or their assistants did, leaving the survivors no way to carry out their duties. Everyone became a law unto himself.

Many people took a middle course, neither too abstemious nor too indulgent, simply following the dictates of natural appetite. They did not isolate themselves, but went about town carrying flowers or sweet-smelling herbs or other spicy plants. These they continually brought to their noses, maintaining that it was good for the brain to be placated with such scents, especially since the air was dense and reeked of death and foul medicines.

There were those people too, hard-hearted but perhaps pragmatic, who insisted that the best way to manage a plague is to get as far away from it as possible. Following this line of thought, men and

women alike in great numbers, concerned with nobody but themselves, fled the city, abandoned their homes and property, not to
mention their own kinsmen, and sought refuge in the countryside, at
houses they owned there or at other people's—the place hardly mattered. They seemed to think that God's wrath would fail to locate
them if they were out of town, and would be content to punish only
those who had not escaped the city-limits. Or they thought that the
city itself was nearing its end, and that nobody ought to remain behind to see it.

Not every member of these different parties died, but neither
did they all survive. Many fell ill, whatever their practice, and were
treated by their companions according to the example they themselves
had set: abandoned by those still well, they were left to die alone.

Granted that people shunned one another and had no kindness
for their neighbors; that even kinsmen rarely visited one another (and
said what they had to say from across the room when they did)—still
worse was the fact that the pestilence had struck such terror into
people's hearts that they forsook their own brothers and sisters, their
nephews and uncles, even their husbands and wives. Most terrible of
all—and hardly believable—, parents refused to visit and care for their
own children, as if these were no better than strangers to them.

Consequently, for a vast number of men and women who fell
ill, the only help to be had was due to the charity of friends (and these
were few and far between) or the avarice of servants, who looked
forward to ludicrously high wages for the attentions they provided. All
the same, the men and women willing to take on such work were few
in number, and not the cleverest people either, lacking ordinary servants' skills. They did little beside reach for things when the sick
called for them—and look on when their employers died. Many of
these people soon died themselves of the service they had done, and
that was their profit in the end.

From all this abandonment of the sick by their neighbors, family
and friends, and from the scarcity of servants for hire, there developed
a practice unheard-of before: once she fell ill, no woman, however
beautiful, alluring or genteel, hesitated to employ a man as her per-

sonal servant, regardless of his character or age—or to expose any part of her body to him without shame, as she would to a woman, if her sickness required it. No doubt this experience left those who did recover from the disease immodest ever after. But it also happened that many others died who might have lived had they the benefit of such attendants. The numbers of those who died day and night in the city, from lack of suitable care and from the sheer power of the plague, were staggering to hear of, more terrible to see. In the face of such things, kinds of behavior necessarily developed among the surviving citizens that ran contrary to the immemorial traditions of the town.

It used to be the practice (as it is now again) for the female relatives and neighbors of the departed to assemble inside his house and lament him alongside his immediate family, while his male neighbors and many other citizens joined other close relatives of his in front of the house. Then, commensurate with the stature of the deceased, representatives of the clergy would arrive; they would burn candles and chant, and the dead man, borne on the shoulders of his peers, would be ceremoniously carried to the church he himself had chosen for his funeral. But as the plague grew more and more fierce, these observances weakened and faded and new practices soon supplanted them. Now there was no throng of women to bemoan one's passing: for many, there was no witness at all. Few indeed had the benefit of their friends' and kinsmen's sorrowful cries and bitter tears, for much of the time there was more laughter and jocularity and capering than there was mourning—behavior which even women, for all their inborn compassion, whole-heartedly adopted for the sake of their own welfare. It became most unusual for more than ten or twelve of a man's neighbors to accompany his body to church, and what funeral procession there was consisted not of members of respectable society, but of a kind of "grave-diggers"—so they called themselves—belonging to the lower classes, who undertook to carry out the burial for money. They hoisted the bier onto their shoulders and trotted it, not to the church designated by the deceased, but to the one closest by. Five or six priests led the way. There was little light, often none at all.

Then, with the aid of these "grave-diggers," and without wearing themselves out with too long or solemn a service, the priests promptly deposited the body in the first unoccupied grave they came upon.

The outlook for the lower class, and, by and large, for the middle class too, was still more miserable, for they were bound to their houses and their immediate neighborhoods—by poverty and by the hope of keeping safe there—and they became sick by the thousands every day, dying uncomforted and uncared-for, with no possibility of rescue. Many met their end in the public street, and many others, having died in their own houses, gave their neighbors belated notice of the fact by the smell of their decaying bodies.

The city was filled with corpses and people adopted a certain routine for dealing with them, more out of fear of contagion from rotting flesh than out of any charity toward the departed. By themselves, or with the aid of any porters they could enlist, they would drag the bodies out of their houses and plant them in front of their doors. It was common, especially in the morning, to see any number of corpses piled up in this way. Biers were ordered (when these were not to be found any available plank of wood served) and not one body, but two or three were laid out on a single board. Often enough a solitary bier carried wife and husband, two or three brothers, a father and son, or other members of a family. It repeatedly happened that, when a pair of priests carrying the cross were leading the way for a corpse, three or four groups of porters carrying biers would fall in behind them, so that the priests, who had started out with one man to bury, now found themselves obliged to six or eight or even more.

Nor were these dead honored with tears or candles or any true company of mourners. Things had reached the point at which the dead commanded no more regard than goats do now. It manifestly proved that, though the occasional small injuries that are part of the natural course of things had never been able to impress upon the cleverest people the necessity of bearing troubles patiently, this great calamity taught even the simplest of men to anticipate and accept the worst. Every day and every hour so many bodies appeared at every church that there was not sacred ground enough to hold them, at least not if the ancient custom of giving each body its own place was to be followed. When the regular grave-sites were filled, large trenches were dug in the church cemeteries and the newly dead stacked up in them like ship's cargo, with some dirt shovelled in to separate the layers.

But I should not dwell on the particulars of our city's past miseries as though they were exceptional, for that evil time did not spare the surrounding countryside either. Among the castle-estates, which in their small way resembled the city, and in the scattered villages and fields, the wretched, impoverished peasants and their families died without attention from doctors or from servants—died at the roadsides, or in their fields, or in their houses, indifferent to where or when, by day, by night, died as animals die, not as men. Those who lived on did as the people in the city did: neglecting established ways, expecting death daily, they applied themselves, not to increasing the future yield of their livestock and fields and all their by-gone labor, but to consuming everything in the fleeting present. The animals— oxen, donkeys, sheep, goats, pigs, fowl—all went free. Dogs, too, ever faithful to their human masters, were driven from their houses and roamed freely through the abandoned wheat-fields, where the crop remained uncut, unharvested. Yet many of these animals, as if they were rational, continued to return undriven to their masters' houses at night, having satisfied their appetites with day-long feeding.

Leaving the countryside and returning to the city, I wonder what more I can say. Such was the cruelty of heaven (to which, to some degree, must be added the cruelty of man) that, from March to the following July, as a result of the ferocity of the plague itself and of the lack of care and outright abandonment of the sick by terrified survivors, there perished within the walls of Florence more than one-hundred-thousand human beings. Before the devastation of the plague, it would not have seemed that the whole population of the city was nearly that large. What grand palaces, what lovely houses, what noble dwellings, once filled with families, with gentlemen and ladies, remained empty now, bereft even of the lowliest servant? How many renowned families, how many rich heritages, how many legendary fortunes were left without an heir? Those valiant men, those captivating women, those pretty youngsters—Galen, Hippocrates and Aesculapius themselves (not to mention less estimable practitioners) would have pronounced them in perfect health. In the morning they had breakfast with their families and friends, but by evening they had joined their ancestors for supper in the other world.

Translated by Richard Tristman.

". . . a watch is constantly kept there night and day to
keep the people in, the plague making us cruel as doggs
one to another."

SAMUEL PEPYS

THE PLAGUE IN LONDON

*The diaries of the civil servant Samuel Pepys (1633–1703), "Clerk of the
King's Ships and Clerk of the Privy Seal," provide a terse though by no
means reticent picture of London life in the later seventeenth century. Pepys
was a man of more than middling sensuality, at once narcissistic and good-
natured. Both traits show to dramatic effect in his day-by-day chronicle of
the bubonic plague which struck the city in 1665 (of which we give a
sampling here). Lodged within a record of his preoccupations with clothing,
food, and fair women, and of his doings at "the office," Pepys's gradual
recognition of the extent of the pestilence and his rising anguish at the
helplessness and despair of his fellow citizens remind us that it is mostly
amid the engaging trivialities of everyday life that mortality insists upon
imposing its distractions.*

*This outbreak of plague was the last of such catastrophic proportions
to affect London. A second catastrophe, the Great Fire, struck the city in the
following year. (Pepys left a gripping chronicle of that deadly experience as
well.) It is likely that the subsequent reconstruction of the City, involving as
it did the replacement of innumerable wood dwellings with new ones of*

stone, did much to put distance between human beings and disease-bearing rats.

April 30, 1665

(Lord's Day.) I with great joy find myself to have gained this month above £100 clear, and in the whole to be worth above £1,400. Thus I end this month in great content as to my estate and gettings: in much trouble as to the pains I have taken and the rubs I expect yet to meet with about the business of Tangier. The fleete, with about 106 ships, upon the coast of Holland in sight of the Dutch. . . . Great fears of the sickenesse here in the City, it being said that two or three houses are already shut up. God preserve us all!

June 7

. . . by water home, where weary with walking and with the mighty heat of the weather, and for my wife's not coming home, I staying walking in the garden till twelve at night, when it begun to lighten exceedingly, through the greatness of the heat. Then despairing of her coming home, I to bed. This day, much against my will, I did in Drury Lane see two or three houses marked with a red cross upon the doors, and "Lord have mercy upon us" writ there; which was a sad sight to me, being the first of the kind that, to my remembrance, I ever saw. It put me into an ill conception of myself and my smell, so that I was forced to buy some roll-tobacco to smell to and chaw, which took away the apprehension.

June 8th

About five o'clock my wife come home, it having lightened all night hard, and one great shower of rain. She come and lay upon the bed; I up and to the office, where all the morning. Alone at home to dinner, my wife, mother and Mercer dining at W. Joyce's, I giving her a caution to go round by the Half Moone to his house, because of the plague. At the Goldsmiths I met with the great news at last newly come from the Duke of Yorke that we have totally routed the Dutch. . . .

June 9th

. . . At noon eat a small dinner at home, and so abroad to buy several things, and among others with my taylor to buy a silke suit, which though I had one lately, yet I do, for joy of the good newes we have lately had of our victory over the Dutch, which makes me willing to spare myself something extraordinary in clothes; and after long resolution of having nothing but black, I did buy a coloured silk ferrandin.

June 10th

In the evening home; and there to my great trouble hear that the plague is come into the City: but where should it begin but in my good friend and neighbour's, Dr. Burnett, in Fanchurch Street, which in both points troubles me mightily. To the office to finish my letters and then home to bed, being troubled at the sicknesse, and my head filled also with other business enough; and particularly how to put my things and estate in order, in case it should please God to call me away, which God dispose of to his glory!

June 11th

(Lord's Day.) Up, and expected long a new suit; but, coming not, dressed myself in my late new black silke camelott suit; and, when fully ready, comes my new one of coloured ferrandin, which my wife puts me out of love with, which vexes me, but I think it is only my not being used to wear colours which makes it look a little unusual upon me. At noon by invitation comes my two cozen Joyces and their wives, my aunt James and he-cozen Harman. I had a good dinner for them, and as merry as I could be in such company. They being gone I out of doors a little to shew, forsooth, my new suit, and back again, and in going I saw poor Dr. Burnett's door shut; but he hath, I hear, gained great goodwill among his neighbours, for he discovered it himself first and caused himself to be shut up of his own accord, which was very handsome.

June 15th

Up, and put on my new stuff suit with close knees, which becomes me most nobly, as my wife says. At the office all day. At noon put on my first laced band, all lace, and to Kate Joyce's to dinner, where my mother, wife, and abundance of their friends, and good usage. . . . The towne grows very sickly, and people to be afeard of it, there dying this last week of the plague 112 from 43 the week before.

June 17th

At the office find Sir W. Pen come home, who looks very well; and I am gladder to see him than otherwise I should be, because of my hearing so well of him for his serviceablenesse in this late great action. It struck me very deep this afternoon going with a hackney coach from my Lord Treasurer's down Holborne, the coachman I found to drive easily and easily, at last stood still, and come down hardly able to stand, and told me that he was suddenly struck very sicke, and almost blind, he could not see. So I 'light and went into another coach with a sad heart for the poor man and trouble for myself lest he should have been struck with the plague, being at the end of the towne that I took him up; but God have mercy upon us all!

June 29th

Up and by water to White Hall, where the Court full of waggons and people ready to go out of towne. To the Harp and Ball, and there drank and talked with Mary. This end of the towne every day grows very bad of the plague.

June 30th

In the afternoon I down to Woolwich and after me my wife and Mercer, whom I led to Mr. Sheldon's to see his house, and I find it a very pretty place for them to be at. So I back again, walking both forward and backward, and left my wife to come by water. Thus this book of two years ends. Myself and family in good health, consisting of myself and wife, Mercer, her woman, Mary, Alice and Susan our maids, and Tom my boy. In a sickly time of the plague growing on. Having upon my hands the troublesome care of the Treasury of Tangier, with great sums drawn upon me and nothing to pay them with; also the business of the office great. Consideration of removing my wife to Woolwich; she lately busy in learning to paint, with great pleasure and success.

July 5th

Up and advised about sending of my wife's bedding and things to Woolwich, in order to her removal thither. . . . By water to Woolwich, where I found my wife come and her two mayds, and very prettily accommodated they will be; and I left them going to supper, grieved in my heart to part with my wife. Late home and to bed, very lonely.

July 6th

By coach to several places, among others to see my Lord Brunkerd, who is not well, but was at rest when I come. I could not see him, nor had much mind, one of the great houses within two doors of him being shut up: and, Lord! the number of houses visited, which this day I observed through the town quite round in my way by Long Lane and London Wall.

July 13th

By water at night late to Sir G. Carteret's, but there being no oars to carry me I was fain to call a skuller that had a gentleman already in it, and he proved a man of love to musique, and he and I sung together the way down with great pleasure, and an incident extraordinary to be met with. Thence after long discourse I and my wife, who by agreement met here, took leave, and I saw my wife a little way down (it troubling me that this absence makes us a little strange instead of more fond), and so parted, and I home to some letters, and then home to bed. Above 700 died of the plague this week.

July 21st

Abroad to several places, among others to Anthony Joyce's, and there broke to him my desire to have Pall married to Harman, whose wife, poor woman, is lately dead, to my trouble, I loving her very much;

and he will consider it. So home and late at my chamber setting some papers in order; the plague growing very raging, and my apprehensions of it great. So very late to bed.

July 30th

. . . It was a sad noise to hear our bell to toll and ring so often to-day, either for deaths or burials; I think five or six times. At night weary with my day's work, but full of joy at my having done it, I to bed, being to rise betimes to-morrow to go to the wedding at Dagenhams.

August 15th

Up by 4 o'clock and walked to Greenwich, where called at Captain Cocke's and to his chamber, he being in bed, where something put my last night's dream into my head, which I think is the best that ever was dreamt, which was that I had my Lady Castlemayne in my armes; and then dreamt that this could not be awake, but that it was only a dream: but that since it was a dream, and that I took so much real pleasure in it, what a happy thing it would be if when we are in our graves (as Shakespeere resembles it) we could dream, and dream but such dreams as this, that then we should not need to be so fearful of death as we are this plague time. By water to the Duke of Albemarle, with whom I spoke a great deale in private. It was dark before I could get home, and so land at Churchyard stairs, where to my great trouble I met a dead corps of the plague in the narrow ally just bringing down a little pair of stairs. But I thank God I was not much disturbed at it. However, I shall beware of being late abroad again.

August 28th

Up, and being ready I out to the goldsmith's, having not for some days been in the streets; but now how few people I see, and those looking like people that had taken leave of the world. In the afternoon I sent down my boy to Woolwich with some things before me, in order to my lying there for good and all.

August 31st

Up, and, after putting several things in order to my removal, to Woolwich. Thus this month ends with great sadness upon the publick, through the greatness of the plague every where through the kingdom almost. In the City died this week 7,496, and of them 6,102 of the plague. But it is feared that the true number of the dead this week is near 10,000; partly from the poor that cannot be taken notice of through the greatness of the number, and partly from the Quakers and others that will not have any bell ring for them. . . . As to myself I am very well, only in fear of the plague, and as much of an ague by being forced to go early and late to Woolwich, and my family to lie there continually. . . .

September 3rd

(Lord's Day.) Up; and put on my coloured silk suit very fine, and my new periwigg, bought a good while since but durst not wear because the plague was in Westminster when I bought it; and it is a wonder what will be the fashion after the plague is done as to periwiggs, for nobody will dare to buy any haire for fear of the infection, that it had been cut off of the heads of people dead of the plague. To church, where a sorry dull parson. I up to the Vestry at the desire of the Justices of the Peace, in order to the doing something for the keeping of the plague from growing; but Lord! to consider the madness of the people of the town, who will (because they are forbid) come in crowds along with the dead corps to see them buried; but we agreed on some orders for the prevention thereof. Among other stories one was very passionate, methought, of a complaint brought against a man in the towne for taking a child from London from an infected house. Alderman Hooker told us it was the child of a very able citizen in Gracious Street, a saddler, who had buried all the rest of his children of the plague, and himself and wife now being shut up and in despair of escaping, did desire only to save the life of this little child; and so prevailed to have it received stark-naked into the arms of a friend, who brought it (having put it into new fresh clothes) to Greenwich; where upon hearing the story, we did agree it should be permitted to be received and kept in the towne.

September 4th

After dinner to Greenwich where I found my Lord Bruncker. We to walk in the Park, and there eat some fruit out of the King's garden, and thence walked home, my Lord Bruncker giving me a very neat cane to walk with; but it troubled me to pass by Coome farme where about twenty-one people have died of the plague, and three or four days since I saw a dead corps in a coffin lie in the Close unburied; and a watch is constantly kept there night and day to keep the people in, the plague making us cruel as doggs one to another.

September 6th

Busy all the morning writing letters to several, so to dinner, to London, to pack up more things thence; and there I looked into the street and saw fires burning in the street, as it is through the whole City, by the Lord Mayor's order. Thence by water to the Duke of Albemarle's: all the way fires on each side of the Thames, and strange to see in broad daylight two or three burials upon the Banke-side, one at the very heels of another: doubtless all of the plague, and yet at least forty or fifty people going along with every one of them.

September 7th

Up by 5 of the clock, mighty full of fear of an ague, but was obliged to go; and so by water, wrapping myself up warm, to the Tower, and there sent for the Weekely Bill and find 8,252 dead in all, and of them 6,978 of the plague, which is a most dreadful number. Thence to Brainford, reading "The Villaine," a pretty good play, all the way. . . .

September 10th

(Lord's Day.) My wife told me the ill news that she hears that her father is very ill, and then I told her I feared of the plague, for that the house is shut up. There happened newes to come to me by an expresse from Mr. Coventry telling me the most happy news of my Lord Sandwich's meeting with part of the Dutch; his taking two of their East India ships and six or seven others, and very good prizes. . . .

September 20th

Up, and after being trimmed, the first time I have been touched by a barber these twelvemonths, I think, and more, went to Sir J. Minnes's and thence to the Duke of Albemarle. But, Lord! what a sad time it is to see no boats upon the River; and grass grows all up and down White Hall court, and nobody but poor wretches in the streets! And, which is worst of all, the Duke showed us the number of the plague this week, brought in the last night from the Lord Mayor; that it is encreased about 600 more than the last, which is quite contrary to all our hopes and expectations, from the coldness of the late season.

October 16th

. . . Lord! how empty the streets are and melancholy, so many poor sick people in the streets full of sores; and so many sad stories overheard as I walk, every body talking of this dead, and that man sick, and so many in this place, and so many in that. And they tell me that in Westminster there is never a physician and but one apothecary left, all being dead; but that there are great hopes of a great decrease this week: God send it!

November 24th

Up, and after doing some business at the office, I to London, and there in my way, at my old oyster shop in Gracious Streete, bought two barrels of my fine woman of the shop, who is alive after all the plague, which now is the first observation or inquiry we make at London concerning everybody we knew before it. So to the 'Change, where very busy with several people, and mightily glad to see the 'Change so full. Off the 'Change I went home with Sir G. Smith to dinner, sending for one of my barrels of oysters, which were good, though come from Colchester where the plague hath been so much. . . .

November 30th

Great joy we have this week in the weekly Bill, it being come to 544 in all, and but 333 of the plague; so that we are encouraged to get to London soon as we can.

November 31st

. . . I have never lived so merrily (besides that I never got so much)
as I have done this plague time. . . . My whole family hath been well
all this while, and all my friends I know of, saving my aunt Bell, who
is dead, and some children of my cozen Sarah's, of the plague. But
many of such as I know very well, dead; yet to our great joy the town
fills apace, and shops begin to be open again. Pray God continue the
plague's decrease! for that keeps the Court away from the place of
business, and so all goes to rack as to publick matters, they at this
distance not thinking of it.

January 5th, 1666

I with my Lord Bruncker and Mrs. Williams by coach with four horses
to London to my Lord's house in Covent-Guarden. But, Lord! what
staring to see a nobleman's coach come to town. And porters every
where bow to us, and such begging of beggars! And a delightful thing
it is to see the towne full of people again as now it is; and shops begin
to open, though in many places seven or eight together and more all
shut, but yet the towne is full compared with what it used to be: I
mean the City end, for Covent Guarden and Westminster are yet very
empty of people, no Court nor gentry being there. . . .

January 9th

Up, and then to the office, where we met first since the plague, which
God preserve us in!

✻

"René . . . so young and robust, ended on the left;
perhaps it was because he has glasses, perhaps because
he walks a little stooped like a myope, but more probably
because of a simple mistake."

PRIMO LEVI

OCTOBER 1944

*Primo Levi (1919–87) arrived at Auschwitz in a transport of 650 Italian
Jews—or "pieces," as the Germans phrased it. Levi was twenty-four years
old.*

*At the end of 1943, after Stalingrad, the shortage of manpower in
Germany was so acute, as Levi explains, that "it became indispensable to
use everybody, even the Jews." At this point, Auschwitz became what he
calls a "hybrid concentration-camp 'empire,' " extending its extermination
function to include "extermination through exploitation." Levi owed his
survival to being pressed into the pool of slave labor at Monowitz, a "work
camp" near Auschwitz where a factory belonging to German industrialists
produced a type of rubber called Buna (the camp itself was thus referred to
as Buna). Imprisoned in the lagers under the control of the SS, slave
laborers worked during the day in the factory under the authority of German industry. The SS anticipated a survival period of three months for
these prisoners.*

This excerpt from Survival in Auschwitz *(1958) describes one of the many processes of selection for the gas chamber employed at Auschwitz and other camps. The term* muselmann, *which appears below, was used by inmates to refer to fellow prisoners whose physical and psychic deteriora-tion was so advanced that they were considered beyond hope—prime for selection. The Ka-Be (abbreviation of Krankenbau), referred to in the pas-sage, is the infirmary. Those who failed to improve at the infirmary were sent to the gas chamber.*

After the war, Primo Levi returned to Italy and his work as a chemist and a writer. He took his own life.

We fought with all our strength to prevent the arrival of winter. We clung to all the warm hours, at every dusk we tried to keep the sun in the sky for a little longer, but it was all in vain. Yesterday evening the sun went down irrevocably behind a confusion of dirty clouds, chim-ney stacks and wires, and today it is Winter.

We know what it means because we were here last winter; and the others will soon learn. It means that in the course of these months, from October till April, seven out of ten of us will die. Whoever does not die will suffer minute by minute, all day, every day: from the morning before dawn until the distribution of the evening soup we will have to keep our muscles continually tensed, dance from foot to foot, beat our arms under our shoulders against the cold. We will have to spend bread to acquire gloves, and lose hours of sleep to repair them when they become unstitched. As it will no longer be possible to eat in the open, we will have to eat our meals in the hut, on our feet, everyone will be assigned an area of floor as large as a hand, as it is forbidden to rest against the bunks. Wounds will open on everyone's hands, and to be given a bandage will mean waiting every evening for hours on one's feet in the snow and wind.

Just as our hunger is not that feeling of missing a meal, so our way of being cold has need of a new word. We say "hunger," we say "tiredness," "fear," "pain," we say "winter" and they are different things. They are free words, created and used by free men who lived in comfort and suffering in their homes. If the Lagers had lasted longer a new, harsh language would have been born; and only this language could express what it means to toil the whole day in the wind, with the temperature below freezing, wearing only a shirt, underpants, cloth jacket and trousers, and in one's body nothing but weakness, hunger and knowledge of the end drawing nearer.

In the same way in which one sees a hope end, winter arrived this morning. We realized it when we left the hut to go and wash: there were no stars, the dark cold air had the smell of snow. In roll-call square, in the grey of dawn, when we assembled for work, no one spoke. When we saw the first flakes of snow, we thought that if at the same time last year they had told us that we would have seen another winter in Lager, we would have gone and touched the electric wire-fence; and that even now we would go if we were logical, were it not for this last senseless crazy residue of unavoidable hope.

Because "winter" means yet another thing.

Last spring the Germans had constructed huge tents in an open space in the Lager. For the whole of the good season each of them had catered for over a thousand men: now the tents had been taken down, and an excess two thousand guests crowded our huts. We old prisoners knew that the Germans did not like these irregularities and that something would soon happen to reduce our number.

One feels the selections arriving. *"Selekcja"*: the hybrid Latin and Polish word is heard once, twice, many times, interpolated in foreign conversations; at first we cannot distinguish it, then it forces itself on our attention, and in the end it persecutes us.

This morning the Poles had said *"Selekcja."* The Poles are the first to find out the news, and they generally try not to let it spread around, because to know something which the others still do not know can always be useful. By the time that everyone realizes that a selection is imminent, the few possibilities of evading it (corrupting some doctor or some prominent with bread or tobacco; leaving the hut for Ka-Be or vice-versa at the right moment so as to cross with the commission) are already their monopoly.

In the days which follow, the atmosphere of the Lager and the yard is filled with *"Selekcja"*: nobody knows anything definite, but all speak about it, even the Polish, Italian, French civilian workers whom we secretly see in the yard. Yet the result is hardly a wave of despondency: our collective morale is too inarticulate and flat to be unstable. The fight against hunger, cold and work leaves little margin for thought, even for this thought. Everybody reacts in his own way, but hardly anyone with those attitudes which would seem the most plausible as the most realistic, that is with resignation or despair.

All those able to find a way out, try to take it; but they are the minority because it is very difficult to escape from a selection. The Germans apply themselves to these things with great skill and diligence.

Whoever is unable to prepare for it materially, seeks defense elsewhere. In the latrines, in the washroom, we show each other our chests, our buttocks, our thighs, and our comrades reassure us: "You are all right, it will certainly not be your turn this time,   *du bist kein Muselmann* . . . more probably mine . . ." and they undo their braces in turn and pull up their shirts.

Nobody refuses this charity to another: nobody is so sure of his own lot to be able to condemn others. I brazenly lied to old Wertheimer; I told him that if they questioned him, he should reply that he was forty-five, and he should not forget to have a shave the evening before, even if it cost him a quarter-ration of bread; apart from that he need have no fears, and in any case it was by no means certain that it was a selection for the gas chamber; had he not heard the *Blockältester* say that those chosen would go to Jaworszno to a convalescent camp?

It is absurd of Wertheimer to hope: he looks sixty, he has enormous varicose veins, he hardly even notices the hunger any more. But he lies down on his bed, serene and quiet, and replies to someone who asks him with my own words; they are the command words in the camp these days: I myself repeated them just as—apart from details—Chajim told them to me, Chajim, who has been in Lager for three years, and being strong and robust is wonderfully sure of himself; and I believed them.

On this slender basis I also lived through the great selection of October 1944 with inconceivable tranquillity. I was tranquil because I managed to lie to myself sufficiently. The fact that I was not selected depended above all on chance and does not prove that my faith was well-founded.

Monsieur Pinkert is also, a priori, condemned: it is enough to look at his eyes. He calls me over with a sign, and with a confidential air tells me that he has been informed—he cannot tell me the source of information—that this time there is really something new: the Holy See, by means of the International Red Cross . . . in short, he personally guarantees both for himself and for me, in the most absolute manner, that every danger is ruled out; as a civilian he was, as is well known, attaché to the Belgian embassy at Warsaw.

Thus in various ways, even those days of vigil, which in the telling seem as if they ought to have passed every limit of human torment, went by not very differently from other days.

The discipline in both the Lager and Buna is in no way relaxed: the work, cold and hunger are sufficient to fill up every thinking moment.

Today is working Sunday, *Arbeitssonntag*: we work until 1 P.M., then we return to camp for the shower, shave and general control for skin diseases and lice. And in the yards, everyone knew mysteriously that the selection would be today.

The news arrived, as always, surrounded by a halo of contradictory or suspect details: the selection in the infirmary took place this morning; the percentage was seven per cent of the whole camp, thirty, fifty per cent of the patients. At Birkenau, the crematorium chimney has been smoking for ten days. Room has to be made for an enormous convoy arriving from the Poznan ghetto. The young tell the young that all the old ones will be chosen. The healthy tell the healthy that only the ill will be chosen. Specialists will be excluded. German Jews will be excluded. Low Numbers will be excluded. You will be chosen. I will be excluded.

At 1 P.M. exactly the yard empties in orderly fashion, and for two hours the grey unending army files past the two control stations where, as on every day, we are counted and recounted, and past the military band which for two hours without interruption plays, as on every day, those marches to which we must synchronize our steps at our entrance and our exit.

It seems like every day, the kitchen chimney smokes as usual, the distribution of the soup is already beginning. But then the bell is heard, and at that moment we realize that we have arrived.

Because this bell always sounds at dawn, when it means the reveille; but if it sounds during the day, it means *"Blocksperre,"* enclosure in huts, and this happens when there is a selection to prevent anyone avoiding it, or when those selected leave for the gas, to prevent anyone seeing them leave.

Our *Blockältester* knows his business. He has made sure that we have all entered, he has the door locked, he has given everyone his card with his number, name, profession, age and nationality and he has ordered everyone to undress completely, except for shoes. We wait like this, naked, with the card in our hands, for the commission to reach our hut. We are hut 48, but one can never tell if they are going to begin at hut 1 or hut 60. At any rate, we can rest quietly at least for an hour, and there is no reason why we should not get under the blankets on the bunk and keep warm.

Many are already drowsing when a barrage of orders, oaths and blows proclaims the imminent arrival of the commission. The *Block- ältester* and his helpers, starting at the end of the dormitory, drive the crowd of frightened, naked people in front of them and cram them in the *Tagesraum* which is the Quartermaster's office. The *Tagesraum* is a room seven yards by four: when the drive is over, a warm and compact human mass is jammed into the *Tagesraum,* perfectly filling all the corners, exercising such a pressure on the wooden walls as to make them creak.

Now we are all in the *Tagesraum,* and besides there being no time, there is not even any room in which to be afraid. The feeling of the warm flesh pressing all around is unusual and not unpleasant. One has to take care to hold up one's nose so as to breathe, and not to crumple or lose the card in one's hand.

The *Blockältester* has closed the connecting-door and has opened the other two which lead from the dormitory and the *Tages-*

raum outside. Here, in front of the two doors, stands the arbiter of our fate, an SS subaltern. On his right is the *Blockältester,* on his left, the quartermaster of the hut. Each one of us, as he comes naked out of the *Tagesraum* into the cold October air, has to run the few steps between the two doors, give the card to the SS man and enter the dormitory door. The SS man, in the fraction of a second between two successive crossings, with a glance at one's back and front, judges everyone's fate, and in turn gives the card to the man on his right or his left, and this is the life or death of each of us. In three or four minutes a hut of two hundred men is "done," as is the whole camp of twelve thousand men in the course of the afternoon.

Jammed in the charnel-house of the *Tagesraum,* I gradually felt the human pressure around me slacken, and in a short time it was my turn. Like everyone, I passed by with a brisk and elastic step, trying to hold my head high, my chest forward and my muscles contracted and conspicuous. With the corner of my eye I tried to look behind my shoulders, and my card seemed to end on the right.

As we gradually come back into the dormitory we are allowed to dress ourselves. Nobody yet knows with certainty his own fate, it has first of all to be established whether the condemned cards were those on the right or the left. By now there is no longer any point in sparing each other's feelings with superstitious scruples. Everybody crowds around the oldest, the most wasted-away, and most "muselmann"; if their cards went to the left, the left is certainly the side of the condemned.

Even before the selection is over, everybody knows that the left was effectively the *"schlechte Seite,"* the bad side. There have naturally been some irregularities: René, for example, so young and robust, ended on the left; perhaps it was because he has glasses, perhaps because he walks a little stooped like a myope, but more probably because of a simple mistake: René passed the commission immediately in front of me and there could have been a mistake with our cards. I think about it, discuss it with Alberto, and we agree that the hypothesis is probable; I do not know what I will think tomorrow and later; today I feel no distinct emotion.

It must equally have been a mistake about Sattler, a huge Transylvanian peasant who was still at home only twenty days ago; Sattler does not understand German, he has understood nothing of what has taken place, and stands in a corner mending his shirt. Must I go and tell him that his shirt will be of no more use?

There is nothing surprising about these mistakes: the examination is too quick and summary, and in any case, the important thing for the Lager is not that the most useless prisoners be eliminated, but that free posts be quickly created, according to a certain percentage previously fixed.

The selection is now over in our hut, but it continues in the others, so that we are still locked in. But as the soup-pots have arrived in the meantime, the *Blockältester* decides to proceed with the distribution at once. A double ration will be given to those selected. I have never discovered if this was a ridiculously charitable initiative of the *Blockältester,* or an explicit disposition of the SS, but in fact, in the interval of two or three days (sometimes even much longer) between the selection and the departure, the victims at Monowitz-Auschwitz enjoyed this privilege.

Ziegler holds out his bowl, collects his normal ration and then waits there expectantly. "What do you want?" asks the *Blockältester:* according to him, Ziegler is entitled to no supplement, and he drives him away, but Ziegler returns and humbly persists. He was on the left, everybody saw it, let the *Blockältester* check the cards; he has the right to a double ration. When he is given it, he goes quietly to his bunk to eat.

Now everyone is busy scraping the bottom of his bowl with his spoon so as not to waste the last drops of the soup; a confused, metallic clatter, signifying the end of the day. Silence slowly prevails and then, from my bunk on the top row, I see and hear old Kuhn praying aloud, with his beret on his head, swaying backwards and forwards violently. Kuhn is thanking God because he has not been chosen.

Kuhn is out of his senses. Does he not see Beppo the Greek in the bunk next to him, Beppo who is twenty years old and is going to the gas chamber the day after tomorrow and knows it and lies there looking fixedly at the light without saying anything and without even thinking any more? Can Kuhn fail to realize that next time it will be his turn? Does Kuhn not understand that what has happened today is an abomination, which no propitiatory prayer, no pardon, no expiation by the guilty, which nothing at all in the power of man can ever clean again? If I was God, I would spit at Kuhn's prayer.

Translated by Stuart Wolf.

⁊ఈ

"Those who were able walked silently toward the suburbs
in the distant hills, their spirits broken,
their initiative gone."

ROBERT JAY LIFTON

IMMERSION IN DEATH

*Psychiatrist and social historian Robert Jay Lifton has written widely on
what he terms "the extreme historical situations characteristic of our era."
He interviewed survivors of the atomic bomb in Hiroshima for several
months in 1962 for a book he would call* Death in Life *(1967). The
Japanese use the term* hibakusha *for "explosion-affected persons"; this
category includes those who were in utero at the time of the bombing. In
this excerpt, Lifton gives special attention to the imagery and the character
of memories of the event—seventeen years earlier. For many, the world
appeared to have come to an end—and to have survived was to be a part
of nothing. By their own accounts, some survivors experienced doubt about
whether they were alive or dead. The social order, along with nature itself,
seemed to have dissolved, so that whatever remained of this decimated
city belonged, as Lifton puts it, to a "supernatural or unnatural" world.
This loss of a sense of human continuity can produce different patterns
of emotional defense. Survivors sometimes make "a psychic bargain,"
Lifton writes, "to live at a devitalized level in return for the right to live
at all."*

Only those at some distance from the explosion could clearly distinguish the sequence of the great flash of light accompanied by the lacerating heat of the fireball, then the sound and force of the blast, and finally the impressive multicolored cloud rising high above the city. This awesome spectacle was not without beauty—as recorded by [a] history professor, who witnessed it from a suburb five thousand meters (a little more than three miles) away:

> A blinding . . . flash cut sharply across the sky. . . . I threw myself onto the ground . . . in a reflex movement. At the same moment as the flash, the skin over my body felt a burning heat. . . . [Then there was] a blank in time . . . dead silence . . . probably a few seconds . . . and then a . . . huge "boom" . . . like the rumbling of distant thunder. At the same time a violent rush of air pressed down my entire body. . . . Again there were some moments of blankness . . . then a complicated series of shattering noises. . . . I raised my head, facing the center of Hiroshima to the west. . . . [There I saw] an enormous mass of clouds . . . [which] spread and climbed rapidly . . . into the sky. Then its summit broke open and hung over horizontally. It took on the shape of . . . a monstrous mushroom with the lower part as its stem—it would be more accurate to call it the tail of a tornado. Beneath it more and more boiling clouds erupted and unfolded sideways. . . . The shape . . . the color the light . . . were continuously shifting and changing. . . .

Even at that distance, he and others experienced what is called the "illusion of centrality," as is succinctly suggested by a later poem originally written in the classical tanka style:

> Thinking a bomb must have fallen close to me, I looked up, but it was a pillar of fire five kilometers ahead.

This illusion, usually attributed to the sudden loss of a sense of invulnerability, is actually an early perception of death encounter, a perception which the atomic bomb engendered at enormous distances.

The bomb was completely on target and exploded, with a force equivalent to twenty thousand tons of TNT, eighteen hundred feet in the air near the center of a flat city built mainly of wood. It created an area of total destruction (including residential, commercial, industrial, and military structures) extending three thousand meters (about two miles) in all directions; and destroyed sixty thousand of ninety thousand buildings within five thousand meters (over three miles), an area roughly encompassing the city limits. Flash burns from the heat generated by the release of an enormous amount of radiant energy occurred at distances of more than four thousand meters (two and a half miles), depending upon the type and amount of clothing worn and the shielding afforded by immediate surroundings. Injuries from the blast, and from splintered glass and falling debris, occurred throughout the city and beyond.

The number of deaths, immediately and over a period of time, will probably never be fully known. Variously estimated from 63,000 to 240,000 or more, the official figure is usually given as 78,000, but the city of Hiroshima estimates 200,000—the total encompassing between 25 and 50 per cent of the city's then daytime population (also a disputed figure, varying from 227,000 to over 400,000). The enormous disparity is related to the extreme confusion which then existed, to differing methods of calculation, and to underlying emotional influences, quite apart from mathematical considerations, which have at times affected the estimators. An accurate estimate may never be possible, but what can be said is that all of Hiroshima immediately became involved in the atomic disaster. . . .

Two thousand meters (1.2 miles) is generally considered to be a crucial radius for susceptibility to radiation effects, and for high mortality in general—from blast, heat, or radiation—though many were killed outside of this radius. Within it, at points close to the hypocenter, heat was so extreme that metal and stone melted, and human beings were literally incinerated. The area was enveloped by fires fanned by a violent "firewind"; these broke out almost immediately within a radius of more than three thousand meters (up to two miles). The inundation with death of the area closest to the hypocenter was such that if a man survived within a thousand meters (.6 miles) and was out of doors (that is, without benefit of shielding from heat or radiation), more than nine tenths of the people around him were fatalities; if he was unshielded at two thousand meters, more than eight of ten people around him were killed. Mortality indoors was lower, but even then to have a 50-per-cent chance of escaping both death or injury, one had to be about twenty-two hundred meters (1.3 miles) from the hypocenter.

Those closest to the hypocenter could usually recall a sudden flash, an intense sensation of heat, being knocked down or thrown some distance, and finding themselves pinned under debris or simply awakening from an indeterminate period of unconsciousness. The most striking psychological feature of this immediate experience was the sense of a sudden and absolute shift from normal existence to an overwhelming encounter with death.

. . . In the case of a psychologist, then a university student, who found himself pinned under the heavy beams of a collapsed house at two thousand meters, and abandoned by two friends who had unsuccessfully attempted to pull him out:

> I began to see my mother's image before me. . . . I regretted that I was going to die. I thought I was young, and had just been successful in very difficult academic competition . . . I wanted to study more in the life ahead of me. . . . And I was dying without seeing my parents.

This kind of maternal image was reminiscent of reports about Japanese soldiers in World War II: trained to go to their deaths with the phrase "Long live the Emperor" on their lips, they instead called out, "Mother!" Both cases suggest an effort to reassert the ultimate human relationship in the face of death's severance, along with (as the psychologist made clear) a protest against what is perceived as premature death.

Beyond these feelings was the sense that the whole world was dying.

. . . A woman writer, Yoko Ota:

I just could not understand why our surroundings had changed so greatly in one instant. . . . I thought it might have been something which had nothing to do with the war, the collapse of the earth which it was said would take place at the end of the world, and which I had read about as a child. . . .

. . . There was a widespread sense that life and death were out of phase with one another, no longer properly distinguishable—which lent an aura of weirdness and unreality to the entire city.

. . . Part of this aura was the "deathly silence" consistently reported by survivors. Rather than wild panic, most described a ghastly stillness and a sense (whether or not literally true) of slow-motion: low moans from those incapacitated, the rest fleeing from the destruction, but usually not rapidly, toward the rivers, toward where they thought their family members might be, or toward where they hoped to find authorities or medical personnel, or simply toward accumulations of other people, in many cases merely moving along with a gathering human mass and with no clear destination. Some jumped into the rivers to escape heat and fire, others were pushed into the water by the pressure of crowds at the river banks; a considerable number drowned. Many seemed to be attracted to the disaster center, overcoming numerous obstacles—such as spreading fire and, later on, guards posted at various points to prevent any influx of people—and made their way through the debris, often losing sight of their ostensible rescue missions in their aimless wandering.

As Dr. Hachiva described the scene in his classic, *Hiroshima Diary*:

Those who were able walked silently toward the suburbs in the distant hills, their spirits broken, their initiative gone. When asked whence they had come, they pointed to the city and said, "That way" and when asked where they were going, pointed

away from the city and said, "This way." They were so broken
and confused that they moved and behaved like automatons.

Their reactions had astonished outsiders who reported with
amazement the spectacle of long files of people holding stolidly
to a narrow, rough path when close by was a smooth, easy road
going in the same direction. The outsiders could not grasp the
fact that they were witnessing the exodus of a people who
walked in the realm of dreams.

One of these "automatons" walking in the "realm of dreams," a
watch repairman, at the time of the bomb in his twenties and three
thousand meters from the hypocenter, describes his own mindless
merging with a group of victims:

> All the people were going in that direction and so I suppose I
> was taken into this movement and went with them. . . . I
> couldn't make any clear decision in a specific way. . . . so I
> followed the other people. . . . I lost myself and was carried
> away. . . .

The phrase he and others used, *muga-muchu,* literally "without
self, without a center," suggests an obliteration of the boundaries of
self. The physical state of many greatly contributed to this obliteration: complete or near-nakedness (partly because of clothes blown off
by the blast and partly through being caught in an early-morning state
of undress), various injuries and forms of bleeding, faces disfigured
and bloated from burns, arms held awkwardly away from the body to
prevent friction with other burned areas. Fellow survivors characterized such people (and by implication, themselves) as being "like so
many beggars," or "like so many red *Jizo* standing on the sides of the
road," implying that their identity as living human beings had been
virtually destroyed.

Indeed, a few hibakusha described being rendered literally un-
recognizable: one girl of thirteen, whose face was so disfigured by
burns that when she returned home, her parents did not know who
she was—until she began to cry; and another, one year older, was not

only similarly disfigured but also unable, probably on a psychological basis, to see or speak:

> My mother and I were taken to [a nearby] island. . . . I couldn't see and couldn't say anything—that is what I heard later. . . . My eyes were not injured. I think I closed my eyes when the bomb fell. My face was so distorted and changed that people couldn't tell who I was. After a while I could call others' names but they couldn't recognize me. . . . We were considered the very worst kind of patients. . . . Of the thirty-five people put on this island, only two survived.

Dr. Hachiya also noted the "uncanny stillness" permeating the hospital where he was, for a time, both director and patient:

> An old woman lay near me with an expression of suffering on her face; but she made no sound. Indeed one thing was common to everyone I saw—complete silence. . . . Miss Kado [a nurse] set about examining my wounds without speaking a word. No one spoke. . . . Why was everyone so quiet? . . . It was as though I walked through a gloomy, silent motion picture.

Yoko Ota referred to this silence right after her description of the "end of the world," and more explicitly equated it with a general aura of death:

> It was quiet around us . . . in fact there was a fearful silence which made one feel that all people and all trees and vegetation were dead. . . .

And a grocer, himself severely burned, conveyed in his description this profound sense of death in life, of ultimate death-life disruption:

The appearance of people was . . . well, they all had skin blackened by burns. . . . They had no hair because their hair was burned, and at a glance you couldn't tell whether you were looking at them from in front or in back. . . . They held their arms bent [forward] like this [he proceeded to demonstrate their position] . . . and their skin—not only on their hands, but on their faces and bodies too—hung down. . . . If there had been only one or two such people . . . perhaps I would not have had such a strong impression. But wherever I walked I met these people. . . . Many of them died along the road—I can still picture them in my mind—like walking ghosts. . . . They didn't look like people of this world. . . . They had a special way of walking—very slowly . . . I myself was one of them.

The other-worldly grotesqueness of the scene, the image of nei-ther-dead-nor-alive human figures with whom the survivor closely identifies himself, is typical. One man put the feeling more directly: "I was not really alive."

OUR PLAGUE:
AIDS

_____

A fiction about soft or easy deaths . . . is part of the mythology of most diseases that are not considered shameful or demeaning.

SUSAN SONTAG
AIDS and Its Metaphors

"Dying in the war against AIDS . . .
contributes nothing to the enemy's defeat. . . ."

EMMANUEL DREUILHE

MORTAL EMBRACE

Mortal Embrace, *by Emmanuel Dreuilhe (1949–88), was published in this country just months before its author's death of AIDS. Dreuilhe described the book as a "medico-literary undertaking," as reliant for its success upon the efforts of his doctors as on himself. Susan Sontag has observed that military metaphors for diseases, besides being inaccurate, contribute to the stigmatizing of the ill. Dreuilhe, however, employs them insistently to track and investigate his feelings, to make his experience fathomable to others, and to help him brave the disease, and their poignancy is increased for him by the paradoxes caused by their imperfect fit.*

Dreuilhe, who was born in Cairo and lived much of his life in France, spent his last ten years in New York City, where he was a translator for the United Nations.

I've recently discovered in myself a hitherto unsuspected interest in war films, which have given me useful lessons in keeping my sense of perspective: though I may sometimes venture out into the unknown,

I've never had to advance against an intelligent and crafty enemy, as real soldiers do. I don't have to keep calmly lobbing grenades while my comrades get their insides or their brains blown to bits before my very eyes. During the Klaus Barbie trial in Lyons, the testimony of the tortured Jews and Resistance fighters showed me that there was one dimension still lacking—fortunately—in my martial metaphor: pain, the kind of torment that brings you to your knees, robs you of your dignity, drags you down to the level of an animal. I know that I would have spilled my guts, told them absolutely everything at the mere sight of the torture chamber. My illness seems to have kept this weapon in reserve and only rarely forces me to admit that I'm completely at its mercy. Others aren't as lucky as I am: they feel the iron grip of the disease crushing their lungs, twisting their entrails. No tranquilizer can dispel their splitting headaches; no lotion can soothe the ferocious itching of the lesions festering on their bodies. In their situation, with an illiterate brute twisting my arm like that, I'd never have been able to write a single line.

Our enemy is using live ammunition, there's no doubt about that, but the panic I sometimes feel when I wake up from a bad dream, for example, isn't as terrifying as the fear that enveloped soldiers fighting in Vietnam. Those of us with AIDS kill no other human beings except our former selves. We'll never shed anyone else's blood. My recurring nightmares, at least the ones I can remember, all have to do with my doctors and medicines. I once dreamed that one of my intravenous drug pouches was filled with a dark, reddish-brown liquid instead of the usual transparent fluid, but my nurse kept reassuring me that it was all right for me to put this substance in my veins. When I finally gave in, I awoke bathed in sweat. And I've been waking up like that every morning for the past few months, whatever the reason. Soldiers must also have disturbing dreams, in which they're threatened and deceived by their own officers or the enemy. Paradoxically, when I open my eyes and look around at all the hospital equipment by my bed, I still think: "Well, it was just a nightmare. I've only got AIDS and I'm not trapped in all that horror I was dreaming about." Isn't a soldier similarly relieved to find, when he awakens, that it's only war out there, and not his own, even more terrible, hallucinatory universe? How can I find rest at night when I'm under such pressure, day after day, month after month? Soldiers go on having war dreams for years after the fighting is over; my unconscious will always be marked by AIDS, if I ever get over it. I'll never be able to see a hypodermic without thinking of "it," or hear the word "diapers" without remembering Oliver's skeletal body in those adult swaddling clothes, like a bulky, rustling pair of rompers. For me, the neighborhood around St. Luke's Hospital is like one of those innocent fields of vegetables near Verdun that evoke memories of terrible bloodshed only in the soldiers who once fought there for months. Thousands of dead and wounded have passed that way, leaving an indelible mark visible only to me and my fellow AIDS patients.

I'm also visited almost every evening by my lost companion, killed in action before his time. I struggle so furiously during the night against these imaginary enemies, about whom I don't dare think in my waking hours, that by morning my pillows and blankets are scattered all over the floor, leaving me shivering without so much as a sheet to protect me from my nocturnal visitors. My bed winds up so rumpled that it suggests prolonged erotic acrobatics when in fact I've simply been defending myself, like Monsieur Seguin's poor goat. I was traumatized as a child by Alphonse Daudet's story, and profoundly disturbed by its sad conclusion. When I first read the tale I was still accustomed to Hollywoodian happy endings, so I expected the goat to survive the wolf's attack after having fought him off all night long. It was only logical to assume that she would be saved and rewarded by the arrival of Monsieur Seguin in the morning. And yet the unhappy animal seems to have fought in vain, since she finally surrenders, panting with exhaustion, at sunrise. I was so angry with the author for having refused the easy way out and for having tried to teach me to fight for the principle of the thing, to preserve my dignity, whatever the outcome might be. The AIDS wolf and General Franco may win in the end, but what counts is fighting honorably at Madrid or withstanding the siege at St. Luke's. That's when one turns to one's childhood heroes, like the frontier woodsman Davy Crockett, the man who knew no fear. He could beat the Indians at their own game and waged his personal war in a strange new world. Like a trapper, I must learn

to recognize the tracks of each opportunistic illness and adapt myself
to the material conditions of the moment, however difficult they may
be—a stay in the hospital, a sleepless night, the insertion of a new
catheter—whistling all the while in the chilly solitude of that dark
forest where I wander without hope of ever finding a sympathetic
Virgil.

.   .   .

We succumb easily to the myth of the Golden Age. The prewar life we
often found monotonous becomes in retrospect a period of unalloyed
prosperity and happiness. One misses not just the sexual escapades,
the free and easy ways, but the quiet evenings as well, the romantic
moments, the walks along a beach—relaxed, a trifle bored, vaguely on
the lookout for some excitement but without a care in the world
beyond the normal concerns of an ordinary life. Like a sword of
Damocles hanging over all our heads, AIDS cuts us off from both the
present and the future. The constant threat of surprise bombing raids
drains enjoyment from those pleasures still within our reach. It's unthinkable to dream of ever returning to those blessed, golden days,
and impossible to imagine that some people back on the home front
may perhaps go on enjoying life the same way we did, as if nothing at
all has happened. That's why a certain bitterness may sometimes show
in what I write. Unjustly, irrationally, I feel that the party's still going
strong elsewhere while I'm sitting here shaking with fever. The Viet-
cong used to tell themselves, as they slogged through the mud, that in
Saigon many of those for whom they were supposedly fighting were
enjoying the good life, living off the Americans, while the women they
wanted for themselves were eagerly pursuing foreigners and their col-
laborationists. My diehard mentality goes hand in hand with a certain
puritanism—recent, in my case—that rankles in those who suffer
from a kind of Cinderella complex, the feeling that everyone has gone
off and left them behind to do the dirty work. My Prince Charming
would be a return to health, but I'm well aware that when this is over,
nothing will bring back the dead, or the carefree innocence we once
knew.

———

Victory or defeat is as hard to envision as recovery or death. We find the image of decay in the physical or social body repulsive, and shrink from the grief of those left widowed, the mourning of orphaned friends. Whenever war is declared, the humiliation of defeat is never officially considered, unless it be to rally flagging spirits at a particularly critical moment in the fighting. Soldiers will die believing in the ultimate triumph of their cause, regretting only that they will never live to see the day of victory. Dying in the war against AIDS, however, contributes nothing to the enemy's defeat, unless one has participated in the experimental testing of new drugs.

People with AIDS ask each other a naive question, one that helps us, perhaps, to carry on: When AIDS has been wiped out, what is the first thing you'll do if you get "through" it? I don't know what to answer. I'm trapped in the mental universe of the disease. AIDS has become second nature to me.

Translated by Linda Coverdale.

THOM GUNN

TERMINAL

The eight years difference in age seems now
Disparity so wide between the two
That when I see the man who armoured stood
Resistant to all help however good
Now helped through day itself, eased into chairs,
Or else led step by step down the long stairs
With firm and gentle guidance by his friend,
Who loves him, through each effort to descend,
Each wavering, each attempt made to complete
An arc of movement and bring down the feet
As if with that spare strength he used to enjoy,
I think of Oedipus, old, led by a boy.

><

"It's been engraved too long on my brain
that my epitaph should proclaim—DIED OF HOMOPHOBIA."

PAUL MONETTE

3275

*Author Paul Monette (1945–95) published this heartbreakingly vital essay
just a year before his death of AIDS. Monette's distinguished contributions
to the literature of AIDS includes a collection of poems,* Love Alone:
Eighteen Elegies for Rog *(1988) and* Borrowed Time: An AIDS Memoir
*(1988). In this essay, Monette recounts his commission, too often repeated,
of finding final resting places for those he loves—and for himself, already
diagnosed with AIDS. He takes us on a tour of graves and epitaphs (his
"very own* National Geographic *special"), from Père-Lachaise to Forest
Lawn, where he returns again and again to the grave of his lover Roger
Horwitz, dead of AIDS at forty-four.*

There are two perfect graves. Well, actually three, but I haven't the
wherewithal or the strength these days to travel as far as Samoa. Stevenson himself was sicker than I when he made his voyage there, a
last-ditch flight to paradise. Or did he see it as his own *Treasure Island*

at last, a chance to consult with parrots and pegleg castaways? Free from Edwardian clutter and the satanic mills of England, perhaps he expected to stumble on a pirate's map. Which in turn would lead him to a sheltered cove, the strongbox hidden in a sea cave whose entrance lay underwater except at the ebb of lowest tide. A boy's adventure for a dying man, hammocked in coconut shade as his own strength ebbed.

His grave is on a promontory overlooking a thousand miles of ocean, so vast you can see the curve of the planet, but maybe that's another boy's illusion. Cut into the slab of stone—granite? quarried where?—is what amounts to the granddaddy of fin-de-siècle epitaphs:

> THIS BE THE VERSE
> YOU GRAVE FOR ME.
> HERE HE LIES
> WHERE HE LONGED TO BE;
> HOME IS THE SAILOR
> HOME FROM SEA,
> AND THE HUNTER
> HOME FROM THE HILL.

Exquisite, that use of "grave" for "engrave," as if the action of the stonecutter and the place itself are one. A lookout, surely, worth a journey halfway round the world. I can see myself there, one foot planted on Stevenson's brow, the trade wind billowing my sailor's blouse as I lift my brassbound spyglass and comb the lordly Pacific. My very own *National Geographic* special.

But not to be realized in the flesh, not in my time anyway. I leave it to stauncher travelers to make the trek to Stevenson's summit, there perhaps to deconstruct the romantic gush of fantasies like mine. Happily no one can desecrate or diminish my other two totems, because I've actually been to them. To the snowbound chapel where Lawrence is buried, in the Sangre de Cristo foothills, on a perch that looks across the high desert beyond the Rio Grande all the way to Arizona. And to the Protestant Cemetery in Rome, where Keats is buried with a half-strung lyre on his tombstone and that final statement written in fire. Surrounded by a meadow of shaggy grass, electric-green, an echo of England in April, the spring that never arrived for the choking poet.

It's only half-true to say that I became a seeker of graves because of AIDS. I grew up in a town pocked with graveyards, old church burial-grounds whose tilted slates have long since lost their graven names. Even then as a melancholy boy I'd sit on a stone, chin in hand, and contemplate the cosmos. Or these country graveyards fenced in iron staves and overhung with willows, the family plot no bigger than a farmhouse bedroom. If they were meant to be a *memento mori,* it was all unconscious to me. Though I daresay I looked like a spook out of Edward Gorey, I don't remember ruminating on death exactly. Rather they constituted a sort of safety zone, where I could indulge my secret longing to be a poet, the chokeless kind.

The first grave I ever tracked down for writerly reasons was Edmund Wilson's. Nothing personal. I'd read an account of the woodland spot where he lay buried with all his honors. A discreet white marble slab two feet high, rounded at the top like the curve of grief itself, and bearing beneath the writer's name three Hebrew letters, which, roughly translated, exhorted the scholar's soul to *Go on from strength to strength.* I carried all of this on a tattered newspaper clipping in my wallet, waiting for the next trip Roger and I made to Provincetown.

The village of Wellfleet is hardly even a detour, the Cape is so narrow beyond the elbow. We found the hillside graveyard without any map or questions asked. Wilson is off by himself under the trees, and it happened that a single daffodil bloomed yellow in front of the stone. It is a detail which at the time cheered me immensely, the opposite of a wilting bouquet, the widow's work of planting a bulb like spitting in Death's face. Mixed up in my head by then—stuffed as it was by overeducation—were fragments of Gray's "Elegy in a Country Churchyard" and Lowell's "Quaker Graveyard in Nantucket." But all of it was still in the realm of the picturesque, no muffled echo of a bell that tolled for me. If anything, this high literary take on darkness managed to push the thing itself away, an amulet of prettied-up quotes safely recorded in Bartlett's.

One visited such places politely, if not piously—like Harold and Maude attending the funerals of strangers, transported by the organ prelude and checking out everyone's hat. Trying on other people's survivors like so many veils, and underneath it all learning how to cry. The first public event I went to after moving to L.A. was Howard Hawks's funeral. I didn't know anyone there, couldn't even have said what movies the man had directed. But I sat next to Angie Dickinson, feeling quite swank, and listened with rapt attention as John Wayne gave the eulogy. I felt faintly ashamed afterward, dissatisfied and incomplete, the way I used to feel in the closet. Thereafter I avoided the obsequies of stars.

Then in the fall of '83 Roger and I were in Rome, having wound our way through Tuscany, waiting overnight to catch a plane back to L.A. We only had a single free afternoon, and decided to track down the Keats-Shelley Memorial House, overlooking the Spanish Steps. A most fussy and eccentric place, chockablock with memorabilia in the Victorian manner, cut-paper silhouettes and locks of everyone's hair. The whole presided over by a sunken-cheeked vicar who didn't appear to want visitors at all.

It took us a while to get our bearings, no help from the vicar. But soon we were reading Joseph Severn's diary under glass, a rending account of the poet's last days. We realized that the tiny room in the front corner was where Keats had actually died, with a window onto the Steps and the Bernini fountain in the piazza. Bernini's conceit was a simple stone boat with gouts of water pouring from its sides, a leaky vessel the sound of whose plashing reached us in the death-room. By all accounts the poet in his final hours was calm and resigned, though agitated at the end by a letter from Fanny Brawne which he couldn't bring himself to open, much less read. He asked that Severn place it in the folds of his winding sheet.

And then that final night, Severn sketching beside the bed to keep himself from going mad with grief. *28 Janry 3 o'clock mng*, he has scrawled in charcoal beneath the sketch of the poet's head lolling on a pillow. *Drawn to keep me awake, a deadly sweat was on him all this night.* And framed above the glass cabinet of Severn's memory, an artist's ink drawing of the grave they bore him to. You couldn't get through

college English, in my time anyway, without some passing reference
to the name that was *writ in water*. But somehow the full text had
escaped me until now, and it brought me up extremely short.

THIS GRAVE CONTAINS ALL THAT WAS MORTAL
OF A YOUNG ENGLISH POET,
WHO, ON HIS DEATH BED,
IN THE BITTERNESS OF HIS HEART,
AT THE MALICIOUS POWER OF HIS ENEMIES,
DESIRED THESE WORDS TO BE ENGRAVEN ON HIS TOMB STONE:

HERE LIES ONE
WHOSE NAME WAS WRIT IN WATER.

FEB 21ST, 1821

I turned to Roger and said with a kind of fevered resolve: "We
have to go there. Right now."

But it was already growing dusk in the piazza below, nearly five
o'clock and the vicar squirming to be rid of us. The Protestant Cemetery was too far away, its gates padlocked at nightfall. No time in the
morning either, since we had to be up at dawn to make the airport.
"Next trip," I said to myself, dissatisfied and suddenly full of portent,
a shiver of mortality and the roads that don't lead back.

. . .

. . . In the winter after Italy, I conceived the reckless scheme of
writing a play about Keats's final week. A nine-days'-wonder of a
notion, to take place in that very apartment above the Spanish Steps.
With Severn and a landlady to care for him, and the landlady's ripe
peasant daughter bringing up milk and hearty soups. . . . And to
vary the setting I'd show the outing Keats and Severn made to the
Protestant Cemetery, before the poet was too ill to leave his bed. The
meadow was pocked with violets that day. Keats sighed when he saw
them, expressing a longing to pull the cover of grass over him, so the
violets would carpet his heart.

But I only got as far as checking the books out of the library. By the time I'd read twenty pages of Walter Jackson Bates's huge biography, weighty as a tombstone itself, my eyes had glazed over. . . . Let John Keats die in peace.

Before another year was out, all my friends were dying instead. But by some quirk of coincidence, none of them was buried in a cemetery. Scattered ashes and memorial services were the fashion, all too often without any reference to AIDS or even gay. We let loose our balloons and made a final circuit through the house of the deceased— where the final battle was already taking place between the "blood" family and the lover, fighting over the towels and the lamps and the bibelots.

The morning after Roger died, his half-brother came bustling into my room and stirred me from my Dalmane twilight. "You've got work to do," he said, and when I frowned in confusion, added, "Where's he going? You've got to pick a place."

The Protestant Cemetery in Rome, I thought irrelevantly, sitting slumped in the back of the car as we toured the city's cemeteries. When we got to Forest Lawn, Hollywood Hills division, the only thing left in my heart besides the grief was a horror of finding myself in *The Loved One.* For this was surely the very place envisioned by Waugh— the sweep of grass like a Palm Springs golf course, no gravestones permitted, only bronze plaques in the ground. Nothing to mar the founder's vision of a Park of Death, joyous with children playing and family picnics, all the dead having gone to heaven. Anchored at one end by a white clapboard village church, or at least the Disney equivalent, and on the other by a half-scale replica of the Old North Church in Boston, of course with generous parking. Dotted about the landscape were white marble statues of stupefying vulgarity, Moms and Dads and kids in frozen groups, little tykes on their knees praying.

But at least no Jesus shit that I could detect. And as it turned out, when we entered the Tara reception center, the theme of the Hollywood Hills division was God Bless America—a garden of patriots as its centerpiece, full-scale bronzes of Washington and Jefferson, and a huge outdoor mural of the signing of the Declaration. Hallmark meets *My Weekly Reader.* Our Comfort Counselor, Mr. Wheeler, was not quite Rod Steiger in a powdered wig, though his nails were lugubriously clean. He moved in a cloud of Aramis that stung the eyes within ten feet of him.

Real estate came first, as it always does in California. Roger's parents and I were driven about in Mr. Wheeler's Cadillac, two miles an hour, as he pointed out each section from Heavenly Rest to Resurrection. I directed him up the winding hill to the highest plots, where the lawn verged on undeveloped chaparral. Atheists all, we abandoned the car and trudged uphill in Mr. Wheeler's wake, the hillside shaded by umbrella pines and with a view across the valley to the San Bernardinos if the smog was light. Wheeler carried a big book like a survey map, the whole acreage divided into numbered plots.

They were sold in pairs, side by side. Puffing from the climb, we decided we liked where we were. A deal: Plot 3275, Spaces 1 and 2, on the hill called Revelation. Delicately Wheeler inquired which space I wanted Roger in. I shrugged. What did it matter? Roger's mother touched my arm and said, "He wants to know which side you boys slept on in bed." Oh. As a matter of fact it went either way, depending on who needed to be closest to the alarm clock. Let Roger have the right side shell. "Excellent," said Mr. Wheeler, circling it on his chart. Then, offhandedly, "This section used to be reserved just for Mormons, but we've opened it up."

I looked around in dismay, only now picking out the Mormon Temple engraved on several bronzes. "Hey, this isn't going to work, Mr. Wheeler. They don't want us up here."

He was shocked. "We're all one family in death," I think he said, and I let it go for the parents' sake. "One thing I should tell you, though," he continued. "At night the deer come down and steal the flowers. We can't stop them." He pointed with dismay to the undeveloped scrub on the hillside above, clearly an affront to the manicured lawns of the dead. "Some people don't like it, having their flowers scattered. Sometimes we have to move their loved ones further down the hill. The deer will only go so far."

Al and Bernice were sporting the same dreamy smile I was. "Don't worry, Mr. Wheeler," I assured him. "We like the deer just fine. What kind of flowers do they prefer?"

He gave a bewildered shrug. His expertise lay elsewhere, in the coffin-and-hearse department. By week's end we had buried Roger there, and I still didn't understand that I'd bought the spot where I'd be spending most of the next year and a half.

There was no place else to go, really. Friends would call with an invitation to lunch, or an extra ticket to the Philharmonic, in one ear and out the other. Not that I wasn't grateful to pass the time, but I knew where I needed to be. Usually from three to five in the afternoon, till closing time. Mostly I sat on my own grave—my permanent side of the bed now—and mostly didn't cry. Cried most of the day and night at home already, so this was my break. Seven days a week. On Saturdays I'd bring up café au lait and croissants at noon and read the paper, just as we always used to do. I'd talk out loud to Roger, reciting him poems. Or I'd lie down and fold my hands across my chest, looking up through the trees and trying to adjust to my last address.

From my perch on the hill I could see the day's funerals, straggling out of the churches. A line of slow cars to the gravesite, the mourners standing in a half circle as the coffin was laid on the lowering hoist, the mounded dirt on either side covered with sheets of Astroturf. They don't do the filling in till after everyone's gone. And I don't know if this constitutes a statistical sample, but almost nobody seemed to wear black anymore. Pastels, a lot of lilac and lavender.

I began to wonder which of the dead had died of AIDS. So I undertook a methodical survey of the whole acreage, moving row by row for the better part of a week, checking out every inscription. At the time there were eighty thousand in residence, with room for another fifty thousand. Here and there I'd find them, young men dead at thirty or thirty-five, with a stray quotation from *Hamlet* or *Pooh*. A silent scattered tribe, the first wave of the plague.

Are you reeling from the mawkishness? Because it gets worse. I had almost made a full circuit by now, having come round again to the western ridge where Roger lay, but still two hundred yards to go. And I realized I had stumbled onto the babies' section. Annabelle, two days old; William Jr., May 25–June 16, 1985. Acres of this, the bronze plaques carved with teddy bears and a lot of Christian singsong. Bronze is not an easy medium to write in, but curiously the cliches seem to help. You learn that it's none of your business what other people choose to memorialize, the inadequate words that mark the scar in their heart.

It takes about six weeks to order the bronze and set it in place. They send you a rubbing of the first casting (a hundred bucks extra), on which I made a myriad of fussy changes. It was finished mid-February and laid in place. I came that day nearly faint with trepidation, fearing somehow the finality, the want of exactly the right word. Or perhaps I'd tried to cram too much in. And still I couldn't say whom it was meant to address, what sort of declaration to the future—as if anyone would even notice it except for an obsessive like me. But here it was, the final word on the final hill. I dropped to my knees and read it through over and over, making sure nothing was off.

> ROGER DAVID HORWITZ
> 1941–1986
> MY LITTLE FRIEND
>
> WE SAIL TOGETHER
> IF WE SAIL AT ALL
>
> BELOVED SON AND BROTHER
> THE WISEST AND JUSTEST AND BEST

The last phrase being Plato's final words on Socrates—in his prison cell, the poison having done its work, history's most compelling argument against capital punishment. But here I'm getting it out of sequence. First came the Christmas crisis, when Forest Lawn relaxes its rule against gaudy tributes and NO ARTIFICIAL FLOWERS. Suddenly the gravesites are decked with Christmas trees and tinsel and wreaths and even battery lights. I'd just begun to get used to the quiet of the place, even looked fondly now on the Old North Church, and here I was confronted by a Macy's load of gewgaws.

I wanted to hide somewhere till Christmas was removed. As it happened, Star and Craig flew out from New York to spend the holiday with me, to get me through it. Star convinced me to take a few days with her over New Year's in New Mexico, where I had never been. "As long as we can visit Lawrence's grave," I replied, setting myself a pilgrimage. The second day we headed north of Taos, blinding sun on the snow, to Kiowa Ranch. Off the road on a rutted track, heading uphill and deep into the trees. To the modest cluster of ranch buildings, the whole of it deeded to David and Frieda Lawrence by Mabel Dodge, in exchange for the autograph manuscript of *Sons and Lovers*.

You must climb a steep hill to reach the chapel, but it wasn't the altitude pounding my heart. My first glimpse of it stung my eyes. Simple, more like a stuccoed shed than a church because crafted by hand. The rose window above the door is the hub of a tractor's tire, the one above the altar inside is a wagon wheel. The altar itself is painted silver, with just the letters DHL incised on the front. A few painted leaves and sunflowers by Dorothy Brett, the painter who was their boon companion, who had to put down her ear trumpet to pick up her brushes.

But it's so silent up there anyway, just the breeze through the piñon trees and my blubbering relief. I felt as if I were standing on the Everest of death. In the warped guestbook several pilgrims had scribbled notes beside their names: *fellow pagan; a worshiper of the God of free love.* Then you step out the door into the delirious vastness of the desert below, all ochre and streaks of purple, and yes the curve of the earth besides. I had managed to come to a new place where Roger and I had never been, without expiring of loneliness. And I had the peculiar feeling that Lawrence had given this view to me, sightless himself in the urn of ashes sealed in the altar.

. . .

We went back to the chapel the next day, by which time I managed the visit without tears. But there was something else going on now, a sudden compulsion to get back to Forest Lawn and our place—as if this whole visit were a kind of betrayal, sleeping in somebody else's bed before the funeral meats were cold. Abruptly Star and I left, and I stopped at the first payphone to change my reservation, bringing me back to L.A. that night, which was New Year's Eve.

I raced over to Forest Lawn next morning, full-crazy by now, terrified that Roger's grave might have vanished, or else that it had lost the magic closeness it engendered—the nearest I could get to him now except in dreams. Though still laden with Christmas, the cemetery was practically deserted, everyone staying home today to watch football. I dropped to my knees at 3275, announcing that I was home again. Whimpering rather than crying, I buried a Zuni ring I'd picked up on the plaza in Santa Fe, buried it over his heart.

And then I began to keen, rocking back and forth on my haunches. I realized I was trying to match the sound of Roger's moaning when I arrived in his room at UCLA the day he died. A sound I barely understood at the time, a lament of terrible urgent sorrow calling out but without any words. The cryptococcus had swelled his brain in the night and stolen his center of speech. "Why is he doing that?" I asked the nurse, but she couldn't say. I asked for a shot to calm his agitation, then realized he could answer me by blinking his eyes when I asked him questions. I called his sister and held the phone to his ear as she talked, and he blinked and blinked.

Now ten weeks later, a stillborn year before me, I finally understand that the bleating sound on that last day was Roger calling my name. Through the pounding in his head, the blindness and the paralysis, all his bodily functions out of control, he had somehow heard me come in. Had waited. And once I understood that, I went mad. My moaning rose to a siren pitch, and I clawed at the grass that covered him. Possessed with a fury to dig the six feet down and tear open the lid and clasp him to me, whatever was left. I don't even know what stopped me—exhaustion, I guess, the utter meaninglessness of anything anymore.

Grief is madness—ask anyone who's been there. They will tell you it abates with time, but that's a lie. What drowns you in the first year is a force of solitude and helplessness exactly equal in intensity to the love you had for the one who's gone. Equally passionate, equally intimate. The spaces between the stabs of pain grow longer after a while, but they're empty spaces. The clichés of condolence get you back to the office, back to your taxes and the dinner table—and for everyone else's sake, you collaborate. The road of least resistance is paved with the gravel of well-meaning friends, rather like the gravel that cremation leaves.

Most of my friends would have said I was doing quite well as we passed the first anniversary. I finished the draft of *Borrowed Time* and set off with Craig for Italy, spending the first night in Rome just off the Piazza Navona where Roger and I had spent the *last* night of our trip in '83. I had no plans to visit Keats's grave, having given over the sum of my graveyard vigil to 3275. But the jet lag woke me wired at dawn, and Craig was a slower riser even than I. Our train to Florence wasn't leaving till eleven.

I scribbled a note and left on foot, my map of the city blown to shreds by the wind off the Tiber. No taxis in sight, but maybe I just needed to get there on my own. I had no idea what the hours were, and got sidetracked in my confusion by a military cemetery, across the way, immaculate and precise as a full-dress drill. A wizened gardener put me right with a lot of gesticulating, and at last I found the crooked side street and the door in the weed-chinked wall.

Open, even so early, and utterly deserted. It seemed at first a typical urban burial-ground, no vacancy and no breathing space, crammed with the marble monuments of another age. But there was a sign nailed to a tree that said KEATS AND SEVERN, with an arrow pointing past the caretaker's office. Beyond that point the tenement crowded-ness opened out onto a pristine lawn, only a handful of graves, some-one having made a shrewd Protestant decision to stop any further burial here, for Keats's sake perhaps. An acre of green bordered on one side by the Cestius pyramid—erected 16 B.C. The Christian in the shadow of the pagan, my sort of place.

I took the pebbled path around to Keats and Severn, already crying, sobbing hysterically—well, histrionically, then—and fell to my knees in the patch of ivy that fronted the graves. I hadn't cried so much since the madness of New Year's Day. I cried for all those who'd died too young, none of their promises kept, whose tombstones bore no name. These days everyone I knew seemed *writ in water*. Severn lay beside him, the painter having lived into his eighty-fifth year, yet still remembered most for those fevered days and nights nearly sixty years before.

> TO THE MEMORY OF
> JOSEPH SEVERN
> DEVOTED FRIEND AND DEATH-BED COMPANION
> OF
> JOHN KEATS
> WHOM HE LIVED TO SEE NUMBERED AMONG
> THE IMMORTAL POETS OF ENGLAND

When I was sufficiently composed again I took my leave. . . .

And when I returned to L.A. ten days later, my vigils at 3275 grew more and more intermittent. Not a conscious thing, or indeed a happy turn of events. I'd finally shifted ground, and knew at last that Roger wasn't there in Forest Lawn at all. Or anywhere else. It would mostly now be a journey for the sake of memory, the marking of his birthday or his deathday or the anniversary of our meeting. A special cortege if his parents or sister were in town, but that was only once a year. I suppose I came to rely on the mail instead, letters from readers of *Borrowed Time* to whom Roger was vividly alive, more alive than to me.

I met Stephen. Everyone said I'd moved on. After the October action in Washington, and Stephen's arrest at the FDA, we gave ourselves a few days' downtime in the Shenandoah Valley. We picnicked in the ruins of a brick plantation house, and later stumbled onto a Confederate graveyard. Buried where they'd fallen, it seemed, tombstones marking the end of soldiers who were only seventeen, some as young as fourteen. And may the gods forgive me, I'd passed once more into the realm of the picturesque. For this was as pretty a place as the old New England family plots fenced by iron staves, where I used to maunder away the afternoons of my adolescence.

Two months later, over New Year's on Kauai, we fulfilled a pledge to Adam Savage, Stephen's former roommate, who wanted his ashes scattered on a very specific beach. The northeast coast of the island, a dirt road winding down along the bank of a stream that was fed by a mountain rainforest—from deep in the interior where the rain never stopped. The stream debouched at Aliomanu Bay, an un-marked palmy strand where the sand was like powdered sugar. Pic-ture-perfect.

We opened the box of ashes, difficult to scatter in the gusting breeze that white-capped the breakers. As Stephen poured the crushed bone into the maelstrom just where the fresh water met the salt, I intoned Edna Millay's "Dirge Without Music," trumpeting it into the wind. All in all an impressive ceremony, to us anyway, till we were confronted by a pair of natives carrying six-packs. "What're you guys dumping in that water?" one of them demanded, his anger barely suppressed. He had a hundred pounds on me.

"It's just a ritual," I replied pleasantly.

"Bullshit," his partner growled.

Stephen was done with the pouring, the last bits blown across the rippling current. We backed away to the car, smiling and nodding. They glared us out of there but made no move to attack. I understood the beach was theirs, no matter who held the deed. But I also knew in my own bones that they'd kill us for the trespass if they knew we'd dumped AIDS in the water. I thought back to them two years later, when my father told me a hospice had been denied a site in one of the Boston suburbs, because the townsfolk feared the runoff of rain from the roof would taint the groundwater with AIDS. This was before the fundamentalists began to picket AIDS funerals in the Midwest, mock-ing and spitting on the mourners.

My mother died the next winter, after what seemed a lifetime of struggling with emphysema. ("I know what it's like," she used to wheeze, "to have people treat you like your illness is all your own fault.") I flew into Boston in a blizzard, and was fishtailed the twenty miles north to Andover by an intrepid Sikh cabdriver. The funeral next morning, blue sky and a blinding snowscape, began with a ser-vice at Christ Episcopal. They opened the coffin one last time in the vestibule, so my father and brother and I could have a final some-thing. I grazed her hand with my fingers, flinching from the icy cold, the waxen flesh. My father kissed her lips.

We buried her in the churchyard, in the snow behind the chan-cel—the gravediggers having huddled and decided the ground wasn't too frozen for the backhoe. My parents had acquired the plot the previous summer, proudly taking me there on my last visit home, so they could "show off the property." It was at the crest of a knoll, which fell in gentle terraces lush with the humid green of June, overlooking a hundred years of slate and granite markers in no particular ranks, faithful parishioners having settled in for the duration. Across on the next rise, separated by a country lane, was the Congregational grave-yard, neighborly but a bit more trim, less shaggy than the Episcopal. You'd never believe you were fifty yards from the center of town.

"It's beautiful, isn't it?" declared my mother excitedly. "Daddy'll be able to come down and visit me and read his paper."

Beside the grave my father has set a small stone bench for just that purpose. For six months after she died, I felt nothing. I'd tell my friends, "As soon as I have a feeling, I'll let you know." Not that the numbness wasn't a feeling, but it gave no access back to her.

It was sometime in early summer that I was driving with Ste-phen and his mother, riding in the back so they could talk. At one point he turned to her and asked, "Mom, do you need a place to visit?" We all knew what kind of place he meant. Dolores shook her head slowly: "No, it's not important to me."

I leaned forward and put in my two cents. "I need it," I said. And slick as a Bible salesman I made a pitch for Forest Lawn, the hill they called Revelation. We'd have to check to see if they allowed ashes to be buried up there, instead of in the safe-deposit boxes of the Columbarium. Otherwise the matter was settled, both of them leaving it up to me.

But it wasn't a detail we ever followed up on, the business of ashes in the ground. He got sick so unexpectedly on Labor Day, none of us really believing he was on his way out. Within ten days he was sealed in a mask, his lungs fed by a noisy oxygen push. He beckoned for paper and pen and scribbled these notes:

9/13/90

Cremated by After-Care (if possible) and if poss. *buried* (in the ground) close to you.

Would've wanted to convert to Living Trust but it seems a little
late now, doesn't it?

Oh yes, later and later every hour. And the *déjà vu* a week later, riding
five miles an hour at Forest Lawn with our Comfort Counselor, then
abandoning the car for the steep walk up Revelation hill. Dolores and
Ted, Stephen's father, accompanied me, along with his sister Susan
and Victor, our staunchest friend. I'd already determined to buy the
highest plot of all, maybe fifteen feet above Roger, because our row
was already filled. The family was pleased with the prospect and let
me make the arrangements. There was in fact no problem about burying an urn of ashes in the ground.

   "We usually sell these plots in pairs," purred the Counselor,
thinking to make some room for me.

   "Oh no, I'm going down there with Roger," I declared, pointing
toward my own spot.

   There was a beat of the purest confusion, as the Counselor tried
to grapple with the meaning here. Slowly he began to put it together
that I was widowed twice, a notion that clearly struck him as rather
indelicate. Like that daft moment in *The Importance of Being Earnest,*
when Jack's revelation that he's orphaned meets with the arch disap-
proval of Lady Bracknell:

   To lose one parent, Mr. Worthing, may be regarded as a misfortune; to lose both looks like carelessness.

   And then Dolores stepped into the breach, turning to Victor to
inquire, very no-nonsense: "Well, do you have a place?"

   After a moment's left-footed dancing among us, we decided
Victor would go beside Stephen. So we informed the Counselor that
after all we would take the two-fer deal, which he duly recorded in his
book of deeds, however questionable the arrangement seemed to him.

   The funeral was three days later, with the burial after the service. I carried the porcelain urn, too small, it seemed, to hold all of
him, for I was a connoisseur of ashes by now. Wondering if the remainder had been left in the oven, since the mortuary hadn't really
liked us providing our own non-regulation urn, brought by Susan's
Marine husband from his posting in Japan.

Numb again, number than even my mother had left me. The thing that sparked the tears was hearing from my friend Dan, who'd stood behind the scenes at the funeral to cue the music. Near him in the doorway lounged a pair of cemetery employees—polyester suits, not diggers—having a smoke. And trading fag jokes and AIDS jokes. Dan hissed at them to be quiet.

I reported them, of course, and of course they denied it. The Boss Comfort Counselor assured me over the phone that Forest Lawn had been the first to accept the dead of AIDS. In fact, she added smoothly, Forest Lawn was proud of having regular consciousness-raising sessions for all their employees, where the demonization of "all non-Christians" was rigorously discouraged. I thought I was going to puke if I didn't get off the phone fast.

I visited every day for a month, bringing with me a folder of pictures of Stephen—running through them like flash cards for a foreign tongue, except here they were wordless. My last jolt of rage had been spent ordering the bronze, on which I proposed to engrave:

STEPHEN F. KOLZAK
MY GUERRILLA, MY LOVE
1953–1990

DIED OF HOMOPHOBIA
DIED A HERO

BELOVED SON AND BROTHER
REAL ISN'T HOW YOU ARE MADE

YOU BECOME

It seemed the least I could give him by way of defiance, since he'd made it clear often enough that he wanted his body dumped on the White House lawn. The family protested as tactfully as it could. I excised *died of homophobia* and said I would have it on my grave instead. We retained the final quotation from *The Velveteen Rabbit*.

After a week or two I could cry a little, pricked by the weird juxtaposition of paying respects to Roger first, then the final climb to Stephen. Yet by the time Victor and I took off for Europe—a month to the day after burying Stevie—the pain had frozen over again. I'd hoped I might get through the grief weeping in cathedrals, but they pretty much left me cold. I even took Victor to the Protestant Cemetery in Rome, but Keats's grave had become just another story by then. More exalted than Forest Lawn, to be sure, where the Counselor had puffed with pride in the neighborhood, pointing out how close we were to Rick Nelson.

I think I've been to Revelation just three times in the last two years, in every case as an escort for one or the other family. The conversations on the hill are mostly suffused with memories—the good ones. In this the parents are wiser than I, who watch my body change and dwindle and seem able to recall only the suffering of the men I loved. These memories pursue me everywhere: the radiation table, in the tunnel of an MRI, half my life in waiting rooms. I don't know where the certainty went, the solidity of the ground beneath me during the first year's visits to Roger. No matter what happened I'd end up here, the compass point of my journey's end. Surcease from the pain at last. Now that seems like another pretty story, no real comfort.

Last October Winston and I went to Paris, a city he'd never seen before. It was his idea to take the Métro out to Père-Lachaise, the permanent address for so many stellar Parisians. Mostly decrepit, not kept up, chockablock with phonebooth chapels whose stained-glass windows were kitsch to the max. Parisians being the least Catholic of Catholics, but with a sentimental streak a mile wide when it came to burying the dead.

They had just sandblasted Oscar Wilde, so the great Egyptian monument by Jacob Epstein—a Deco angel rampant, hovering in stone—was clean of all graffiti. No evidence of violence except the angel's privates, hacked away in the twenties and never replaced. Then Gertrude Stein, an unadorned slab with just her name and dates, very bourgeois. "But where's Alice?" I wondered aloud, thinking I'd misremembered their lying together. Then we walked around behind the slab through the unkempt ivy and found Alice's name in smaller letters, as if she'd averted her face from the spotlight one last time.

Around the next corner was Piaf's plot. Fortunately we had a

map to find it, because she is listed first on the grave as Edith Gio-
vanna Gassion (*dit* Piaf), her sparrow nickname consigned to paren-
theses. In any case it's a family plot, her own name no more prominent than the others. And we couldn't get too close, because she had a
guardian attendant that day, a little man with a henna-rinsed rug and
Poirot mustache who seemed profoundly offended by our presence.
He was cleaning up the place, bearing away the withered floral tributes and dumping them in a *poubelle*. October tenth had been the
twenty-ninth anniversary of her death, and people remembered still.
Was this peculiar man, pushing seventy now, some member of the
Gassion family? Or more likely one of the forty thousand mourners
who broke through police barricades at the funeral, just to be closer to
her.

The afternoon was sharp as an apple, clouds breaking up after
days of rain, as we made our way around to the entrance again—one
eye peeled for Proust and Isadora Duncan. We passed the line of
memorials to those who'd died in the camps: Sachsenhausen, Buchen-
wald-Dora, Auschwitz, Ravensbruck, Mauthausen, each monument
more horrorstruck than the last. Beseeching figures reaching their
bony limbs to the sky, that the agony might lift. At the Mauthausen
memorial there are 186 steps carved in the stone, to represent the
Sisyphean task of the inmates, carrying rocks from the quarry—186
steps to reach level ground, only to be sent back for more rocks.

We walked on somberly, mocked by the flashing sunlight
through the chestnut trees, the necropolis having been washed clean
by the rain. And then we entered a quarter that was overrun with
graffiti, on every grave on every side. But not the urban graffiti we
were used to, the hieratic mock-Cyrillic of the spray can. Here the
notes and tributes were rather more formal: SEX DRUGS AND ROCK N
ROLL; WE LOVE YOU, JIM; THE MUSIC NEVER DIES. Intensifying in volume as
we neared the grave itself, scarcely a bare spot left on the bourgeois
marble—useless to sandblast such a torrent.

At Morrison's place was a curious assembly of punk Eurokids
and retro American hippies, sitting about and smoking but altogether
subdued and respectful. Hard to tell the difference, frankly, between
this ragtag troupe and the fussy man with the henna job, as far as the

fervor of memory went. There's no one way to visit such places, no prescribed amount of tears. But always it seems we make the journey to enter a river of memory larger than our poor tributaries, the brooks of spring that have dried up by summer's end.

Inevitably, Père-Lachaise is defined by its most distinguished residents, so many and so varied that one cannot help but move through its alleys like a tourist. As long as you're there you might as well check out Proust. No disrespect in that, but hardly the level of pilgrimage that brings you to Kiowa Ranch or the Protestant Cemetery.

My own touchstone in Paris lies at the center of the city—the hub of France, in fact, from which all distances and road signs take their measure. If you are a hundred kilometers from Paris, it means you are just so far from the west portal of Notre Dame. At the stern tip of the Ile de la Cité, just behind the brawny cathedral, lies the monument to the French deported to the camps. It's barely identified, easy to miss, a gated garden in front of what looks like a fortress wall. On either side a pair of steep stairways lead down to a walled courtyard at the level of the river.

A concrete holding pen, it feels like, with a single opening onto the river, a barred gate like a portcullis. You are meant to feel that here is where they will board you under guard, onto prison ships that will carry you to your doom. If you turn away you're confronted by the narrow entrance that pierces the fortress wall and beckons you into a kind of cave.

The first thing you see, directly in front of you, is a dimlit tunnel receding deep under the island. The tunnel is paved with tiny glass beads of light, one for each of the two hundred thousand deportees. On the end wall of the tunnel is a bright light, almost a searchlight, which I've been told is intended to represent hope. But it's hard not to see it as the beam of a train, bearing down on all of us. At your feet there's a sort of bronze sarcophagus, containing the remains of an *inconnu,* an unknown inmate.

You are not permitted to enter the tunnel, only to wander around the vestibule. On the walls are carved quotations from the writers of the Resistance—Sartre, Camus, St. Exupéry, Vercors. But the carver's alphabet is jagged, as if every letter had been etched in the stone with a sharpened spoon handle. Defacement of a very high order, the graffiti of the damned. Curiously uplifting in its way, because there isn't a false step anywhere, no Disney simplification, no tidying up. As you walk out into daylight again, incised above the doorway in the same prisoner's alphabet is the final admonition:

> FORGIVE BUT
> DON'T FORGET.

I wasn't numb there at all. No tears exactly, but a sense in which I was centered by my grief. All my dead around me bearing me up. We were in Paris seven days, staying in a small hotel on the Ile Saint Louis, barely a hundred yards from the monument. I paid a visit every day and usually had the place to myself. Like some version of the man with the henna wig, I grew quite proprietary, gladly offering simultaneous translations of the words in the stone to American tourists struggling with their high school French. One afternoon I was joined by an old man who told me he had survived two years at Bergen-Belsen. After a half-hour of showing *me* the monument I wasn't sure whether he'd be offended if I offered him a gratuity. When I did, he accepted it heartily and gave me a bear hug, then took off to have himself a glass.

All of which somehow leads me back to 3275. I will probably die without forgiving anyone, certainly not the *Kapos* and the Commandants of Reagan/Bush and their genocidal politics of AIDS. It's been engraved too long on my brain that my epitaph should proclaim—

> DIED OF HOMOPHOBIA
> MURDERED BY HIS GOVERNMENT

Still room of course for a line or two of uplift, a scrap of Shakespeare, but I haven't settled on that yet. My heart is too exhausted to sustain the bitterness anymore, not even against the calumnies of my enemies. The writer who trashed me twelve years ago in the *Native* has kept up his campaign. "It isn't even English," he remarked to an interviewer last summer, shuddering at my prose. He has a friend who calls him, he says, and reads whole paragraphs of me, reducing them both to whinnies of laughter.

But his malice has lost its power to make me feel *writ in water*. AIDS has taught me precisely what I'm writ in, blood and bone and viral load. I can't tell anymore whom I am addressing with my epitaph. The accidental tourist? Or my own grieving friends who can't even parse their losses anymore, who don't need bronze to recall me. And after all, I've been visiting my own grave for years now—*pre-need,* as they call it at Forest Lawn—and I don't require any further vigil from anybody.

Unless it is some kind of safety zone. And as long as there's no piety in the gesture. I don't like flowers, but the deer do. Keats and Lawrence and Stevenson all died of their lungs, robbed by a century whose major products were soot and sulfur. We queers on Revelation hill, tucking our skirts about us so as not to touch our Mormon neighbors, died of the greed of power, because we were expendable. If you mean to visit any of us, it had better be to make you strong to fight that power. Take your languor and easy tears somewhere else. Above all, don't pretty us up. Tell yourself: *None of this ever had to happen.* And then go make it stop, with whatever breath you have left. Grief is a sword, or it is nothing.

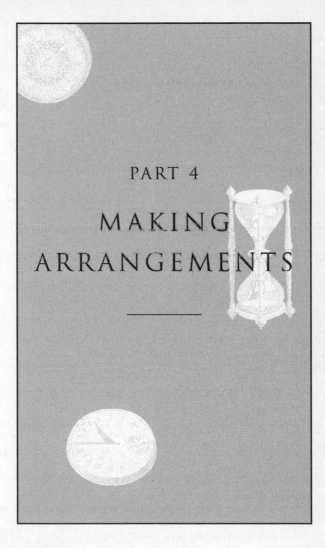

PART 4

MAKING ARRANGEMENTS

U̲nlike fiction, endings in life don't come at the end. A life ceases— but rarely has it ended. In the funeral service and in the final disposition of the remains, a sense of closure is sought and often found. Perhaps in ceremony, as in fiction, we find what is missing in experience, a beginning, middle, and end.

Anthropologists have observed that procedures for tending and disposing of the dead show a fluctuating history instead of the stability we might expect of it. "From this," writes A. L. Kroeber, "follows the generalization that intensity of feeling regarding any institution is likely to be a poor criterion, if any, of its permanence." Our burial or cremation practices may acquire for us the solemnity of the inviolable—so that we would find any deviation or alternative abhorrent— and yet such observances can pass out of practice within a relatively short span of time.

Perhaps it is the customary itself that draws us at such times. Faced with the disorienting task of making funeral arrangements—not to mention the addling task of dying—customs (secular and religious) provide bearings, resolutions for unanticipated and distressing choices. However we understand our attraction to ritual, certainly the ceremonious allows an unwonted regard and courtesy to human suffering—albeit often in the name of another order of meaning. And in its imperturbable pace, it can get us from here to an unimaginable there.

In the section that follows we offer some distinguished examinations of premodern and modern rites and rituals for greeting death and bidding the dead farewell.

THE
"FORMAL FEELING"
RITES AND RITUAL

———

From man's blood-sodden heart are sprung
Those branches of the night and day
Where the gaudy moon is hung.
What's the meaning of all song?
"Let all things pass away."

W. B. YEATS
Vacillation

"The dead . . . need comfort or mothering
like infants, from mother or wife, to close the eyes,
straighten the limbs, fix the jaw shut."

EMILY VERMEULE

A VERY ACTIVE DEAD

The archaeologist Emily Vermeule is distinguished for her many fertile works on the art and culture of Bronze-Age Greece. Her Aspects of Death in Early Greek Art and Poetry, *grounded in the most expert archaeology, is anything but remote in its delving and urbane account of a distant culture's efforts to establish, through ritual and art, an intimate alliance of the living and the dead. Vermeule's crisp eloquence, and her ability to find lively truths in long-buried practices, call Montaigne and Sir Thomas Browne to mind. In the following passages from this rich work, Vermeule examines Greek funeral customs and the beliefs about life and death which they ratify.*

The dead themselves, or parts of them, are not at all fugitive. The earth's crust is filled with them, in the forms of bones, dust, oil, monuments, memories, myth—with different techniques of access. On the physical side it is easy to disturb them and to learn how the human race has cared to bury its dead in the past. Artists recorded the ceremonial gestures of grief, and the forms of funeral. Poets created the images of love and longing, and views of another land where the dead might still move and talk in a persistent weak imitation of life. When the different kinds of evidence and testimonies about death in the Greek world—about body and soul, about the grave and the underworld, about mortality and immortality, loss and creativity—are drawn together, it is entirely natural that they should conflict and refuse to be drawn into any easy harmonious picture.

More than any other experience, death engenders uncertain feelings and confused thoughts. Life and death are the most obvious opposites, even to children, and the most obvious unity, in untutored instinct as well as in old poetic and religious tradition: irreconcilable principles insistently held together like twins in a nurse's arms. In this naturally illogical sphere, where body and soul lead separate but linked lives and deaths, Greek logic was only gradually and precariously applied, with minimal success. From Herakleitos to Lucian, whenever reason was brought to bear upon the unknowable, a sense of self-mockery was produced which, almost inevitably, cured itself only by slipping sideways into mythical fantasy, where opposites are so often congenial.

It is nearly impossible to recreate any general "Greek view of death," although Greek practical behavior when confronted with death is well known, and was not very different from practice in other cultures. Early Greeks took death extremely seriously, as we all do. If they were less elaborate in their ceremonies and less optimistic in their beliefs than the Egyptians, perhaps less creative in ritual than the Hittites, they still had powerful emotional and religious feelings about burying the dead, for which there is the most persuasive and moving evidence in Greek epic and tragedy. A significant part of their artistic energy was focused on themes of death, and on burial as a partial solution to the problems of death.

"Burial" is used here, perhaps wrongly, as a general term for the permanent disposal of a corpse. It does not seem to affect either ceremony or views of the afterlife, whether the corpse was put dressed directly in the ground, or was burned on a pyre with the ashes and bones collected later. Students of Greek culture have long tried to detect differences in how the different generations understood the psyche or the *soma* according to whether the prevailing fashion was to bury or burn. It does not seem to matter; any form of burial marks the family or community action which transfers the body to a new state of belonging, and the absent element of individuality called the *psyche* always is absent, and so "elsewhere." The ideas about what happens when someone dies are too deep to be affected by physical techniques of disposal, just as they extend beyond the limits of languages and cultures which may modify them.

A death is not completed in an instant. . . .

The body from which an essential element has departed, and which is itself no longer stable or quite clean, must be cleaned and prepared and dressed; the family and larger clan must come together, the grief felt for one whose absence deprives them of familiar comforts must be lifted from the heart by gesture and mourning, with public and private farewells. There must be a processional escort to the burial place, a permanent separation of the group from the visible body, which is concealed or dispersed, and replaced, in a sense, by a tomb-stone or a mound. There is a practical control of ceremonies meant for purification and family unity, and whatever further support, from time to time, the dead family member is thought to need. The cere-mony of burial confirmed the value of the efforts a man had made during his lifetime, and in some way released him from any further effort.

What cultured Greek individuals really thought about death is hidden from us except through literary interpretation. The Solonian legislation against excessive mourning is guarantee that the ceremonial aspects of burial in archaic Athens were protracted, expensive, and enjoyable to aristocrats. A good funeral has always been a lot of fun, a reunion stirring open emotions and bringing news to exchange, the periodic intersection of the family, the clan, and the city. Beyond behavior, private thoughts are harder to discover, except as they were like our own. Statements on tombstones of the archaic period are not sentimental; the family is proud of the deceased and will miss him. There is no other real source for individual thoughts except poetry, which is surely atypical. . . .

The Greek poet's concern with death was at once practical and mythical. Some form of poetry was necessary to launch the dead on their way, the mourning song which relieved the living and confirmed the excellence of the dead. . . . The simple evocative phrases we know—"you were my dearest child . . . ," "you were kind to me . . . ," are designed to assure the dead person that he has been loved and will still be loved, and that memory of him is vivid while his family lives. This memory is freshened both by attendance at his burial place and by repeated narrative of his past words and actions. In this direction, the practical and mythical coincide, for an obvious part of the poet's work is to keep the past, that is the dead, alive by quotation and interview. . . .

. . .

Most people preserve the dead and learn from them. We like to distinguish ourselves from the simpler beasts by declaring that we are the only animals to bury our dead and so to rescue the past. Elephants may put branches on a dead friend, or sprinkle him with dust; bears will bury another animal to ripen it for eating; dolphins hold formal mourning rites, as even cows do. Still, human speculation about death has been historically self-centered and self-flattering, rejoicing in unique anguish and burden. What other animals may do has seemed unimportant, because to us they have neither history nor myth, which our dead have given us. . . .

. . .

The Greeks are a very active dead: no living person has the power of even a minor nameless hero, whose power flows simply from the fact that he is dead and angry about it, and cannot sleep still. Not even the Great King had the power of some of the named heroes, Achilles, or Herakles or Orpheus, who lived in poetry and managed later minds, with poets and prophets and politicians as their mouthpieces. These dead figures stalking through myth, history, and figured art were the major sources of meaning for most Greeks—most human experience could be understood in their terms. As models they embodied the fear of death and the courage of facing it frankly, of flight and acceptance. They were shown in scenes of mourning, of murder, of attack by enemies and lovers (although seldom succumbing to disease and accident, since their lives were to be significant and so not trivially lost). They were strongly suggestive of life after death, both in the way they were held in memory as active figures, and in the way they were often treated in cult as having the power to respond to the living. Many cultured Greeks represented themselves as anxious to get down to the underworld and talk to the fabled dead, who could illuminate the lost past and the truths of life. A surprising number of the dead, as they lived again in mythical tales, demonstrated how a man might get past his appointed day of death and destiny . . . by intelligence and the faculty of love, or at least how he might retain a spark of *nous* or *thumos*, perception and feeling, which could help the intercourse with the other dead.

From the great range of ancient testimonies about the dead a few elements of thought may be selected. The Greeks made a clear distinction between body and soul, between the flesh that decayed and must be buried, and the wind-breath *psyche* that left the carcass and went elsewhere into a pool of personalities which could be activated by memory. The distinction was clearest at the moment of death itself, when from the mouth or from a wound a little element or fragment of a breath or wind passed, small and nearly unnoticed, from the body. Yet when the dead were considered as figures of the past, this bit of wind grew curiously substantial. In both literature and ceremony we detect a feeling among the early Greeks that there is a deeper concern for the body than for the soul, and that the body is perceived as double: one stays in the grave where it retains particular powers, and one goes to the kingdom of the dead, where it can still be hurt.

When the Greeks considered sin at all they punished it, in the dead, in an oddly physical manner. For a thousand years after Homer the scene of the underworld tortures of the dead in the *Odyssey* remained corporeal, in the absence of *corpora,* physical for those who had not much physique left to speak of. As Tantalos is punished with hunger and thirst, appetites alien to the *psyche;* as Tityos has his liver ripped out and Sisyphos sweats rolling his stone, we encounter an enduring folktale element in the vision of the afterlife which runs counter to the theoretical distinctions between body and soul. . . . These themes stress an old feeling that the body was, in fact, existence; that if existence continued it would to some degree be bodily; and that wrong treatment of a dead body was, as Greek tragedy constantly demonstrates, a major wickedness. That is why so much Greek poetry and art which touches on death naturally focuses on burial and mourning.

. . .

The *psyche* is real, not fiction. When someone dies, a man or woman who had just hours before been a recognizing friend now fails to respond to normal stimuli; the eyes do not focus but do not close as in sleep either; the body temperature drops, the flesh is cold and pale, the limbs have no power and the blood stops flowing; it is clear that something activating—breath or strength of concentration, intelligence and feeling—has vanished. The Greeks did not know that this little element would ever be weighed by modern science, although its images were often weighed in Greek and Egyptian art. Now a doctor in Dusseldorf has succeeded in quantifying the soul by placing the beds of his terminal patients on extremely sensitive scales. "As they died and the souls left their bodies, the needle dropped twenty-one grams." Homer's successors would have enjoyed this scientific accuracy, although the doctor does not tell us if something like a puff of smoke went past him, or if he heard any slight batlike noise. The Greek psyche picked up qualities of strength from the living individual; its poetic representation had necessarily to be ambiguous.

. . .

. . . It was best to die at home, although the heroic and military code proclaimed that it was also best to die on the battlefield with honor. At least one should be mourned at home if possible. The recovery of the dead in wartime was a constant value in Greek history, as it is now. In the *Odyssey,* the bodies of those murdered suitors who came from beyond Ithaka were shipped home by fishing boat. If a man died away from home he might be brought back to his parents and wife, or at least be buried with honors by his friends on an alien battlefield. The Greeks who died at Troy may have accepted this burial in foreign earth the more easily because the old grave-mounds in the Trojan plain belonged to heroes who were still remembered in local legend. The new . . . tombs among them, visible to sailors on the Hellespont, guaranteed that their occupants would be drawn into this world of antique fame. The worst was not to be buried, not to be mourned by mother or wife, or to have your body dallied with by the careless dogs and birds on land and the fish at sea. When the body was really lost, as when a man died at sea, it was often felt best to prepare a cenotaph and a stone *sema* [a sign or representation] to replace the body.

The religious ceremonies of mourning and farewell to the dead were simple, probably the oldest and least changing art-form in Greece. They marked the practical steps any family must take, and the stages in the slow process of transitions between the body's faltering and the soul's stabilized condition in another world. The *psyche*'s departure from the body was only the beginning of death, in both poetry and fact. Hades accepted only the man whose death had been completed, not the starting dead man. To join with full rank the "renowned tribes of the dead" required the three obvious phases it still does: the washing and preparation of the body and the house; the *prothesis* or vigil wake over the prepared body, at which the major mourning was expressed; and the *ekphora* or procession to the cemetery, by chariot or cart or on foot, our automobile cavalcade. Around these practical steps the ordinary duties of greeting guests, collecting gifts, cleansing possible contaminations and singing the laments fell into place.

The body was washed and dressed first. The warm baths were necessary for removing stains of blood and sickness, preventing corruption and contagion; they were also ceremonial as for all the greater passages like birth and marriage. The washing gave rise to the persistent connection between bathtubs and coffins, cauldrons and urns.

The body was anointed with oil, wrapped from head to foot in a cloth, spread with another cloth, and laid on a bed or bier, usually with the feet toward the door, facing the journey. The house was hung with wreaths and sprays of leaves, and these were also offered to the dead man. There was special use of marjoram and celery, myrtle and laurel leaves. A bowl of water from a source outside the house might be offered to anyone who touched the corpse, although the Greeks did not in general believe that death was contagious. The bier was usually dressed like a bed with mattress, blanket and pillows, part of the old association between sleep and death which is still natural for us.

These are family responsibilities of the women in the household who loved the dead dearest and miss him most. The dead are helpless, and need comfort or mothering like infants, from mother or wife, to close the eyes, straighten the limbs, fix the jaw shut. "My bitch of a wife would not even close my eyes or fix my jaws," complained murdered Agamemnon in the underworld, a refusal of family duty which was a clear measure of her distaste for him. The pleasant presentation of the body was partly prompted by feelings that it might appear in the underworld as it had left the upper world, a matter quite separate from the theory of the *psyche*. This is clear with the chin band, of gold, leather or linen often seen in funeral paintings and occasionally surviving in gold; sometimes . . . the dead person runs down to Hades still wearing it, a natural confusion of body and soul.

As in modern wakes, the dead are instinctively felt capable of hearing the funeral lament, and perhaps even of noting the ceremonial funeral gestures of striking the head, tearing out the hair, beating the breast, and scratching the cheeks till the blood runs. Lucian complains of the contrast between the peaceful dead and the convulsed mourners: "The living are more to be pitied than the dead. They roll on the ground time after time and crash their heads on the floor, while he, decent and handsome, lies high and crowned with ornamental wreaths, exalted and made up as though for a procession" (*On Funerals* 12).

The key role in this mourning was played by women through song, because the center of the ceremony was the expression of love, made memorable by form. The tradition of the lament scarcely changed between the Bronze Age and the Hellenistic period. The singer-woman usually cradled the head of the dead between her two palms as Thetis clasped Achilles' head when she foresaw his death, crying sharply. . . .

There are several forms of funeral songs. . . . Of these the *goos* is most intense and personal, its theme the memory of the lives the two shared and the bitterness of the loss. It survived brilliantly from Homer until the early twentieth century. . . . "Hektor most dearest to my heart of all my children . . . now you lie dewy and fresh for me in the hall"; "Hektor, you leave your time young and leave me a widow; . . . you did not reach out your arms to me from your bed when you died, or tell me a word I could always remember at night." So now:

> For if the sea won't swell and rise the rock's not wrapped in
> foam,
> and if your mother mourns you not the world won't weep
> you home. . . .

> ". . . death had superseded sex as a taboo subject and
> one surrounded with a morbid and
> furtive fascination. . . ."

GEOFFREY GORER

DEATH, GRIEF,
AND MOURNING IN
CONTEMPORARY BRITAIN

The British anthropologist Geoffrey Gorer (1905–85) wrote extensively on death and mourning rituals. In his influential essay "The Pornography of Death" (1955), Gorer argued that "Whereas copulation has become more and more 'mentionable,' particularly in the Anglo-Saxon societies, death has become more and more 'unmentionable.'" In Death, Grief, and Mourning in Contemporary Britain (1965), from which this excerpt is taken, Gorer reflects upon the dramatic decline of shared public rituals of mourning. As death has become a more covert, even shameful matter, grief has grown more isolating, of longer duration. After the period of shock and disorganization, the bereaved in our deritualized cultures have no clear prescription for what to do next. Mourning rituals or "grief work," Gorer maintains, assist us in giving expression to and working through our loss.

This piece holds an added interest, in presenting a brief autobiography glimpsed through the deaths that shaped the author's life.

Some of the most vivid memories of my early childhood are concerned with the death of Edward the Seventh. I had just turned five in May, 1910. On the Sunday morning after his death, our nanny took my brother Peter (two years my junior) and me for our customary walk on Hampstead Heath. It was a fine morning and the Heath was crowded. As we came out of Heath Street to the White Stone Pond we could see a mass of people out to enjoy the sun; and practically every woman was dressed in full mourning, in black from top to toe. Nearly all the men were in dark suits too, but that was customary for "Sunday best." This mass of black-garbed humanity struck me as a most depressing sight.

We used to have Sunday lunch with our parents; and there was Mother, too, dressed in black. I grizzled and nagged at Mother to get out of those horrid clothes, and finally she agreed to wear "half-mourning"—grey or purple—in the house; but, she explained to me, she *had* to wear black when she went out. King Edward was a good king, we were very sorry that he had gone, and wearing black was a sign that we respected and missed him and shared the grief of his family. I think this made some sense to me, for I think that I knew then that Queen Mary—Princess May—was a client of my father, and so it was right that Mother should do what pleased her. But I didn't understand why everybody else had to too.

This is my first clear recollection of death and mourning. There were no deaths in my family of which I was conscious during my childhood . . . ; but I was certainly conscious of the fact of death. The parade of funerals—horse-drawn, of course, with black plumes and all the trimmings—was a constant feature of street life; and we children had to keep an eye out for them and take off our hats or caps for the whole time that the funeral procession passed us; it was very *rude* not to, and showed a lack of respect for people in their great trouble. And when people were dressed in mourning—they might be visitors or servants or shop-assistants—we had to be quiet, and not fidget or make a noise. As small children we learned that mourners were in a special situation or state of mind and had to be treated differently from others, with more consideration and more respect; and I think our education on this subject was typical of that period.

I have no memory of being puzzled about death; it was something which happened to all people and to animals too. Our dear bulldog Billy was smothered on one of the spring transfers from town to country; I remember being unhappy and angry at his unnecessary death; but not surprised. . . . A family anecdote recounts that I was found in tears on my tenth birthday, and when asked why I was crying, explained that I had got into two figures, and so few people got into three! On some level I had accepted the fact that I was mortal, and so were all those I loved; but the only death that I contemplated was natural death. Violent death was exotic, a thing which happened in books—I was an avid reader of Conan Doyle and, particularly, of Rider Haggard—and did not represent any sort of domestic threat.

My father was drowned in the *Lusitania* on his return from a business trip to the United States in May, 1915. As we learned later, he died heroically, giving up both his seat in one of the lifeboats and his life-belt to two women passengers, both of whom survived and visited my mother. His death was completely unforeseen, for at that period only soldiers in the firing line and Belgians were thought to be in any danger.

I learnt of the sinking of the *Lusitania* at breakfast at school. We sat at long tables, I near the bottom end, one of the masters at the head; the master would read out the war news from his newspaper, and the headline would be passed down the table. I can well remember the almost physical shock with which I heard the news, a short period during which every sound seemed to have gone out of the world; then I burst into uncontrolled sobbing and it was, it seemed, quite a time before I could explain to anybody what I was crying about. When I could be understood, I was treated with great kindness, but like an invalid; no demands were made on me, I was indulged, conversation was hushed in my presence. I cannot remember anyone, master or boy, talking seriously to me about death in general or the death of my father in particular; nor can I remember any of them making a joke in my presence.

Of course, my father's death was not confirmed immediately.

There were days of agonized waiting, as survivors were picked up and brought to land, chiefly to Irish ports; even now I can barely reconstruct the agony my mother must have gone through as she waited outside the Cunard office. I think I must have been in a sort of daze during that period. . . .

I do not remember how soon I was given black ties and had bands of crepe sewn on to the sleeves of my suits; but I remember the first days I wore these insignia of woe, feeling, despite my unhappiness, somehow distinguished, in nearly every sense of the word. I was set apart; and this was somehow fitting and comforting.

As rational hope diminished, I constructed elaborate fantasies that my father was surviving on some desert island in the Atlantic; for at least some months I put off the acceptance of his final disappearance by these dreams. . . .

. . .

My mother came down to see me about three weeks later, a tragic, almost a frightening figure in the full panoply of widow's weeds and unrelieved black, a crepe veil shrouding her (when it was not lifted) so that she was visibly withdrawn from the world. She had become very pale and very thin, her eyes appearing enormous in her face. All I remember of this visit, besides her appearance, was her asking me where we should spend the summer holidays; and when I said I should like to be in our country house near Windsor, she sighed and said she did not think she could manage it. I realized that this was an emotional, not a financial statement. This is the only decision I was asked to make, or participate in, then. As a child I never saw my mother cry.

. . .

In the summer of 1915 and thereafter, widows in mourning became increasingly frequent in the streets, so that Mother no longer stood out in the crowd. She followed scrupulously the customary usage in the modification of her outdoor costume, the shortening and abandoning of the veil, the addition of a touch of white at the proper calendrical moments. It would have been unthinkable at that date for a respectable woman to do otherwise. In early 1917, when she could otherwise have worn some colour, her father died at a ripe age and she had to return to black for a further six months. His funeral was the first I had ever attended; the sound of the earth on the coffin impressed me very much, but it was a general melancholy rather than a poignant grief; he had always seemed to me so very old, with his white hair and beard, that his actual death made little impression. . . .

. . .

I cannot from my own memory recall when the full panoply of public mourning became exceptional, rather than general; but the evidence suggests that it was towards the end of the war, in 1917 and 1918. It was not much later that I heard, in one of the first musical comedies I ever saw—called, I think, *Yes, Uncle*—a song which shocked me then, and, on recollection, shocks me still, which began:

> Widows are wonderful,
> You must admit they're wise . . .

One can see the point, of course. The holocaust of young men had created such an army of widows; it was no longer socially realistic for them all to act as though their emotional and sexual life were over for good, which was the underlying message of the ritual mourning. And with the underlying message, the ritual too went into the discard. There was too, almost certainly, a question of public morale; one should not show the face of grief to the boys home on leave from the trenches.

. . .

With the armistice, my preoccupation with and expectation of death diminished, virtually disappeared; so too did my experience of death. My maternal grandmother died a year or so later, during term-time;

my mother was indignant that I was not allowed to go to her funeral;
but I only recollect a faint sorrow. I wore a black armband for Grannie
for three months.

. . .

I saw a dead body for the first time in 1931, purely by accident, in a
hospital in the U.S.S.R. My brother Peter and I had (rather adventur-
ously for the time) gone on an Intourist tour of most of European
Russia; and, since he was just qualified as a doctor, he was particularly
interested in visiting hospitals. At Kiev, as I recall, the naked corpse of
a young woman was carried past us on a rough stretcher. I was star-
tled; and Peter reproached himself that he had not foreseen the possibility of such a confrontation. The picture remains vivid in my mind
to this day; she had been a very beautiful girl. But it was only by an
effort of imagination that I could conceive that she had ever been
alive; the corpse was a thing; only intellectually did I realize that it had
once been a person. . . .

. . .

The outbreak of the Second World War was violently redintegrative of
all the gloom and apprehension that I had felt during my childhood,
even though I was intellectually convinced that the war was a necessary one. . . .

     My brother Peter married for the first time during the war and
lost his wife (from undiagnosed tuberculosis) on the day that the
armistice was signed. I never met her; but when I returned to England
later in the year Peter's melancholy, emaciation and relative apathy
demonstrated vividly the profound physiological and psychological
modifications of the personality which deep mourning produced. I
did not consciously, at that time, make a connection between the
prolongation of his mourning and the lack of any social ritual to ease
it. I thought in the conventional terms of a change of scene as a cure
(or palliative) for the desolation of grief. I arranged for him to come to

the United States, first for a holiday and then to work; this was eventually effective, and he found his second wife there.

I was more conscious of the lack of support which contemporary British society gives to the bereaved when I visited Olive S. in the spring of 1948. Her husband John, one of my very good friends, had died unnecessarily from a cancer of the throat, undiagnosed until the terminal stage; and Olive was left with three young children, the youngest a babe in arms. When I went to see her some two months after John's death, she told me, with tears of gratitude, that I was the first man to stay in the house since she had become a widow. She was being given some good professional help from lawyers and the like who were also friends; but socially she had been almost completely abandoned to loneliness, although the town was full of acquaintances who considered themselves friends.

My mother was starting to turn senile and during the last four years of her life—she died in 1954—degenerated into a helpless, incontinent and almost completely incoherent parody of a human being, one of the most distressing transformations one could witness; her death, when it finally came, was consciously seen as a release and a relief. Intellectually, I had never quite forgiven her for having so overburdened my childhood and adolescence with responsibility; but I wept for her after her cremation. She had been dying over so long a time that the chief difference her actual death made was the abandonment of the flat in which she had spent the last years of her life and the distribution between my brothers and myself of the family chattels. Apart from the gathering at the cremation service and letters of condolence there was no social ritual.

. . .

In 1955, I had put into words my awareness that death had superseded sex as a taboo subject and one surrounded with a morbid and furtive fascination for many people, according to the evidence of the horror comic and the "X" film; I called my essay *The Pornography of Death*. I had also explored in some detail the beliefs about the afterlife held by a considerable cross-section of English people and had documented the virtual disappearance of the beliefs in judgment or damnation or of any of the terrors which, the evidence suggests, made the fear of death so poignant to believing Christians in former generations. Although a variety of unorthodox beliefs about the afterlife were voiced, they were predominantly bland.

When I had wound up all the estates for which I was executor at the beginning of 1960 it seemed as though my personal preoccupation with the sequels to death had, as far as one could foresee, come to a halt; nor were my scientific interests then further directed to the subject.

Then, in April, 1961, Dr. X, who had been a friend and colleague of my brother since they were medical students together, telephoned me the appalling news that Peter, who had gone for a medical check-up because of slight pains in his right shoulder, had been diagnosed as suffering from irremediable cancer: not only were his lungs affected . . . , but also his spine; the prognosis was absolutely hopeless, a probable twelve months of increasing debility and pain before an agonized death. He asked me to decide whether his wife, Elizabeth, should be informed; he had already decided to hide the truth from Peter; and he and his colleagues engaged in the most elaborate and successful medical mystification to hide from Peter's expert knowledge the facts of their diagnosis.

I was emotionally completely unprepared. I had (have) long believed that I was likely to die of cancer, since my father's parents and his brother and sister had all died of cancer and a brother of my mother of leukemia; I had accepted that I carried a diseased inheritance. But, quite illogically, I had never intellectually considered that my brothers had the same inheritance as myself, perhaps in part because I resemble my father in features and colouring, whereas Peter and Richard took much more after my mother's family. It is probable too that, in the same way that I had intellectually accepted responsibility for my mother and brothers after my father's death, I had unconsciously thought that I would take the burden of our cancerous heredity away from the others.

Peter was at the happiest and most successful period of his life, blissfully married and enjoying his two children, innocently delighted with his election as a Fellow of the Royal Society and the growing international recognition of his scientific work, and looking forward to having his own department created for him. In the 1930's when I had a certain success as a writer, he was frequently asked whether he was related to me; in the last years of his life I was being asked whether I was related to him.

The fact that he was engaged in very original scientific work added extra qualms to my collusion in the kindly meant deception that his colleagues at Guy's Hospital were practicing on him. I felt sure that, under similar circumstances, I should wish to be informed so that, if at all possible, the scientific ideas and unrealized projects could be transmitted to others to carry though; we shared a respect for the values of scientific knowledge which I felt were being transgressed. Further, I foresaw (for my wartime work had taught me the burden of secrets) that my relationship to him, and that of anybody else so informed, would be progressively falsified by the inevitable continuous dissimulation. I fully intended to argue about the ethics of such deception with Dr. X at a slightly later date; but he and his colleagues had persuaded Peter that he was run down and slightly arthritic and needed a good holiday; and I was willing that he should have this relatively carefree period.

Whether Elizabeth should be informed was a much more pressing and perplexing problem. The knowledge would, I knew, reduce her to despair, for she was completely devoted to Peter; apart from her garden she had no interests which were not also his, her English friends and acquaintances were almost all his colleagues and their spouses.

In my perplexity I consulted Dr. Y. He is the wisest British man I know concerning human relations (our mutual friend and my former collaborator, the late Dr. John Rickman, was such another), and I thought that he would see the situation more clearly than I could in my deep distress; by good fortune he and his wife were coming to see me some four days after I had spoken to Dr. X. His advice was that Elizabeth should be told; one of the arguments he advanced was that, if she were ignorant, she might show impatience or lack of under-standing with his probably increasing weakness, for which she would reproach herself later; she could use the final months of their marriage better if she knew them for what they were. That night, and for many months afterwards, I cried myself to sleep, rather noisy sobs.

Elizabeth was told by Dr. X, and took the terrible news with magnificent courage and common sense. Her role in the deception was infinitely harder than mine, for she could never let up, never safely abandon herself to grief; I doubt if she could have supported the continuous presence for long.

It was arranged that, on his discharge from Guy's, Peter and Elizabeth should come and spend a week with me in the country, and then go on to Blagdon for some fishing, a pastime to which Peter was passionately addicted. He breakfasted in bed, and rose late, but other-wise he seemed in the highest of spirits, indeed rather euphoric; he was continuously elaborating plans for a future which Elizabeth and I knew he would never see. I thought the euphoria might in part be due to the analgesics of which Dr. X had given him a considerable supply; but Elizabeth did not think so.

In the evening of May 10th, 1961, I had a dinner engagement in London which I kept; when I returned home a little before midnight Peter and Elizabeth were still up, happy and mellow. We went to bed rather late. In the morning when their breakfast was brought to them Elizabeth rushed into my room, saying Peter was either in a coma or dead. He was very clearly dead, his face cyanosed and his body cool-ing. Elizabeth collapsed into my bed.

The rest of the day was a busy nightmare, though I could find at least intellectual comfort in the knowledge that Peter had been spared the increasing pain and weakness which the prognosis had foreseen; he had died in his sleep, without any signs of pain, from what the autopsy showed to have been oedema of the lung. . . .

Dr. Z got in touch with the undertakers for me, and it was arranged for a pair of ex-nurses to come to lay out the body. They imparted a somewhat Dickensian tone; they were fat and jolly, and asked in a respectful but cheerful tone, "Where is the patient?" One of them was out a couple of minutes later to ask if he had a fresh pair of pyjamas; I could not bring myself to go through his clothes, and showed them his suitcase.

Some half-hour later their work was done and they came out saying, "The patient looks lovely now. Come and have a look!" I did not wish to, at which they expressed surprise. I gave them a pound for their pains; the leader, pure Sarah Gamp, said, "That for us, duck? Cheers!" and went through the motions of raising a bottle and emptying it into her mouth. I sat with Elizabeth when, shortly afterwards, the undertaker's men came to take the body away; the noise of their feet on the uncarpeted stairs was slow and sinister. Later, I had to go to the mortuary to make a formal identification of the corpse, before the autopsy could be made. I was frightened of fainting, for I felt nearly exhausted. I did not, however, though I slumped into a chair as I confirmed that it was my dear brother. The layers-out had done a good job; he was composed, colorless and waxen. The two pictures of his corpse remain completely vivid in my memory.

Besides all the problems connected with the disposal of the body, there were many people to be informed of his death, and complicated arrangements to be made to tell the children of their father's death and arrange for them to come to me. These arrangements Elizabeth thought out with great clarity; she was completely prostrate—it was hours before she felt strong enough to walk across the hall to another room I had had prepared for her; and I also had to tidy up their previous room and pack away Peter's clothes and belongings into a suitcase, lest their sight distress Elizabeth, or the children who would occupy the room on the morrow. Although I was crying much of the time while I performed these tasks, it was only in the evening, when Elizabeth was hopefully sleeping under sedation, that the full extent of our loss overwhelmed me. . . .

Owing to the necessity of an autopsy, there was a longer delay than customary between Peter's death and his cremation; the interval passed in a daze, interrupted with bouts of busyness for me. . . . Elizabeth decided not to come to the cremation herself—she could not bear the thought that she might lose control and other people observe her grief; and she wished to spare the children the distressing experience. As a consequence, their father's death was quite unmarked for them by any ritual of any kind, and was even nearly treated as a secret, for it was very many months before Elizabeth could bare to mention him or have him mentioned in her presence.

In his will, Peter had requested a Church of England service for his cremation, I presume because this would cause the least trouble; none of us had any sort of religious belief. Neither of the clergymen who were personal friends was available to conduct the service; the crematorium supplied a handsome cleric, dressed in a sky-blue robe, with dramatic, even theatrical, gestures. The moment, in a cremation service, when the coffin disappears through the folding doors still seems (despite frequent exposure) a moment of the most poignant finality. Many of Peter's friends and nearly all our surviving relatives were present.

The only time that I felt near to collapsing was on the return from the cremation (it involved a two-hour motor-drive each way); I had to go to bed, to be by myself, for a few hours. With enormous courage, Elizabeth assured me that she and the children had had a good day; they had taken a picnic to the fields where the grass was being cut for silage. . . .

We all went for a few days to friends in Frome; and then life had to be resumed. It was the experience of the following months which suggested to me that our treatment of grief and mourning made bereavement very difficult to be lived through.

In my own ease, I was able to mourn freely, to indulge in passionate bouts of weeping without self-reproach. I lost about twenty pounds in weight over the following three months, and my sleep tended to be disturbed. I had frequent dreams of Peter, many of them about our early childhood; waking from them was very distressing. I did all the routine work necessary, but felt disinclined for anything which demanded prolonged concentration. I wore a black tie for about three months. I had great pleasure in seeing real friends, but was unwilling to meet strangers. A couple of times I refused invitations to cocktail parties, explaining that I was mourning; the people who invited me responded to this statement with shocked embarrassment as if I had voiced some appalling obscenity. Indeed, I got the impression that, had I stated that the invitation clashed with some esoteric debauchery I had arranged, I would have had understanding and jocular encouragement; as it was, the people whose invitations I had refused, educated and sophisticated though they were, mumbled and hurried away. They clearly no longer had any guidance from ritual as to the way to treat a self-confessed mourner; and, I suspect, they were frightened lest I give way to my grief, and involve them in a distasteful upsurge of emotion.

This would certainly seem to be the explanation of the way in which Elizabeth was avoided by her and Peter's friends; they treated her, she said, as though she were a leper. Only if she acted as though nothing of consequence had happened was she again socially acceptable.

This fear of the expression of grief on the part of the English professional classes unfortunately matched Elizabeth's New England fear of giving way to grief, of losing self-control. She did not wear black clothes nor ritualize her mourning in any way; she let herself be, almost literally, eaten up with grief, sinking into a deep and long-lasting depression. At the period when she most needed help and comfort from society she was left alone.

As an anthropologist, I knew that the vast majority of recorded human societies have developed formal rituals for mourning. Typically there are communal ceremonies from the period immediately after the death until the disposal of the body; typically, the bereaved are distinguished by a change in their physical appearance, such as special clothes, shaving the hair or letting it grow and so on, so that all who come into contact with them know they are mourners and treat them in a specified ritualistic fashion; and, typically, a mourner goes through what van Gennep called a *rite de passage*—a formal withdrawal from society, a period of seclusion, and a formal re-entry into society.

"I . . . needed to hold him, to look at him, to
find out where he was hurting. These instincts
don't die immediately with the child."

SHEILA AWOONER-RENNER

I DESPERATELY NEEDED
TO SEE MY SON

*Sheila Awooner-Renner, a British health-care worker, directed this article
to other health professionals, recommending that they stop their practice of
keeping the family away from the deceased's body, and begin to allow the
grieving to attend to washing and preparing the body. This final care,
Awooner-Renner feels, is a privilege and consolation. Beyond this, she describes, with documentary precision, her tragedy—and every parent's
nightmare.*

Recently my child was killed in a road accident. He was 17. The
journey had begun at 1 P.M. and he died at 3:28 P.M. I was told at 7:10
P.M. I couldn't quite understand why they had travelled such a short
distance in six hours. My mind must have thought that it happened
just before I was told. As the policeman who came to tell me of my
son's death said that they were unable to take me to the hospital it
took me some time to find someone to take me to him. The police at

first seemed relieved that I had a car and could drive, but in the circumstances that was impossible. They were then anxious for me to find a relative to take me, and when I failed then a friend. I failed at friends, too. By now they were getting desperate—what about neighbours? I didn't know them either. In fact, there was a huge gulf between my [own] . . . and their understanding. . . . I needed someone close enough to be able to reveal myself safely who would not take over and do the right thing and say the right words and with whom I would have to behave as they were projecting I should behave. The people I needed are rare and were away. Therefore what I wanted was someone impersonal, a stranger—someone with no expectations of me. The police would have done nicely. I also needed someone with a good reliable car and without children who could just drop everything to take me to a place 50 to 60 miles away in the middle of an ordinary evening. Eventually, though shocked and barely able to function, I found somebody able to take me. The police were to tell the hospital of our intended arrival.

On arrival at the hospital just after 10:15 P.M. no one was expecting us. "Everybody has gone now, and I should have gone too by now," a social worker said. My friend and I were put in a small anteroom and the door was closed. We had been put in a box with the lid closed to spare us the sight of panicky people rushing to and fro, telephone calls being made, etc., while the system was being re-assembled for us. I wouldn't have that. I behaved myself for three to four minutes, then I opened the door. I still couldn't see anything but felt better. What would have made me feel much better was to have seen and shared the panic. That would have been human: being put in a small, quiet, impersonal room behind a closed door was not.

Eventually the system assembled itself again. It seemed that I had not after all come to see my son but to identify him. The hospital manager was kind and caring with a woman's warmth. She knew what I needed or nearly knew. What I desperately needed was to see my son. But it was explained that I couldn't see him until I had been interviewed by the coroner's officer, who, not knowing I was to arrive, was somewhere else. Eventually he arrived. By now I was getting nicely institutionalized. I was behaving myself. I put him at his ease when he asked his questions—well, I tried to. He, poor man, knew the formula and knew each question had to be put with a sympathetic preamble. He was unctuous. He was sorrowful. And I wanted to see my son. He knew what to do with grieving relatives. He knew the formula, so he did it—to the end. He had no idea who, in reality, I was. I said that I wanted to see my son alone—no, I asked permission to see my son alone. Permission was granted on condition that I "didn't do anything silly."

With no idea what "anything silly" was I acquiesced, imagining he meant "don't touch and don't disturb anything." He disappeared. Apparently there was great rushing about preparing Timothy for viewing. Putting a piece of gauze over a graze on his forehead was regarded as important so that I should not be offended or frightened or disgusted. We walked along a corridor. We arrived at a door. It was opened. No more hope; no more thinking it might not be Timothy. Incredibly, it was my Timothy. It was him, my lovely boy.

He was lying on an altar covered by a purple cloth, which was edged with gold braid and tassels. Only his head was visible. Such was the atmosphere of constraint I either asked permission or was given permission to enter. I can't remember. I entered, alone. The others stayed watching through the open door. I reached him and stroked his cheek. He was cold.

Timothy was my child, he had not ceased to be my child. I desperately needed to hold him, to look at him, to find out where he was hurting. These instincts don't die immediately with the child. The instinct to comfort and cuddle, to examine and inspect the wounds, to try to understand, most of all, to hold. But I had been told "not to do anything silly." And they were watching me to see that I didn't. So I couldn't move the purple cloth. I couldn't find his hand by lifting the cloth. I couldn't do anything. I betrayed my instincts and my son by standing there "not doing anything silly." Because I knew that if I did my watchers would come in immediately, constrain me, and lead me away.

Why did they do this? No doubt they thought that they were acting for the best. We, as a society, have lost contact with our most basic instincts. The instincts we share with other mammals. We marvel at cats washing and caring for their kittens. We admire the protection an elephant gives to her sick calf, and we are tearful and sympathetic when she refuses to leave her offspring when he dies, when she examines him, and nuzzles him, and wills him to breathe again. And we have forgotten that that is exactly what the human mother's most basic instinct tells her to do. And we deny her. If a human mother is not able to examine, hold and nuzzle her child she is being denied her motherhood when in extremis.

We have come to think that we are protecting her when we are really protecting ourselves. We have forgotten that this is the mother who has cleaned up the vomit, who has washed his nappies, who has dealt with and cleared away his diarrhoea. She has cleaned the blood from his wounds, she has kissed him better, and she has held him in his distress. She has done all of this since the day he was born. If he has been a patient in hospital she has possibly fed him by tube, she may have changed his dressings, she may have given him his injections. She will certainly have washed him and helped him to dress and combed his hair. And she will have held him.

Again I ask, who are we protecting when we deny her this last service which she can do for her child? We are not protecting the child. There is nothing she can do to harm her child. We are not protecting her: the fact of her child's death is not altered by the denial of her instincts.

Having nursed my mother through her last illness at home I was privileged to bathe her after death, to redress her wounds with clean dressings, to remove her catheter and drainage. It was a tearful and loving last service that my sister and I were privileged to perform for her. And it helped to heal our grief.

But my lovely boy was draped on an altar, covered with a purple robe, and all expressions of love and care which I had were denied to me. And I don't know when that wound will heal.

The time has come when we in the caring services should think again about how we serve the bereaved. A cup of tea and an aseptic look at the body does not serve. If it is their wish and instinct to wash the body, to hold the body, and to talk to the dead loved one then they should be helped to do this. They will be distressed and they may frequently need to stop to wipe the tears. But they will be helped in their healing. How ironic that we will have to retrain ourselves to help in this most basic service, but this is something which we must do.

❧

". . . she would have enjoyed it enormously."

GEORGE BERNARD SHAW

ON THE CREMATION
OF HIS MOTHER

George Bernard Shaw (1856–1950) describes the funeral service and cremation of his eighty-three-year-old mother in a letter to Stella Campbell, an actress with whom he was romantically connected. In an earlier letter to Lady Gregory he wrote: "my mother is dying, they say, but won't die—makes nothing of strokes—throws them off as other women throw off sneezing fits." Lucinda Elizabeth (Bessie) Shaw's final illness lasted for some time; she had been unconscious for sixteen weeks when she "passed out in her sleep . . . quietly and imperceptibly . . . ," George's sister Lucy wrote. Perhaps Shaw's satisfied description of the furnace doing its work can be traced in part to his long-standing advocacy of cremation as a part of his public hygiene campaign. Later, on the day of the funeral, Shaw made a note to himself to buy some shares in the cremation business.

The Mitre, Oxford.
22nd February 1913

What a day! I must write to you about it, because there is no one else
who didn't hate her mother, and even who doesn't hate her children.
Whether you are an Italian peasant or a Superwoman I cannot yet find
out; but anyhow your mother was not the Enemy.

Why does a funeral always sharpen one's sense of humor and
rouse one's spirits? This one was a complete success. No burial horrors. No mourners in black, snivelling and wallowing in induced grief.
Nobody knew except myself, Barker and the undertaker. Since I could
not have a splendid procession with lovely colors and flashing life and
triumphant music, it was best with us three. I particularly mention the
undertaker because the humor of the occasion began with him. I went
down in the tube to Golders Green with Barker, and walked to the
Crematorium; and there came also the undertaker presently with his
hearse, which had walked (the horse did) conscientiously at a funeral
pace through the cold; though my mother would have preferred an
invigorating trot. The undertaker approached me in the character of a
man shattered with grief; and I, hard as nails and in loyally high
spirits (rejoicing irrepressibly in my mother's memory), tried to con-
vey to him that this professional chicanery as I took it to be, was quite
unnecessary. And lo! it wasn't professional chicanery at all. He had
done all sorts of work for her for years, and was actually and really in
a state about losing her, not merely as a customer, but as a person he
liked and was accustomed to. And the coffin was covered with violet
cloth—not black.

I must rewrite that burial service; for there are things in it that
are deader than anyone it has ever been read over; but I had it read
not only because the parson must live by his fees, but because with all
its drawbacks it is the most beautiful thing that can be read as yet.
And the parson did not gabble and hurry in the horrible manner
common on such occasions. With Barker and myself for his congrega-
tion (and Mamma) he did it with his utmost feeling and sincerity. We
could have made him perfect technically in two rehearsals; but he was

excellent as it was; and I shook his hand with unaffected gratitude in my best manner.

At the passage "earth to earth, ashes to ashes, dust to dust" there was a little alteration of the words to suit the process. A door opened in the wall; and the violet coffin mysteriously passed out through it and vanished as it closed. People think that door the door of the furnace; but it isn't. I went behind the scenes at the end of the service and saw the real tiling. People are afraid to see it; but it is wonderful. I found there the violet coffin opposite another door, a real unmistakable furnace door. When it lifted there was a plain little chamber of cement and firebrick. No heat. No noise. No roaring draught. No flame. No feel. It looked cool, clean, sunny, though no sun could get there. You would have walked in or put your hand in without misgiving. Then the violet coffin moved again and went in feet first. And behold! The feet burst miraculously into streaming ribbons of garnet coloured lovely flame, smokeless and eager, like pentecostal tongues, and as the whole coffin passed in it sprang into flame all over; and my mother became that beautiful fire.

The door fell; and they said that if we wanted to see it all through, we should come back in an hour and a half. I remembered the wasted little figure with the wonderful face, and said "Too long" to myself; but we went off and looked at the Hampstead Garden Surburb (in which I have shares), and telephoned messages to the theatre, and bought books, and enjoyed ourselves generally.

By the way I forgot one incident. Hayden Coffin [a comedian and light-opera singer] suddenly appeared in the chapel. *His* mother also. The end was wildly funny, she would have enjoyed it enormously. When we returned we looked down through an opening in the floor to a lower floor close below. There we saw a roomy kitchen, with a big cement table and two cooks busy at it. They had little tongs in their hands, and they were deftly and busily picking nails and scraps of coffin handles out of Mamma's dainty little heap of ashes and samples of bone. Mamma herself being at that moment leaning over beside me, shaking with laughter. Then they swept her up into a sieve, and shook her out; so that there was a heap of dust and a heap of calcined bone scraps. And Mamma said in my ear, "Which of the two heaps is me, I wonder!"

And that merry episode was the end, except for making dust of the bone scraps and scattering them on a flower bed.

O grave, where is thy victory?

In the afternoon I drove down to Oxford, where I write this. The car was in a merry mood, and in Notting Hill Gate accomplished a most amazing skid, swivelling right round across the road one way and then back the other, but fortunately not hitting anything.

The Philanderer, which I came down to see (Mona Limerick as Julia), went with a roar from beginning to end. Tomorrow I drive to Reading and thence across Surrey into Kent to the Barkers. The deferred lunch at the German Embassy will take place on Monday. Unless I find at Adelphi Terrace before 1:15 a telegram forbidding me ever to see you again, I *know* I shall go straight from the Embassy to your bedside. I must see you again after all these years.

Barrie is in bed ill (caught cold in Oxford a week ago) and ought to be petted by somebody.

I have many other things of extreme importance to say, but must leave them until Monday. By the way you first said you were leaving Hinde St on the 23rd; but you said last time to Lady Jekyll "Another ten days." If you are gone when I call I shall hurl myself into the area and perish.

And so goodnight, friend who understands about one's mother, and other things.

G.B.S.

❧

"Let the worms sign my ribs, and the pretty foot
of a lizard imprint my mandible. . . ."

RICHARD SELZER

REMAINS

*Richard Selzer practiced and taught surgery for twenty-five years. After
publishing four books, he turned in 1985 to writing as a full-time occupa-
tion. He remarked that surgery and writing "have become incompatible
because the surgeon must be anesthetized, but the writer must feel everything." Never without consciousness that the surgeon's cure is only temporary, Selzer has written beautifully, memorably about mortality—as well
as about the shock wave of stillness when the body stops its work under the
surgeon's hands. His books include* Mortal Lessons: Notes on the Art of
Surgery *(1976); an account of his near-fatal bout with Legionnaires' disease,* Raising the Dead *(1993); and* Letters to a Young Doctor *(1982),
from which the following is taken.*

*For Selzer, nature makes no mistakes; there is "not one natural
object in existence that ought not to be," and this includes disease, defor-
mity—and our "remains." In this piece, Selzer evokes the mysteries of the
body as he contemplates his own remains and their disposal. In conversations with author Peter Josyph, published as* What One Man Said to
Another *(1984), Selzer observed, "There are all kinds of immortality. The*

*immortality of the flesh in whatever progeny you produce. The immortality
of the flesh in another sense is that, like all matter, it cannot be created or
destroyed. If it's cremated . . . why then there's smoke, and the smoke is
a kind of soot that falls to the earth and becomes part of the earth again,
from which crops grow. . . ."*

From the flavor of your last letter, I infer that you have attended your
first autopsy. It is only natural that while studying Pathology you
dwell upon death. Nor ought you to be embarrassed to be caught red-
handed in an act of philosophy. Where, if not in a morgue, would a
man's thoughts turn toward his mortality? It will do your patients no
harm to have their doctor feel fraternal about dying. When there is
nothing else to do for a patient, the doctor functions as Charon, medi-
ator between the living and the dead. He offers to the dying, if nothing
else, his familiarity with death. But you must not peer too much into
your own grave. It is self-indulgent and wasteful. Take your cue from
the men who work in the morgue. They are of a marvelously cheerful
nature. It is always so in every hospital. And, truly, it does no more
good to think of a tumorous tree gnawed by termites than of a tree in
full and shimmering leaf. The autopsy he performs each day, to the
pathologist, is no mere matter of death, but most intensely a matter of
life. Just see how the glow has not wholly relented from the body on
the slab. The grand implication of an autopsy is of the abounding life
to come. The dissector in the morgue rummages in this hotel of bones
with its corridors and lobbies, and windows curtained with lace,
searching for the legacy of the newly dead. He is the deliverer of
wisdom.

Lately, I, too, have been dwelling on the end of my days. This is
no morbid turn of the mind, I assure you, no fit of melancholia. I do
but obey the advice of Montaigne, who insisted that to learn Philosophy is to learn to die. Make no mistake, I am in no way restless for the
next world. I like it fine right here. I only wish to lose the sight from
my eyes when I have lost the desire to see anything. And had I influence in Heaven, I would bend the ear of God for longevity. Should
that request be denied (and say what you will about the power of

prayer, sometimes the answer is just plain "No!"), only then would I lower my sights to resignation.

It is all very well for the clergy to intone the certainty that Death is not the end, but just a new beginning, a "pleasant potion of immortality," as Sir Thomas Browne put it. But I myself admit to a bit of skepticism about that. After all, how do they know? Frankly, I'd rather spend the next ten years dining on slugs and bitter vetch than the next ten minutes licking my chops in the back of a hearse at the prospect of ambrosia. Besides, I have watched too many of my fellow men squeeze through that small tunnel whose narrow girth restricts the breath to quick, shallow huffs, suffuses and darkens the lips, glazes the eyes and presses forth groan upon groan from the poor wheezy thing caught in midpassage.

Such is the prettiness that comes to me as I lie in my bed and cannot sleep. Why is it that the airy persiflage of the clergy is so much more palatable during the daylight hours? While at night the smallest allusion to mortality scrapes through the brain like a grappling hook dragging for a drowned man? I am reinforced in my prejudice against matters funerary by having just resumed from the still-open grave of a colleague. All during the prayers, stalking from headstone to headstone, and wearing a terrible smirk—the fattest cat I have ever seen.

The whole matter of departure was brought on by an attack of la grippe, which explains my tardiness in answering your letter. . . .

. . .

"Bundle up," my wife had said. "You'll catch your death." And so I almost did. Though catch may be the wrong verb here as I have no mind to run after it, even though the absence of a belief in a Hereafter is of some comfort. One can die without the anxiety of the believer, secure in oblivion, ready for Nothing.

. . . By the way I hereby charge you with the disposal of my remains.

Yes, you don't look so pale. I am not asking you to hold my sword for me to run upon, though had I the choice of my dispatch, I should ask to die by the sword rather than by the nursing home, as I much prefer a good, clean, lancinating pain to a long listlessness. There is a danger of becoming angry at death as though it were less a friend than an adversary when, in truth, it is neither one more than the other. . . .

Now to the business: I shall not be dogmatic about the method of disposal. In this, at last, you shall be on your own. If it is to be burial, I reject embalming, and would prefer to remain unboxed. Take care that the earth be packed snugly all around, an even pressure that will afford the coziness I love, and would also prevent any slippage away. I should not like to face eternity with a piece missing. You know how I am about cozy. Give me a chimbly cottage with a feather of smoke and, outside, all around, snow on the prowl, sniffing at the windows.

Justest, I suppose, for an unregenerate smoker, would be cremation. To be inhaled by God—his tobacco. After the ignition, you could watch from a neighboring ridge while "me" wafts toward the pines, spreading out thin before going over to the other side. At the last, only a bit of ash for you to blow away.

But if it is to be interment, I shall allow you a bit of wit. Secure, if you like, one of my long bones—the left femur, I think—and after a sensible period of time, whittle from it a sort of flute with finger holes and all, and lacquer it to a fare-thee-well. What fun to think of Rimski-Korsakov blown out of what once occupied my pants. Yeats wanted to be a mechanical bird hammered out of gold, so he could be immortal. Me, I'd rather be of my own stuff. Then with a bit of breath and some finger work, I'd sing on and on. Flesh liquefies into the occasional tears of the bereaved, while bone dawdles away eternity, powdering off a grain at a time. In the durability of his workstuff, the orthopedist owns the longest calling.

The more I think about it, the better I like burial in the ground. People are of two kinds, you know. Those that love nothing more than to be wrapped up snug by their environs, and those who yearn to be unfettered, airborne, wafted. Knowing this, it is not at all amazing that some prefer interment while others opt for cremation. It is not a reasoned choice; it is a matter of temperament.

You agree? Then burial it is. Let the worms sign my ribs, and the pretty foot of a lizard imprint my mandible, fossils for some as yet unborn anthropologist. These creatures—ants, lizards, worms—do but ransack the corpse in hopes of finding what is hidden there a jewel or a soul or some bit of evidence that this man has loved. Nothing lasts as it is anyway, but advances toward hard stability from which it can be retrieved one day by curious and wondering fingers. An anthropologist, sifting through the sands of Arabia, comes upon King Solomon's finger bone. He slips a ring from the dead white phalanx, slides it onto his own finger and all at once there is the faint enduring scent of frankincense. It has all returned. The found object is lit by memory. It lives again.

Intellectually, I admire the Zoroastrians, whose method of disposal is to serve up their dead alfresco to the vultures that line the rooftops waiting for just such a feast. It seems both tidy and sensible. These vultures are truly in the service of man. The recycling of animal matter is economical. But where, I wonder, are the creatures who dine on the vultures in their time? Are there any? Lice, I suppose. Heaven, in its wisdom, made the flesh of the buzzard unpalatable to all but the most ravenous of jackals, thus assuring sufficient attendance at Zoroastrian banquets of these sweeps and chars.

Not a pretty sight, you say? I have seen worse, most having to do with the deprivation of love. Still, my admiration for this Asiatic practicality is tempered by Occidental sentiment. I confess to a love of graveyards. There is nothing so romantic as a rose garden where the bodies of young soldiers are buried. The roses there are celestial. They glow as no others do. You gaze at them, inhale their fragrance . . . and you remember old faces and old deeds. It is the next thing to reincarnation.

Now, as to the matter of my own autopsy. Hmmm . . . I have thought of it . . . and I prefer not to.

"Hypocrite!" you cry. "You, above all others—you should see the need!"

"Yes, but there is a greater need. To myself."

"But why not?" you ask. You are indignant, outraged.

"With homage to Bartleby the Scrivener," I answer, "I just prefer not to."

All this dwelling on remains! By the time Death comes to claim me, I shall already have been dead for many years—from long immersion in the habit of it.

DEATH CULTURES

When the young Dawn with finger-tips of rose
made heaven bright, the Trojan people massed
about Prince Hektor's ritual fire.
All being gathered and assembled, first
they quenched the smoking pyre with tawny wine
wherever flames had licked their way, then friends
and brothers picked his white bones from the char
in sorrow, while the tears rolled down their cheeks.
In a golden urn they put the bones,
shrouding the urn with veiling of soft purple.
Then in a grave dug deep they placed it
and heaped it with great stones. The men were quick
to raise the death-mound. . . .
            When they had finished
raising the barrow, they returned to Ilion,
where all sat down to a banquet in his honor
in the hall of Priam king. So they performed
the funeral rites of Hektor, tamer of horses.

HOMER, *Iliad*
translated by Robert Fitzgerald

"People went to visit the tomb of a dear one
as one would go to a relative's home. . . ."

PHILIPPE ARIÈS

THE MODERN CEMETERY

*The modern cemetery and modern burial preparation are the subjects of
these two brief excerpts from* Western Attitudes Toward Death *(1974), by
Philippe Ariès, the renowned historian of death.*

    *In eighteenth-century France the centuries-old practice of burial in
unmarked church graves went out of favor, and individual grave markers
and private tombs, where "visits" could be made, began to catch on. In the
United States, a shift of a slightly different order is described, as embalming
and "viewing" of the remains became common practice in the middle of the
nineteenth century. Intrigued and slightly mystified by this still popular
American morticians' art, Ariès writes in an essay called "Death Inside
Out" (1975): "The idea of making a dead person appear alive as a way of
paying one's last respects may well strike us as puerile and preposterous.
. . . But it . . . testifies to a rapid and unerring adaptation to complex
and contradictory conditions of sensibility. This is the first time in history
that a whole society has honored the dead by pretending they were alive."
In Ariès's view, the modern practices of private burial and of embalming
point to a number of specifically modern attitudes about death: a "Roman-*

tic cult of memory" and subtle refusal to accept the departure of a loved one, a new conception of the "dignity" of the dead, and, particularly in the United States, a conspicuous profit motive.

In the Middle Ages the dead were entrusted to or rather abandoned to the care of the Church, and the exact location of their place of burial was of little importance, most often being indicated neither by a monument nor even by a simple inscription. Certainly by the fourteenth century and especially since the seventeenth century, one can discern a more pronounced concern for marking the site of the tomb, a good indication of a new feeling which was increasingly being expressed, without being able to impose itself completely. The pious or melancholy visit to the tomb of a dear one was an unknown act.

In the second half of the eighteenth century, things changed, and I have been able to study this evolution in France. The accumulation of the dead within the churches or in the small churchyards suddenly became intolerable, at least to the "enlightened" minds of the 1760s. What had been going on for almost a millennium without arousing any scruples became the object of vehement criticism. An entire body of literature bears witness to this. On the one hand, public health was threatened by the pestilential emanations, the unhealthy odors rising from the common graves. On the other hand, the flooring of the churches and the ground of the cemeteries, which were saturated with cadavers, and the exhibition of bones in the charnel houses all constituted a permanent violation of the dignity of the dead. The Church was reproached for having done everything for the soul and nothing for the body, of taking money for masses and showing no concern for the tombs. The example of the Ancients, their piety toward the dead as shown by the remnants of their tombs as at Pompeii and by the eloquence of their funeral inscriptions, was called to mind. The dead should no longer poison the living, and the living should form a veritable lay cult to show their veneration of the dead. Their tombs therefore began to serve as a sign of their presence after death, a presence which did not necessarily derive from the concept of immortality central to religions of salvation such as Christianity. It derived instead from the survivors' unwillingness to accept the departure of their loved one. People held on to the remains. They even went so far as to keep them visible in great bottles of alcohol, as in the case of Necker and his wife, the parents of Madame de Staël. Naturally such observances, though they were advocated by certain authors of plans for sepulchers, were not adopted in a general fashion. But the common desire was either to keep the dead at home by burying them on the family property, or else to be able to visit them, if they were buried in a public cemetery. And in order to be able to visit them, the dead had to be "at home," which was not the case in the traditional funeral procedure, in which they were in the church. In the past one was buried before the image of the Virgin or in the chapel of the Holy Sacrament. Now people wanted to go to the very spot where the body had been placed, and they wanted this place to belong totally to the deceased and to his family. It was at this time that the burial concession became a certain form of property, protected from commerce, but assured in perpetuity. This was a very significant innovation. People went to visit the tomb of a dear one as one would go to a relative's home, or into one's own home, full of memories. Memory conferred upon the dead a sort of immortality which was initially foreign to Christianity. From the end of the eighteenth century and even at the height of the nineteenth and twentieth centuries in anticlerical and agnostic France, unbelievers would be the most assiduous visitors to the tombs of their relatives. The visit to the cemetery in France and Italy became, and still is, the great continuing religious act. Those who no longer go to church still go to the cemetery, where they have become accustomed to place flowers on the tombs. They meditate there, that is to say they evoke the dead person and cultivate his memory.

Thus it is a private cult, but also from its very origins, a public one. The cult of memory immediately spread from the individual to society as a result of one and the same wave of sensibility. The eighteenth-century authors of cemetery plans wanted cemeteries to serve both as parks organized for family visits and as museums for illustrious persons, like St. Paul's Cathedral in London.

In America, during the eighteenth and the first half of the nineteenth centuries, and even later, burials conformed to tradition, especially in the countryside: the carpenter made the coffin (the coffin, not yet the "casket"); the family and friends saw to its transport and to the procession itself; and the pastor and gravedigger carried out the service. In the early nineteenth century the grave was still sometimes dug on the family property—which is a modern act, copied from the Ancients, and which was unknown in Europe before the mid-eighteenth century and with few exceptions was rapidly abandoned. In villages and small towns the cemetery most frequently lay adjacent to the church. In the cities, once again paralleling Europe, the cemetery had in about 1830 been situated outside the city but was encompassed by urban growth and abandoned toward 1870 for a new site. It soon fell into ruin and Mark Twain tells us how the skeletons would leave it at night, carrying off with them what remained of their tombs ("A Curious Dream," 1870).

The old cemeteries were church property, as they had been in Europe and still are in England. The new cemeteries belonged to private associations, as the French authors of those eighteenth-century plans had fruitlessly dreamed. In Europe cemeteries became municipal, that is to say public, property and were never left to private initiative.

In the growing cities of the nineteenth century, old carpenters or gravediggers, or owners of carts and horses, became "undertakers," and the manipulation of the dead became a profession. Here history is still completely comparable to that in Europe, at least in that part of Europe which remained faithful to the eighteenth-century canons of simplicity and which remained outside the pale of Romantic bombast.

Things seem to have changed during the period of the Civil War. Today's "morticians," whose letters-patent go back to that period, give as their ancestor a quack doctor expelled from the school of medicine, Dr. Holmes, who had a passion for dissection and cadavers. He would offer his services to the victim's family and embalmed, it is said, 4,000 cadavers unaided in four years. That's not a bad rate for the period! Why such recourse to embalming? Had it been practiced previously? Is there an American tradition going back to the eighteenth century, a period in which throughout Europe there was a craze for embalming? Yet this technique was abandoned in nineteenth-century Europe, and the wars did not resurrect it. It is noteworthy that embalming became a career in the United States before the end of the century, even if it was not yet very widespread. We can cite the case of Elizabeth "Ma" Green, born in 1884, who as a young woman began to help the undertaker in her small town. At the age of twenty she was a "licensed embalmer" and made a career of this trade until her death. In 1900 embalming appeared in California. We know that it has today become a very widespread method of preparing the dead, a practice almost unknown in Europe and characteristic of the American way of death.

One cannot help thinking that this long-accepted and avowed preference for embalming has a meaning, even if it is difficult to interpret.

This meaning could indeed be that of a certain refusal to accept death, either as a familiar end to which one is resigned, or as a dramatic sign in the Romantic manner. And this meaning became even more obvious when death became an object of commerce and of profit. It is not easy to sell something which has no value because it is too familiar and common, or something which is frightening, horrible, or painful. In order to sell death, it had to be made friendly. But we may assume that "funeral directors"—since 1885 a new name for undertakers—would not have met with success if public opinion had not cooperated. They presented themselves not as simple sellers of services, but as "doctors of grief" who have a mission, as do doctors and priests; and this mission, from the beginning of this century, consists in aiding the mourning survivors to return to normalcy. The new funeral director ("new" because he has replaced the simple undertaker) is a "doctor of grief," an "expert at returning abnormal minds to normal in the shortest possible time." They are "members of an exalted, almost sacred calling."

Thus mourning is no longer a necessary period imposed by society; it has become a morbid state which must be treated, shortened, erased by the "doctor of grief."

Translated by Patricia M. Ranum.

※

". . . the funeral men have constructed their own grotesque
cloudcuckoo-land where the trappings of Gracious Living are
transformed, as in a nightmare, into the
trappings of Gracious Dying."

JESSICA MITFORD

THE AMERICAN WAY
OF DEATH

*This classic study by Jessica Mitford (1917–96) was originally published in
1963, at the height of the funeral industry's greatest hold on American
consumers. In 1960, Mitford tells us, Americans set a national and world
record, spending approximately $2 billion on funerals. "Americans spend
more on funerals," Mitford writes, "than they spend on police protection
($1.8 billion) or on fire protection ($1 billion)." Mitford's book may have
contributed to a tightening of government control of funeral-trade practices
and an increase in consumer caution. In many states, for instance, laws
now dictate that inexpensive caskets not be hidden away but put on display
alongside costlier ones; preparation, service, and burial costs must be item-
ized even in package deals; and the next of kin must give permission before
embalming is initiated. To get a sense of today's value of the dollar amounts
Mitford cites, consider that in 1963 the average American-made family car
cost about $2,500.*

> How long, I would ask, are we to be
> subjected to the tyranny of custom and
> undertakers? Truly, it is all vanity and
> vexation of spirit—a mere mockery of woe,
> costly to all, far, far beyond its value; and
> ruinous to many; hateful, and an
> abomination to all; yet submitted to by all,
> because none have the moral courage to
> speak against it and act in defiance of it.
>
> LORD ESSEX

O Death, where is thy sting? O grave, where is thy victory? Where, indeed. Many a badly stung survivor, faced with the aftermath of some relative's funeral, has ruefully concluded that the victory has been won hands down by a funeral establishment—in disastrously unequal battle.

Much has been written of late about the affluent society in which we live, and much fun poked at some of the irrational "status symbols" set out like golden snares to trap the unwary consumer at every turn. Until recently, little has been said about the most irrational and weirdest of the lot, lying in ambush for all of us at the end of the road—the modern American funeral.

If the Dismal Traders (as an eighteenth-century English writer calls them) have traditionally been cast in a comic role in literature, a universally recognized symbol of humor from Shakespeare to Dickens to Evelyn Waugh, they have successfully turned the tables in recent years to perpetrate a huge, macabre and expensive practical joke on the American public. It is not consciously conceived of as a joke, of course; on the contrary, it is hedged with admirably contrived rationalizations.

Gradually, almost imperceptibly, over the years the funeral men have constructed their own grotesque cloudcuckoo-land where the trappings of Gracious Living are transformed, as in a nightmare, into the trappings of Gracious Dying. The same familiar Madison Avenue language, with its peculiar adjectival range designed to anesthetize sales resistance to all sorts of products, has seeped into the funeral industry in a new and bizarre guise. The emphasis is on the same desirable qualities that we have all been schooled to look for in our daily search for excellence: comfort, durability, beauty, craftsmanship. The attuned ear will recognize too the convincing quasi-scientific language, so reassuring even if unintelligible.

So that this too, too solid flesh might not melt, we are offered "solid copper—a quality casket which offers superb value to the client seeking long-lasting protection," or "the Colonial Classic Beauty—18 gauge lead coated steel, seamless top, lap-jointed welded body construction." Some are equipped with foam rubber, some with innerspring mattresses. Elgin offers "the revolutionary 'Perfect-Posture' bed." Not every casket need have a silver lining, for one may choose between "more than 60 color matched shades, magnificent and unique masterpieces" by the Cheney Casket-lining people. Shrouds no longer exist. Instead, you may patronize a grave-wear couturière who promises "handmade original fashions—styles from the best in life for the last memory—dresses, men's suits, negligees, accessories." For the final, perfect grooming: "Nature-Glo—the ultimate in cosmetic embalming." And, where have we heard that phrase "peace of mind protection" before? No matter. In funeral advertising, it is applied to the Wilbert Burial Vault, with its ³⁄₈-inch precast asphalt inner liner plus extra-thick, reinforced concrete—all this "guaranteed by Good Housekeeping." Here again the Cadillac, status symbol par excellence, appears in all its gleaming glory, this time transformed into a pastel-colored funeral hearse.

You, the potential customer for all this luxury, are unlikely to read the lyrical descriptions quoted above, for they are culled from *Mortuary Management* and *Casket and Sunnyside,* two of the industry's eleven trade magazines. For you there are ads in your daily newspaper, generally found on the obituary page, stressing dignity, refinement; high-caliber professional service and that intangible quality, *sincerity*. The trade advertisements are, however, instructive, because they furnish an important clue to the frame of mind into which the funeral industry has hypnotized itself. . . .

If the undertaker is the stage manager of the fabulous production that is the modern American funeral, the stellar role is reserved for the occupant of the open casket. The decor, the stagehands, the supporting cast are all arranged for the most advantageous display of the deceased, without which the rest of the paraphernalia would lose its point—*Hamlet* without the Prince of Denmark. It is to this end that a fantastic array of costly merchandise and services is pyramided to dazzle the mourners and facilitate the plunder of the next of kin.

Grief therapy, anyone? But it's going to come high. According to the funeral industry's own figures, the *average* undertaker's bill in 1961 was $708 for casket and "services," to which must be added the cost of a burial vault, flowers, clothing, clergy and musician's honorarium, and cemetery charges. When these costs are added to the undertaker's bill, the total average cost for an adult's funeral is, as we shall see, closer to $1,450. . . .

. . .

Is the funeral inflation bubble ripe for bursting? A few years ago, the United States public suddenly rebelled against the trend in the auto industry towards ever more showy cars, with their ostentatious and nonfunctional fins, and a demand was created for compact cars patterned after European models. The all-powerful auto industry, accustomed to *telling* the customer what sort of car he wanted, was suddenly forced to *listen* for a change. Overnight, the little cars became for millions a new kind of status symbol. Could it be that the same cycle is working itself out in the attitude towards the final return of dust to dust, that the American public is becoming sickened by ever more ornate and costly funerals, and that a status symbol of the future may indeed be the simplest kind of "funeral without fins"?

Men have been most phantasticall in the
singular contrivances of their corporall
dissolution. . . .

SIR THOMAS BROWNE, *Urne-Buriall*

"The No. 280 reflects character and station in life. It is superb in styling and provides a formal reflection of successful living." This is quoted from the catalogue of Practical Burial Footwear of Columbus, Ohio, and refers to the Fit-A-Fut Oxford, which comes in patent, calf, tan or oxblood with lace or goring back. The same firm carries the Ko-Zee, with its "soft, cushioned soles and warm, luxurious slipper comfort, but true shoe smartness." Just what practical use is made of this footwear is spelled out. Burial footwear demonstrates "consideration and thoughtfulness for the departed." The closed portion of the casket is opened for the family, who on looking see that "the ensemble is complete although not showing. You will gain their complete confidence and good will." The women's lingerie department of Practical Burial Footwear supplies a deluxe package, in black patent box with gold embossed inscription, of "pantee, vestee" and nylon hose, "strikingly smart—ultimate in distinction." Also for the ladies is the "new Bra-form, Post Mortem Form Restoration," offered by Courtesy Products at the demonstrably low price of $11 for a package of 50—they "accomplish so much for so little."

Florence Gowns Inc. of Cleveland, Ohio, exhibited their line of "streetwear type garments and negligees" together with something new, a line of "hostess gowns and brunch coats," at a recent convention of the National Funeral Directors Association. (However, the devotional set exhibit at the same meeting, put on by Ray Funeral Supplies of Grand Rapids, Michigan, while it included "The Last Supper" in new paints and finishes, failed to come through with a "Last Brunch.")

The latest in casket styles range from classic (that is, the "urn theme") to colonial to French provincial to futuristic—the "Transition" casket, styled for the future—surely, something here to please everybody. The patriotic theme comes through very strong just now, finding its most eloquent expression in Boyertown Burial Casket Company's "Valley Forge." This one is "designed to reflect the rugged, strong, soldierlike qualities associated with historic Valley Force. . . . Its charm lies in the warm beauty of the natural grain and finish of finest Maple hardwoods. A casket designed indeed for a soldier—one that symbolizes the solid, dependable, courageous American ideals so bravely tested at Valley Forge." The Valley Forge casket is pictured in a full-page color spread in the October 1961 issue of *Casket and Sunnyside,* resting on a scarlet velvet drapery, flanked by some early American cupboards. For all its soldierlike qualities it looks most comfortable, with its nice beige linen pillow and sheets. On the wall behind it hangs a portrait of George Washington who is looking, as usual, rather displeased.

For the less rugged, the bon vivant who dreams of rubbing shoulders with the international smart set, the gay dog who would risk all on the turn of a card there is the "Monaco," a Duraseal metal unit by the Merit Company of Chicago, "with Sea Mist Polished Finish interior richly lined in 600 Aqua Supreme Cheney velvet, magnificently quilted and shirred, with matching jumbo bolster and coverlet." Set against a romantic background depicting a brilliant Riviera sky, its allure heightened by suggestions of tropical ferns and a golden harp, this model can be had for not much more than the cost of a round-trip flight to Monte Carlo.

. . .

Well, there is a great deal more to it. The observer, confronted for the first time by the treasures and artifacts of this unfamiliar world, may well feel something akin to the astonishment of Bernal Díaz at his first glimpse of the hitherto undiscovered court of Montezuma: "We were amazed," he declared, "and some of the soldiers even asked whether the things we saw were not a dream."

To venture a little further into the baroque wonderland of the mortuary: "The Final Touch that Means so Much" describes Geneva Sculptured Hardware (decorative handles and hinges), with its "natural beauty and mood-setting styles, a completely new concept of sculptured hardware compliment [sic] caskets; for emphasis, to heighten their attractiveness, and above all to make your completed product desirable—the final touch toward increased sales."

. . .

The burial vault is a relative newcomer in funeral wares. As late as 1915 it was used in only 5 to 10 per cent of all funerals—a far cry from today's proud slogan of a leading vault manufacturer, "A Wilbert Burial Vault Every Minute" (based, a footnote tells us, on an eight-hour workday). Since the word "vault" may connote to the uninitiated a burial chamber, a word of explanation is in order. The vault we are describing here is designed as an outer receptacle to protect the casket and its contents from the elements during their eternal sojourn in the grave. Vaults are made of a variety of materials; they may be of concrete, pre-asphaltlined; of aluminum; of a copper, asphalt and concrete mixture; of fiber glass. In any case, a good vault is a "symbolic expression of affection." They are getting more beautiful by the year, may be had in a variety of colors including polished stripes, and are frequently decorated with all sorts of lovely things—foreverness symbols like Trees of Life or setting suns—leading one to speculate as to whether the time may not be ripe for the introduction of a sur- or super- or supra-vault to protect the vault. And so on and on, like those little wooden eggs-within-eggs we used to find in our Christmas stockings.

Cemeteries now compete with the funeral directors for the lucrative vault business. Many today require the use of vaults in all burials, for the ostensible reason that the vault prevents the caving in of the grave due to the eventual disintegration of the casket. The selling point made to the customer is, of course, the eternal preservation of the dead. It seems that the Midwest is a particularly fruitful territory for the sale of metal vaults. "Must be a psychological reason brought about by thoughts of extreme heat and cold, stormy weather, snow, and frozen ground," muses *Mortuary Management*.

An appropriate showcase setting for all these treasures assumes a special importance. Gone forever are the simple storefront undertaking establishments of earlier days. They have been replaced by elaborate structures in the style of English country houses, French provincial chateaux, Spanish missions, split-level suburban executive mansions, or Byzantine mosques—frequently, in a freewheeling mixture of all these. A Gothic chapel may be carpeted with the latest in wall-to-wall two-inch-thick extra-pile Acrilan, and Persian rugs laid on top of this; its bronze-girt door may open onto an authentically furnished Victorian drawing room in one corner of which is a chrome-and-tile coffee bar. The slumber rooms in the same building may stress the light and airy Swedish modern motif.

The funeral home "chapel" has begun to assume more and more importance as the focal point of the establishment. In fact, many now call themselves "chapel." The nomenclature has gradually changed. From "undertaker" to "funeral parlor" to "funeral home" to "chapel" has been the linguistic progression; *chapel* has the additional advantage of circumventing the word *funeral*. Chapel of the Chimes, Chapel of Memories, Little Chapel of the Flower—these are replacing Snodgrass Funeral Home. The chapel proper is a simulated place of worship. Because it has to be all things to all men, it is subject to a quick change by wheeling into place a "devotional chapel set" appropriate to the religion being catered to at the moment—a Star of David, a crucifix, a statue of the Virgin and so on. Advertisements and promotional brochures generally emphasize the chapel and its features: "Enter the chapel. Note how the sun pours its diffused glory through Gothic windows, and how the blue and amber, ruby and amethyst tones of glass play smilingly on walls and ceiling . . ." (Chapel of the Chimes brochure).

The slumber rooms are elusively reminiscent of some other feature of American life. What familiar, recurring establishments also boast such eclecticism of design, from medieval to futuristic, invariably combined with the most minute attention to comfort? In what category of building are you sure to find voluptuous carpeting underfoot, floor-length draw drapes, skillfully arranged concealed lighting to please the eye, temperature expertly adjusted by push button for maximum well-being—the soothing atmosphere of restful luxury pervading all? The answer was suggested by a funeral director with whom I was discussing costs. His prices are, as is customary in the trade, predicated on the cost of the casket, and he was explaining the items which go to make up the total. "So then you've got a slumber room tied up for three days or more," he said. "Right there's a consideration. How much would it cost you to stay in a good motel for three days? Fifty dollars or more, right?"

Motels for the dead! That's it, of course—a swimming pool and TV the only missing features.

. . .

> . . . disposal of the dead falls rather into a
> class with fashions, than with either customs
> or folkways on the one hand, or institutions
> on the other . . . social practices of
> disposing of the dead are of a kind with
> fashions of dress, luxury and etiquette.
>
> "Disposal of the Dead" by A. L. Kroeber. . . .

One of the interesting things about burial practices is that they provide many a clue to the customs and society of the living. The very word "antiquarian" conjures up the picture of a mild-eyed historian groping about amidst old tombstones, copying down epitaphs with their folksy inscriptions and irregular spelling, extrapolating from these a picture of the quaint people and homey ways of yore. There is unconscious wit: the widow's epitaph to her husband, "Rest in peace—until we meet again." There is gay inventiveness:

> Here lie I, Master Elginbrod.
> Have mercy on my soul, O God,
> As I would have if I were God
> And thou wert Master Elginbrod.

There is pathos: "I will awake, O Christ, when thou callest me, but let me sleep awhile for I am very weary." And bathos: "Tis but the casket that lies here; the gem that fills it sparkles yet."

For the study of prehistory, archeologists rely heavily on what they can find in and around tombs, graves, monuments; and from the tools, jewels, household articles, symbols found with the dead, they reconstruct whole civilizations, infer entire systems of religious and ethical beliefs.

Inevitably some go-ahead team of thirtieth-century archeologists will labor to reconstruct our present-day level of civilization from a study of our burial practices. It is depressing to think of them digging and poking about in our new crop of Forest Lawns, the shouts of discovery as they come upon the mass-produced granite horrors, the repetitive flat bronze markers (the legends, like greeting cards and singing telegrams, chosen from an approved list maintained at the cemetery office) and, under the ground, the stamped-out metal casket shells resembling nothing so much as those bronzed and silvered souvenirs for sale at airport gift shops. Prying further, they would find reposing in each of these on a comfortable mattress of innerspring or foam rubber construction a standardized, rouged or suntanned specimen of Homo sapiens, U.S.A., attired in business suit or flowing negligee according to sex. Our archeologists would puzzle exceedingly over the inner meaning of the tenement mausoleums with their six or seven tiers of adjoining crypt spaces. Were the tenants of these, they might wonder, engaged in some ritual act of contemplation, surprised by sudden disaster? Busily scribbling notes, they would describe the companion his-and-her vaults for husband and wife, and the approved inscription on these: TOGETHER FOREVER. For purposes of comparison they might recall the words of Andrew Marvell, a poet from an earlier culture, who thus addressed his coy mistress:

> The grave's a fine and private place,
> But none, I think, do there embrace.

"Many people today don't
know what a dead person looks like."

RUDOLF SCHÄFER

PHOTOGRAPHING THE DEAD

*Rudolf Schäfer, a photographer from the former East Germany, discusses
his thoughts on taking a series of photographs at the Pathological Institute
of the Charité in Berlin of the faces of anonymous subjects shortly after
their deaths.*

Photographing the dead is not new—in the last century, it was quite
common—but people do find the idea rather strange. Many people
today don't know what a dead person looks like. In modern society
we are separated from the event of death: somebody becomes ill and
goes into hospital, and then there's a phone call or a telegram informing you of the death, and the body is prepared and put in the coffin,
and the coffin is put in the grave and that's it. There is no direct
experience of what death actually looks like, and people have formed
this notion that it must look terrible because the events leading to it
were terrible.

. . . A full-face portrait, perfectly natural in life, seems unnatural in death. These are ordinary poses. We are constantly bombarded with newspaper and television pictures of catastrophes and wars—violent, extreme pictures—but we defuse one of the implications of these images—our own mortality—with the thought that nothing so extreme will ever happen to us. With these pictures you simply don't have that option.

. . . Of the dead themselves I knew only a few details: when they were born, when they died, what they died of. Nothing more. These people all died of natural causes. People remark that they all look very peaceful. That is the point: there is nothing special about these faces. The peace of this moment, this coming to rest: this is what dead people look like.

Even so, some people react with moral outrage: how could I rob these people of their last remaining possession, their dignity? They have a point and I'm not denying that the moral dilemma exists, but you have to reach beyond it to see what is perhaps more important, namely, the questions the pictures raise in our own minds about ourselves. To me the pictures have a terrible beauty; they are beautiful. At the same time, the question they pose cannot be avoided. The one thing I think I learned during this period is that life is too short to waste on unimportant things. These pictures show what will surely become of us all one day, and we should therefore take a little bit more care over our lives.

Interview conducted and translated by Piers Spence.

"... someone said to me with disdain:
'You talk about Death very flatly.'"

ROLAND BARTHES

CAMERA LUCIDA

The remarkable reflections that make up French literary critic Roland Barthes's (1915–80) essay on the art of photography, Camera Lucida, *were inspired by his discovery, in the days after his mother's death, of an early photograph of her among the mementos she had left him. Barthes's view in this book that photographs are essentially "certificates of presence," uncanny traces of the vitality of what has perished, yields a profound essay in aesthetics which is at the same time a searching meditation on death, time, and memory. Barthes did not survive his mother long:* Camera Lucida *was published posthumously in 1981.*

All those young photographers who are at work in the world, determined upon the capture of actuality, do not know that they are agents of Death. This is the way in which our time assumes Death: with the denying alibi of the distractedly "alive," of which the Photographer is in a sense the professional. For Photography must have some historical relation with what Edgar Morin calls the "crisis of death" beginning in the second half of the nineteenth century; for my part I should prefer that instead of constantly relocating the advent of Photography in its social and economic context, we should also inquire as to the anthropological place of Death and of the new image. For Death must be somewhere in a society; if it is no longer (or less intensely) in religion, it must be elsewhere; perhaps in this image which produces Death while trying to preserve life. Contemporary with the withdrawal of rites, Photography may correspond to the intrusion, in our modern society, of an asymbolic Death, outside of religion, outside of ritual, a kind of abrupt dive into literal Death. *Life/Death*: the paradigm is reduced to a simple click, the one separating the initial pose from the final print.

With the Photograph, we enter into *flat Death*. One day, leaving one of my classes, someone said to me with disdain: "You talk about Death very flatly."—As if the horror of Death were not precisely its platitude! The horror is this: nothing to say about the death of one whom I love most, nothing to say about her photograph, which I contemplate without ever being able to get to the heart of it, to transform it. The only "thought" I can have is that at the end of this first death, my own death is inscribed; between the two, nothing more than waiting; I have no other resource than this *irony*: to speak of the "nothing to say."

The only way I can transform the Photograph is into refuse: either the drawer or the wastebasket. Not only does it commonly have the fate of paper (perishable), but even if it is attached to more lasting supports, it is still mortal: like a living organism, it is born on the level of the sprouting silver grains, it flourishes a moment, then ages. . . . Attacked by light, by humidity, it fades, weakens, vanishes; there is nothing left to do but throw it away. Earlier societies managed so that memory, the substitute for life, was eternal and that at least the thing which spoke Death should itself be immortal: this was the Monument. But by making the (mortal) Photograph into the general and somehow natural witness of "what has been," modern society has renounced the Monument. A paradox: the same century invented History and Photography. But History is a memory fabricated according to positive formulas, a pure intellectual discourse which abolishes mythic Time;

and the Photograph is a certain but fugitive testimony; so that everything, today, prepares our race for this impotence: to be no longer
able to conceive *duration,* affectively or symbolically: the age of the
Photograph is also the age of revolutions, contestations, assassina-
tions, explosions, in short, of impatiences, of everything which denies
ripening.—And no doubt, the astonishment of "that-has-been" will
also disappear. It has already disappeared: I am, I don't know why,
one of its last witnesses (a witness of the Inactual), and this book is its
archaic trace.

What is it that will be done away with, along with this photograph which yellows, fades, and will someday be thrown out, if not by
me—too superstitious for that—at least when I die? Not only "life"
(this was alive, this posed live in front of the lens), but also, sometimes—how to put it?—love. In front of the only photograph in which
I find my father and mother together, this couple who I know loved
each other, I realize: it is love-as-treasure which is going to disappear
forever; for once I am gone, no one will any longer be able to testify to
this: nothing will remain but an indifferent Nature. This is a laceration
so intense, so intolerable, that alone against his century, Michelet
conceived of History as love's Protest: to perpetuate not only life but
also what he called, in his vocabulary so outdated today, the Good,
Justice, Unity, etc.

"Only the knife, guided by the human hand, can perform the transition from life to death in the desired manner."

SIEGFRIED GIEDION

THE MECHANIZATION
OF DEATH

The work of Siegfried Giedion (1886–1968), the architectural historian who for many years headed the Harvard School of Design, introduced the theme of time into a subject more obviously associated with space. His early work Space, Time and Architecture *applied what would be Giedion's lifelong preoccupation with "constancy and change" to the understanding of architectural modernism—a movement of which Giedion was a vigorous champion. His last work sought to discover* The Eternal Present *in the monuments of ancient Egypt and the Near East. But Giedion was also a pioneer of what he called "anonymous history," really the history of everyday life. In his* Mechanization Takes Command *(1948), Giedion observed the effect of the development of machinery in dozens of timeless and commonplace processes, from bathing to bread-making. To observe the mechanization of slaughter, Giedion visited abattoirs and packinghouses, and his chapter on the subject does not conceal his plain horror at what he found there—not because conditions were especially unwholesome, but because, for all its assembly-line efficiency, modern slaughter still requires a lethal laying on of human hands.*

The phenomenon of mechanized death will be regarded here neither from the sentimentalist's point of view nor from that of the food manufacturer. What interests us is solely the relation between mechanization and death; such is our present concern. Both are involved in the mass production of meat.

The development of this murder machinery can best be surveyed in the files of the Patent Office at Washington. There one can follow the manner in which hogs are slowly caught by their hind leg with the help of cunning devices; fed into the machinery, and, suspended in line, moved into the most favorable position for killing; the manner in which cattle are skinned by means of pulleys, ropes, and levers, and hogs scraped by revolving cutters and grippers.

The sole purpose of the drawings in the Patent Office is to illustrate the patent claim as clearly as possible. Yet freely viewed in their continuity, without regard to their technical interpretation and significance, they strike us as a *danse macabre* of our time. Their bare purposiveness is more direct, hence more impressive, than the nineteenth-century portrayals of the relation of life to death. . . .

In the fifteenth century, the Last Judgment, inseparable from death, was a reality as threatening and perhaps more dreaded than death itself. In the nineteenth only death in its biological nakedness remains, and even this is kept closeted. Hence all images of that time dealing with our relation to death . . . have become untrue. They use devaluated symbols unsupported by the living reality of belief.

The greater the degree of mechanization, the further does contact with death become banished from life. Death is merely viewed as an unavoidable accident at the end. . . . It is more honest to picture death in its crassness as the Spaniard, Louis Buñuel, in his motion picture *Le Chien Andalou* [The Andalusian Dog] (1929), did symbolically. There the symbolization of death is found in the play of irrational associations. Trivial everyday happenings and phantastic occurrences are interwoven into an artistic reality: A razor becomes a long-stretched cloud cutting through the full moon in the night sky, and turns into a murderer's knife slicing through a young woman's eye. The scenario runs:

> A balcony in the night.
> Near the balcony a man is sharpening his razor. The man looks at the sky through the window panes and sees . . .
> A slight cloud moving towards the moon, which is full.
> Then the head of a young woman open-eyed.
> The slight cloud now passes before the moon.
> The blade of the razor is drawn through the eye of the young woman, slashing it.

All this is indifferently crass, cruel, and true. Its directness captures something of the eternal terror of death. The horror resides in the sudden, incalculable destruction of an organic creature.

The transition of life to death cannot be mechanized if death is to be brought about quickly and without damage to the meat. What mechanical tools were tried out proved useless. They were either too complex or outright harmful. Most of them hampered satisfactory bleeding. Our habit of eating meat only after it has been cleared of all blood must, it is asserted, be traced back to Jewish precepts, since both Greeks and Romans were anxious to keep the precious liquid in the carcass. They strangled the animals, or pierced them with heated spears, so as to prevent bleeding. Yet people would more likely abstain from meat than give up habits that have grown into instincts. Blood terrifies.

Only the knife, guided by the human hand, can perform the transition from life to death in the desired manner. For this operation craftsmen are needed who combine the precision and skill of a surgeon with the speed of a piece worker. It is established how far and how deep the throat of a hog should be pierced. A false stroke injures the meat product. And it must be done quickly—500 hogs per hour. To sever the jugular vein, the sticker seizes the animal, suspended head downward by its forefoot, turns it properly, and pierces the throat about six inches. The same consummate skill and caution must be applied in butchering sheep; these less lively animals are hoisted to the rail in pairs. The stick is performed with a double-edged stiletto, just behind the ear.

Cows are no longer taken to pens by the carload to be killed with a pointed spear. When they were, the sticker squatted on boards often placed crosswise over the pens awaiting the moment when he could best thrust the spear between the eyes of his victim. Today a four-pound hammer is used to smash in the skulls of the cattle in a narrow knocking pen; once hit, the animals collapse like wooden blocks. It is then that the workmen fasten the chain around the hind legs and hoist them to the rail, head downward. At the same time, the sticker thrusts a knife into the throat of the unconscious animal. The blood is usually gathered in special containers.

Killing itself then cannot be mechanized. It is upon organization that the burden falls. In one of the great packing plants, an average of two animals are killed every second—a daily quota of some 60,000 head. The death cries of the animals whose jugular veins have been opened are confused with the rumbling of the great drum, the whirring of gears, and the shrilling sound of steam. Death cries and mechanical noises are almost impossible to disentangle. Neither can the eye quite take in what it sees. On one side of the sticker are the living; on the other side, the slaughtered. Each animal hangs head downwards at the same regular interval, except that, from the creatures to his right, blood is spurting out of the neck-wound in the tempo of the heart beat. In twenty seconds, on the average, a hog is supposed to have bled to death. It happens so quickly, and is so smooth a part of the production process, that emotion is barely stirred.

What is truly startling in this mass transition from life to death is the complete neutrality of the act. One does not experience, one does not feel; one merely observes. It may be that nerves that we do not control rebel somewhere in the subconscious. Days later, the inhaled odor of blood suddenly rises from the walls of one's stomach, although no trace of it can have clung to the person.

How far the question is justified we do not know, nevertheless it may be asked: Has this neutrality toward death had any further effect upon us? This broader influence does not have to appear in the land that evolved mechanized killing, or even at the time the methods came about. This neutrality toward death may be lodged deep in the roots of our time. It did not bare itself on a large scale until the War, when whole populations, as defenseless as the animals hooked head downwards on the traveling chain, were obliterated with trained neutrality.

" . . . a primordial fear of the dead . . . must have been
much stronger than any 'sense of bereavement.' . . ."

ERWIN PANOFKSY

THE DANGEROUS DEAD

*Erwin Panofsky (1892–1968) brought a legendary compound of prodigious
learning and inspired intelligence to the elucidation of many monuments in
the history of art. He modernized and deepened the study of what may be
called the cultural expressiveness of art, discovering in iconography and
conventions of representation the shared meanings on which individual artistic vision draws. In Tomb Sculpture, the last of his books to be published
in his lifetime, Panofsky poignantly evokes the ideas and feelings surrounding the commemoration of death in four civilizations, ranging from that of
ancient Egypt to that of baroque Europe. The book appeared in 1968, a
little before the historical study of death became the prominent subject it
now is. Our selection is taken from the opening pages of the work, in which
Panofsky delineates his subject matter and discusses some of the most
ancient notions of death still discernible in art.*

. . . There is hardly any sphere of human experience where ratio-
nally incompatible beliefs so easily coexist and where prelogical, one

might almost say metalogical, feelings so stubbornly survive in periods of advanced civilization as in our attitude toward the dead.

The aboriginal fears and taboos of primitive man survive all
around us (even in ourselves), and primitive rituals continue to be
practiced, unbeknownst to those who do so, up to this day. When we
close the mouth and eyes of the dead and arrange them in an attitude
of peaceful repose, their hands often placed crosswise, we do so in the
belief of performing an act of piety; but there is reason to assume that
in these very acts of piety *toward* the dead there survive, in a residual
or sublimated form, measures taken *against* the dead in order to prevent them from harming us: measures such as putting out their eyes,
tying or even mutilating their hands and feet, dismembering them,
putting them in tightly closed vessels, often in postures similar to that
of the embryo (*pace* the psychoanalysts, these customs prevailed long
before the actual position of the embryo was known), or sealing them
up in hollow trees.

The Egyptians did just the opposite from what seems natural to
us. They opened the eyes and mouths of the dead so that these might
be able to see, to speak, and to enjoy whatever life was imputed to
them, and we shall see that there was an amazingly widespread and
long-lived reluctance, overcome only at certain times and in limited
areas, to represent the dead with eyes closed on funerary monuments.
This brings us right *in medias res*.

Animals fear death and experience a sense of privation as a
result of the death of others, at times to the point of dying or seeking
death themselves; most of you have read, I hope, Maupassant's moving short story, *Amour,* where a male teal whose mate has been killed
by a bullet keeps circling above the spot with "short, repeated, heart-
rending cries" until he is shot down himself. But animals do not know
about death. Man, however, has known about it from the remotest
times and in the most primitive conditions. He realized that his life
was limited—in every sense of the term, that is to say, formed as well
as restricted—by death. Yet he could not bring himself to believe that
the extinction of life (viz., of the ability to move, to speak, to eat, etc.)
meant the end of existence—particularly since dreams, hardly distinguished from "apparitions" at an early stage of human consciousness

(see Aeschylus' "the sights of specters appearing in dreams"), seemed to assure the survivors of the continued existence of the dead.

This very belief, however, infused into the living a primordial fear of the dead which must have been much stronger than any "sense of bereavement" and, like all primordial fears, was closely akin to religious worship (we still speak of the fear of God as much as of the love or worship of God, and the borderline between the dead and the gods tends to be fluid). The dead, continuing to live without the opportunities—but at the same time without the limitations—of the undead, could do infinite harm. And to prevent this there were two ways, one negative, the other positive. On the one hand (as has already been hinted at), the living might attempt to render the dead powerless; on the other, they might seek to make the dead happy. But we must remember that, in this strange sphere, not even these extreme possibilities were of necessity mutually exclusive. Even where cremation was adopted as apparently the most effective means of reducing the dead to impotence by destroying the matter as well as the shape of their bodies (or where the bodies were allowed to rot away and only the bones were subsequently collected and buried in what are known as "ossuaries"), the relatively small containers of these remains were shaped like figures, like houses, or even, exceptionally, like both—a procedure which, in a sense, reinstated the very situation destroyed by cremation or decomposition. Even the ash urns could be placed on thrones like living rulers; cherished possessions were added; and special drains were provided through which offerings of wine or blood could reach these receptacles.

Some ways of rendering the dead powerless, and their unnoticed survival in modern civilization, have already been mentioned. It is even possible, I believe, that the Roman ritual of *os resectum*—that curious custom of cutting off a finger from the body to be cremated and throwing earth upon this severed member—is not so much a symbolic re-enactment of burial at a period when interment had been superseded by cremation as it is a survival of the quite primitive custom of cutting off one or more fingers of the corpse in order to prevent the dead from using weapons against the living.

The means of making the dead happy were, of course, to provide them with what may be called the necessities of afterlife, that is to say, with everything they used to need or enjoy when alive: food, drink—particularly drink, for the dead were always thought of as extremely thirsty—shelter, tools, weapons, ornaments or toys, animals, and, if they had been prominent enough, servants. The custom of slaughtering not only horses, dogs, and cattle but also slaves (or, in the case of princes, gentlemen and ladies in waiting) at the grave of their masters—or, worse, of burying them alive together with the corpses—is common to all primitive (and so-called primitive) peoples, to the American Indians as well as to the ancient Germans, to the predecessors of the Greeks (when Achilles sacrificed twelve Trojans at the grave of Patroclus, he probably committed an act not so much of vengeance as of propitiation) as well as to the inhabitants of Ur in Chaldea.

I have always spoken of "the dead." But now we must qualify. At a primitive stage of civilization it was indeed the person as a whole that was believed to survive on some unknown and unknowable plane, and to be capable of "coming back" as what the French so eloquently call a *revenant*. It took a great amount of observation and reflection to realize that the body of the dead individual decays and ultimately vanishes of itself, while his power—for good or evil—remains unimpaired: that what apparently continues to function and to intrude upon the world of the living is something which persists when the body has perished.

When this difference between "that which perishes" and "that which persists" had been recognized, it was, however, not concluded (by way of mathematical subtraction, as it were) that the surviving entity was, so to speak, the living person minus the body. It was not reasoned: the dead person cannot move, breathe, speak, hear, or feel; consequently, that which survives in death must be identical with that which has enabled his body to move, to breathe, to speak, to hear, or to feel in life but has fled away from it at the moment of death. According to immediate experience (in dreams, etc.), the surviving entity was not an invisible and, so to speak, impersonal "life force"; it was, on the contrary, a mysterious but very concrete and individual being that differed from the dead person only in its lack of materiality:

an insubstantial image or shade which, far from being a part of the deceased, was rather a ghostly duplicate thereof.

It took, therefore, a further step to distinguish between this "double" of the dead person—duplicating him in his entirety except for matter—and an invisible and volatile principle that had animated the body when alive: to distinguish, that is, between what I should like to call . . . an "image-soul" and a "life-soul," the latter supposed to reside in the blood or (preferably) in the breath and so completely divorced from the individual shape and personality of the former human being that art attempted to symbolize it under the guise of such small, fast-moving creatures as snakes, butterflies, fishes, and, above all, birds.

When this second step was taken, there resulted a tripartition (occasionally further diversified, as in ancient Egypt) which was to survive for millennia and leave its imprint on art as well as language. In Greek we have, in addition to the words for body, *soma* or *mele,* several words for soul: *skia, eidolon,* and *psyche. Skia* and *eidolon,* needless to say, originally designated the "image-soul" and were, therefore, visually symbolized by human figures, often of small size and dark in color in order to express the lack of life, and winged in order to express incorporeality. *Psyche* (literally: a breeze, a breath) originally designated the "life-soul" and was, therefore, visually symbolized (as has already been mentioned) by butterflies or birds. In Latin a similar contrast is expressed by *manes,* on the one hand, and *anima, animus,* or *spiritus* on the other; and in English by "ghost" (originally only the "image-soul") and "soul" or "spirit." But in all these cases the original distinctions were not consistently respected, so that we can now speak of the Holy Ghost as well as of the Holy Spirit and, if so inclined, may conjure up spirits as well as lay ghosts.

Once the distinction between body and soul (or souls) had been made, it became evident that purely negative measures to render the departed harmless could be of no avail. Neither the "image-soul" nor the "life-soul" could be incapacitated or immobilized by incapacitating or immobilizing the body—with the single exception of souls which for some reason or another had not managed to disengage themselves from their bodies. This was believed to be the case with persons not decently buried, with suicides, and, most important, with maidens who had died between betrothal and marriage (*lamiae*) and sought a belated gratification of their frustrated desires. Persons of this kind were . . . "living-dead," believed to prey upon the living like—or, rather, as—vampires; for it is in Greece and the Balkan countries that the belief in vampires, to which we owe so many haunting works of literature from Goethe's *Braut von Korinth* and Keats's *Lamia* down to Bram Stoker's *Dracula,* remained endemic at all times and became epidemic as late as the eighteenth century. Vampires had to be killed a second time (preferably by driving a stake through their hearts) so that their souls might be freed from their bodies for good and thus come to rest; but the bona fide dead could not be dealt with so harshly. They had to be pacified by providing for the postmortal needs of their surviving souls. Failure to do so was considered the greatest of crimes, while to do it effectively and in perpetuity was the most sacred of duties: a matter of private and public self-preservation.

LEGACIES

———

. . . If thou art rich, thou'rt poor;
For, like an ass whose back with ingots bows,
Thou bear'st thy heavy riches but a journey,
And Death unloads thee.

WILLIAM SHAKESPEARE
Measure for Measure

※

"He was not in a forgiving mood, and he may have been
too ill for his advisers to wish to nudge him. . . ."

E. A. J. HONIGMANN

THE SECOND-BEST BED

"Shakespeare," Keats said, "led a life of allegory. His works are the commentary upon it." The documents that permit scholars to comment upon
the dramatist's literal, everyday existence are not nearly so profuse: a
handful of leases and deeds, some business contracts connected to the theater—and a mysteriously laconic last will and testament, characterized by
many puzzling omissions and at least one enigmatic bequest: that of the
poet's "second-best bed" to his wife, Anne Hathaway.

In the brilliant work of historical and psychological detection that
follows, the noted Shakespearean scholar E. A. J. Honigmann combines a
penetrating account of testamentary practices in Shakespeare's seventeenth-
century milieu with an unorthodox but compelling picture of the poet in his
dying days.

"In the name of God, amen. I William Shakespeare of Stratford upon
Avon in the county of Warwick gentleman in perfect health and memory God be praised do make and ordain this my last will and testa-

ment in manner and form following. That is to say first I commend my soul into the hands of God my creator, hoping and assuredly believing through the only merits of Jesus Christ my Saviour to be made partaker of life everlasting, and my body to the earth whereof it is made."

With these words Shakespeare began his will, shortly before his death in 1616, bequeathing to the world a statement of his assets and of his closest friends. The will appears to adopt the impersonal jargon of lawyers and thus, despite the famous "second-best bed," to conceal rather than reveal the testator. I want to compare the will with others of the period and to suggest that Shakespeare's failure to observe some testamentary conventions makes his a most unusual document, one that gives us unexpected insights into his personality and even into his relationship with his wife, Anne Hathaway.

Placing Shakespeare's will in the cultural traditions of its period, we must compare it not only with London and Stratford wills but, more specifically, with those made by testators belonging to the same social class. After the preamble of a gentleman's will there were often directions for the funeral. John Heminges, the dramatist's colleague for at least twenty-two years, said, "and my body I commit to the earth to be buried in Christian manner in the parish church of Mary Aldermanbury in London," and he requested that "my funeral may be in decent and comely manner performed in the evening, without any vain pomp or cost." Shakespeare commended his soul to God, "and my body to the earth wherof it is made."

In itself this abruptness might have little significance—yet it needs to be seen in a larger context. A gentleman at this time would often leave a sum for the repair of parish church, another sum for a funeral sermon or an annual sermon, and now and then for a monument—not for all but for some of these . . . let us call them social obligations. Shakespeare's colleague Thomas Pope left directions in 1603 for his funeral in the parish church and "towards the setting up of some monument on me in the said church and my funeral £20." Another colleague, Augustine Phillips, asked in 1605 to be buried in the chancel of the parish church and gave "to the preacher which shall preach at my funeral . . . twenty shillings."

Shakespeare left no such bequests and this may indicate a lack of interest, or even disaffection. The haste with which his will was prepared cannot be wholly blamed for such omissions since he found time to add other small bequests, which were interlined. Moreover he did give a generous sum to the poor of Stratford: "Item, I give and bequeath unto the poor of Stratford aforesaid ten pounds." Some testators asked their church wardens to distribute such alms. Shakespeare didn't—is that significant? He remembered only one godchild in his will—is that significant?

Taken singly these points attract no attention; taken together they are a puzzle. Compare John Combe of Old Stratford, gentleman, who directed in 1612, "Item. I give and bequeath to every one of my godchildren before not named five shillings apiece." Combe also asked to be buried in the parish church, left £60 for a tomb, and twenty shillings a year forever "to make a sermon twice a year"— evidently a more committed son of the church than W. Shakespeare.

Before I try to explain other curious omissions it will be helpful to remind you of the story of Judith Shakespeare's marriage and its effect on her father's will. . . . I follow [E. K. Chambers's] narrative. Shakespeare probably first gave instructions for a will in January 1616; a draft was prepared by his lawyer, Francis Collins, consisting of three sheets. On March 25 Shakespeare decided to change his will—"The changes he desired in the opening provisions were so substantial that it was thought best to prepare a new sheet one." Sheets two and three "were allowed to stand with some alterations; and in this form it was signed on each sheet by Shakespeare." Sheet one is "mainly occupied with bequests to Shakespeare's daughter Judith," so "it is reasonable to suppose that it was her marriage on 10 Feb. 1616 which determined the principal changes." A lack of confidence in Thomas Quiney, Judith's husband, could explain these changes, thought Chambers—and a later discovery proved him to be correct.

Others have shown that Shakespeare had cause to mistrust his new son-in-law, for Thomas Quiney was forced to appear in open court in the parish church and confess to "carnal copulation" with one Margaret Wheeler. That was to be on March 26; one day earlier, on the 25th, Shakespeare sent for Collins and had his will redrafted to protect his daughter—in effect to ensure that Quiney received none of his money, except under stringent conditions.

Other wills survive in which a member of the family is sharply rapped on the knuckles, most often a son-in-law, as in Shakespeare's case. Elizabeth Condell, the widow of Shakespeare's colleague, said of one bequest, "Yet so I do intend the same as that my said son-in-law Mr. Herbert Finch shall never have possession of the same; and therefore my will is that my said executors shall keep those goods in their hands for the good of my grandchildren . . . unless my said son-in-law . . . shall first give good security." Jacob Meade, who had an interest in the Hope theater, asked his executors to retain a sum for his daughter,

> the principal to remain unto and for the only use and behoof of my said daughter, so long as it shall please almighty God that she shall live with her husband Michael Pyttes, whom I will shall have nothing to do or meddle therewith.

Shakespeare's unloved son-in-law was put in his place even more humiliatingly. He was not mentioned by name, his very existence was not acknowledged, even though the most carefully hedged clauses of the will were clearly devised in response to his unwelcome arrival in the bosom of the family. The thought is not unlike that of Elizabeth Condell and Jacob Meade, but notice the curious phrasing. Daughter Judith was to have £150, and another £150 after three years

> if she or any issue of her body be living at the end of three years. . . . Provided that if such husband that she shall at the end of the said three years be married unto or attain after do sufficiently assure unto her . . . lands answerable to the portion by this my will given . . . then my will is that the said £150 shall be paid to such husband as shall make such assurance to his own use.

Such husband? Who could be responsible for this phrasing, just six weeks after Judith Shakespeare married her first husband, Thomas Quiney?

. . .

Elizabeth Condell and Jacob Meade named the sons-in-law who had displeased them. Shakespeare's will carefully avoids naming Thomas Quiney . . . —and names omitted, for one reason or another, seem to me a peculiarity of his will as a whole. Bequests to several friends were interlined, therefore were afterthoughts: for instance, those to Hamnet Sadler, William Reynolds, and to "my fellows John Heminges, Richard Burbage and Henry Condell." More astonishingly, there was not a single reference to the testator's wife in the will as first completed. Had it occurred to Shakespeare before the draft was completed that he ought to remember friends and his wife, he could have added more clauses at a later point in the will; instead they were inserted awkwardly, and none too legibly, in between lines that were already written.

I shall return to Anne Hathaway in a moment. First, though, some other "omissions" from the will. Shakespeare, the owner of one of the largest houses in Stratford, must have kept servants. A gentleman usually remembered his servants in his will—individual bequests to some, and very often a year's wages for all the rest. "Item, I give unto those my servants whose names are expressed and declared in the schedule to this my will . . . the several sums to their names written," said William Combe of Warwick. Shakespeare left nothing to his servants. Leading actors left bequests to each other and also, in some cases, to the hired men of the company and to their apprentices; Shakespeare left bequests to just three "fellows," as an afterthought, a smaller number than one might have expected, and nothing at all to hired men or former apprentices, after at least twenty-two years with, basically, the same company.

Another fairly common practice at this time was to forgive all debts in one's will, or at least small debts or the debts of impecunious friends or relations. John Combe of Old Stratford, the "noted usurer" who bequeathed £5 "to Master William Shakespeare," had his own way of forgiving debts—fractionally forgiving them, perhaps inspired by professional instinct. "Item, I give and bequeath to every one of my good and just debtors for every twenty pound that any man oweth me twenty shillings." Shakespeare, who may have been a moneylender and certainly took others to law to recover debts, forgave no debts in his will.

Compared with other testators from the same social class it may appear that William Shakespeare was totally self-centered and shockingly tight-fisted. Before we jump to conclusions I want to mention another omission, for which I blame not the testator but his lawyer. A wise lawyer made sure that the will he helped to prepare would stand scrutiny in a court of law. If there were deletions in a will it was prudent to certify their authenticity, as on the verso of Samuel Rowley's will (1624): "Memorandum that these words, 'and said lease in Plough Alley,' interlined between the eleven and twelfth lines within written, were interlined before the ensealing and delivery hereof"—with the names of four witnesses. Any insertion or deletion in a will could cause trouble. No one took the precaution of authenticating all the changes in Shakespeare's will, a more heavily revised will than any I have seen. More extraordinary still, the date at the beginning was interlined above an almost illegible deletion, without being validated by witnesses, although a changed date could have become a vital issue had the will been contested.

I think that we are driven to two conclusions, one old and one new. The old one is that the testator was a very sick man, thought to be on his deathbed—hence the messiness of the will, only one page of which was rewritten (a most unusual procedure): hence the fact that his seal could not be found. (The will ends, "In witness whereof I have hereunto put my seal," then "seal" was crossed out and "hand" substituted.) In short, the will was a draft, from which a fair copy was to have been made, had there been time—and, just in case time might run out, the testator and five witnesses there and then added their signatures. We happen to know that Shakespeare lived another month: I assume that after March 25 he was in no condition to sign his name again, and that this was the reason why the draft had to serve as his "original will," the definitive document.

My second conclusion, in which I depart from Chambers and other authorities, is that I see all the unusual features of the will as evidence that the testator himself, and not his lawyer, was largely responsible for its wording and structure. . . . One suspects that it was the shock of hearing the news about Thomas Quiney and his misdemeanors that triggered off the rewriting of the will—and, quite possibly, Shakespeare's final illness as well. The testator's first priority on March 25 was to sort out his financial relationship with his new son-in-law—nothing else mattered so much to him. He was not in a forgiving mood, and he may have been too ill for his advisers to wish to nudge him to do whatever else was customary—for the church, for his servants, for debtors, and for other unremembered friends.

Now—back to Anne Hathaway. "Item, I give unto my wife my second-best bed with the furniture"—interlined, evidently an afterthought. Beds figure more prominently in wills of the period than any other kinds of furniture, so there is no need for raised eyebrows. Nor is it significant that she was not called "my loving" or "my beloved" wife, as wives normally were, rightly or wrongly. Unlike most other testators, Shakespeare did not use terms of endearment anywhere in his will. Yet neither did his lawyer, Francis Collins, who signed his own will just a year later, in 1617. Legally speaking it scarcely mattered what you called your wife—though, incidentally, it was most unusual not to refer to her by name. One would have expected "Item, I give unto *my wife, Anne,* my second-best bed. . . ." The only similar case that I remember, of a wife not named, occurs in the will of the actor Alexander Cooke (1614), which was also unusual in one other respect. It begins, "In the name of the Father, the Son, and the Holy Ghost, I, Alexander Cooke, sick of body but in perfect mind, do with mine own hand write my last will and testament. . . ." Wills written by the testator himself are rare, and, as in the case of Alexander Cooke, are likely to depart from some of the customary forms and phrases. Others have recently suggested that Shakespeare penned his own will. I don't agree, yet, as I have said, the thinking and some of the actual words of the will often seem to be the testator's own, not the time-honored rigmaroles of scriveners and lawyers.

Did Shakespeare, perhaps aware that he was on his deathbed, intend a snub to his wife when he left her the second-best bed? Some have argued that it was a gesture of affection: it would be the marital bed, whereas the best bed would be kept in the best room reserved for important visitors. Another probable reference to Anne Hathaway persuades me, however, that the wife who was given only a bed and no jewels or other keepsakes, was not as great a comfort to her husband as he may have wished. On sheet two the will initially said, "Item, I give, will, bequeath and devise unto my daughter Susanna all that capital messuage or tenement with the appurtenances called the New Place wherein I now dwell . . ." etc. At some stage this was changed to, "I give . . . unto my daughter Susanna Hall [and then, interlined] for better enabling of her to perform this my will and towards the performance thereof . . . ," a puzzling insertion.

What can it mean? New Place and the other properties were going to Susanna in any case. The words "for better enabling her to perform this my will and towards the performance thereof" seem to imply that the "performance" might be hindered. How, by whom, for what reason? I can think of one person who might have had different thoughts about the disposal of Shakespeare's "plate, jewels and household stuff" as they are lumped together and collectively bequeathed in the will—a person who would continue to reside at New Place and who might indeed have hindered the "performance." If I am right, this allusion to Mistress Shakespeare, who is not named, resembles the treatment of Thomas Quiney. . . . Shakespeare meant, I take it, that his daughter Susanna *and no one else* was to be the mistress of New Place.

. . .

Shakespeare's relationship with his wife, a major factor in the structure of the will, is not as invisible to us as is often suggested. Is it not significant that John and Mary Shakespeare, the poet's parents, produced children over a span of twenty-two years (with christenings from 1558 to 1580), whereas William Shakespeare and his wife stopped producing children after only three years of marriage? Though not infertile, they stopped when he was twenty-one and she twenty-nine or thereabouts—unusual before the introduction of modern birth control. Biographers are now pretty well agreed that the poet's relationship with the dark lady of the *Sonnets* cannot be waved away as just a literary exercise; if they are right, this too is part of the story of his marriage. And is it not significant, again, that we find not a single reference in the will to any member of Anne Hathaway's family, apart from the terse mention of Anne herself?

When Shakespeare bought the Blackfriars Gate-House in 1613, three co-purchasers or trustees were named with him in the indenture, though he was to be the sole owner. What was the reason for this legal fiction? Legal experts explain that "the use of trustees had the effect of barring Shakespeare's widow from any right to the property." This effect was no doubt intended, and it reinforces the impression given by the will.

Wills were by no means as stereotyped as we are sometimes led to believe, and Shakespeare's must be one of the most truly original of original wills. There are many signs in it of anger or disappointment, obliquely expressed. Apart from Thomas Quiney . . . , let us not forget Master Richard Tyler the elder, who was to have received 26s. 8d. "to buy him a ring" in the first version of the will and whose name was simply struck out, though he was still alive. Perhaps Shakespeare gave nothing to the church because the church had very recently excommunicated his daughter Judith and her husband and was about to humiliate them again. They may have deserved it, yet it would not be too surprising if Judith's father resented this public chastisement of his family. Many details appear to fit into a larger pattern; the treatment of Anne Hathaway may be a part of it. It is not a pretty spectacle, the deathbed scene that I have sketched, with an afflicted testator apparently so unforgiving. We can only hope, though not too confidently, that the dead hand, as George Eliot was to call it, does not point accusingly at Anne Hathaway, as well as so many others.

I have strayed from the cultural traditions of the last will and testament to the deathbed scene, about which, again, we can only speculate. Am I correct in thinking that Shakespeare broke most of the rules? . . . It is reassuring, at any rate, that in the only other record that equals Shakespeare's will in importance as a personal document he also went his own way and made up his own rules: I mean in the account he gave of himself in the *Sonnets*. In the will and the *Sonnets* he emerges as unconventional, and highly critical of those closest to him—the young man, the dark lady, and members of his own family. The traditional image of "friendly Shakespeare," "easy Shakespeare," "gentle Shakespeare," presents him as he struck others when in congenial company; the will, like the *Sonnets,* gives us glimpses of the solitary inner man, and helps—a little—to explain the sustained rage of a Hamlet or a Prospero.

"For those who were close to death, the will legitimized their enjoyment of earthly goods retroactively. . . ."

CARLOS M. N. EIRE

FROM MADRID TO PURGATORY

In sixteenth-century Spain, expectations of the hereafter were extravagantly detailed and precise, historian Carlos M. N. Eire explains in From Madrid to Purgatory *(1995). A routine everyday sinner, for example, looked forward to a purgatory stay averaging two thousand years. Since one day of earthly suffering could knock off a whole year in purgatory, a long and painful death was not necessarily considered a misfortune. In fact, a devout deathbed repentance could not only redeem some purgatory time but save a lifelong hardened sinner from the flames of hell.*

The last will and testament played an important role in determining one's place in the hereafter. Charitable bequests carried unquestioned salvific power, and popular treatises on the art of dying, called Ars Moriendi, *provided instruction for deathbed rituals and preparation of the will. Spanish law also dictated specific requirements for legacies: all testators were required to make arrangements for disposal of their corpse, and for their soul's safe passage to the afterlife—that is, money for prayers, vigils, and masses. When King Philip II died in 1598, he left a bequest in keeping with his wealth and piety, for thirty thousand masses to be said for his soul, and for two monks to be at prayer around the clock interceding for his soul and the souls of the royal family, in perpetuum. "Though few if any of [these] testators . . . hoped to go directly to paradise," Eire writes, "most of them literally pawned part of their earthly fortune in exchange for a briefer passage through purgatory."*

When a notary came to prepare someone's testament at the bedside anywhere in sixteenth-century Spain, he would be drawn into an intimate ritual, both as participant and spectator, for most people died at home then, in their own beds, and had their bodies prepared for burial by their relatives. Moreover, the process of dying was itself marked by many conventions and expectations to which the writing of the will was inextricably linked. To try to understand the mentality of these documents, one must first contemplate the death ritual itself, or at least some idealized portrayal of it.

In the sixteenth century it was taken for granted by most Catholics that one should prepare for death throughout one's life, so that when the inevitable moment arrived, one would know how to act. Crossing over into the afterlife, to a timeless state in which one faced existence in purgatory, hell, or heaven, was far too important a moment to approach unprepared. This was the assumption made by the genre of Ars Moriendi literature. After all, to promote the act of dying as an "art" in which one should become skilled was to assume that, as in any other art, success would be impossible without the proper training.

Ars Moriendi texts were a genre of practical, devotional literature aimed at the laity that first appeared in the early fifteenth century. Though often mentioned in the same breath with the *danse macabre* and other aspects of late medieval interest in funereal realism, the *Ars Moriendi* did not share in the grotesque spirit of dancing skeletons and rotting corpses. The tenor of most of these texts was one of comfort: The *moriens,* or dying person, was seen as a Christian who needed to be prepared for the experience beyond the grave by the assurances of a loving God. On the whole, this literature emphasized the doctrines of grace and forgiveness over those of punishment and damnation but insisted that these benefits could be gained only through deliberate effort and preparation.

These were detailed instruction booklets. The more traditional texts were divided into six sections: (1) a collection of questions on death from Christian authorities; (2) advice to the dying person on ways of resisting the five sins of faithlessness, despair, impatience, pride, and worldliness; (3) catechetical questions that had to be answered correctly in order to gain salvation; (4) prayers and rules to assist in the imitation of the dying Christ; (5) advice to those who were present around the deathbed; (6) prayers to be said by those who were present at the moment of death.

The basic structure and content of these texts remained largely unchanged until the sixteenth century, when the forces of humanism and the Catholic Reformation gave rise to some innovations. The key assumption of the earlier literature had been that one's eternal fate was decided at the moment of death: as the Latin adage put it, *Salus hominis in fine consistit* [A man's salvation depends upon his end]. The purpose of the manual was to allow the dying to escape hell, or even purgatory, by helping them to repent as deeply and thoroughly as possible. . . .

. . .

But what, exactly, did these treatises have to say about dying well? The step-by-step instructions were clear and detailed, the advice easy to comprehend. Because dying was considered to be a social process, the advice was aimed not just at the dying person but at family and neighbors as well. . . .

Once someone's illness or injury was determined to be serious enough to threaten death, a notary and a priest would be sent for, a will would be drawn up, and preparations for the death watch would begin. But this was no passive vigil. Helping one's relatives and neighbors to die well was considered a serious obligation, for the temptations that the dying person faced were considered to be the most awful and terrifying of all, and it was generally believed that one could aid the dying to resist them. To assist the dying, in fact, was considered a highly meritorious act of charity: it was better than offering suffrages for those who were already dead. Friends and relatives would arrive. Some would begin to assist the dying person in the recitation of prayers; others would read devotional literature, possibly from an *Ars Moriendi* book. Confraternities might be summoned to pray for the soul of the *moriens,* or dying person. If he or she belonged to a confraternity, their fellow members were obliged to come and remain throughout the ordeal; if not, the confraternity could be paid to come. Their procession and arrival were often underscored in the streets with the tolling of bells and the chanting of hymns. The priest, too, would often make a ceremonial approach and entrance, carrying the consecrated host through the streets, as in a small-scale Corpus Christi procession, causing bystanders to drop to their knees and sometimes even drawing out people from the churches.

The priest administered to the dying three indispensable sacraments known as the last rites and served other functions as well. First, he heard their final confession and granted them absolution, allowing them to face death with a clean soul: this was supposed to be the most thorough and most contrite confession of one's whole life. For many people it was not only their last confession but the first one they had made in years, and it could take a considerable amount of time to do it well. Next, the priest gave them communion, their last one on earth, known as the *viaticum,* literally the "take-it-with-you," which fortified them for the final death struggle and helped ensure a safe passage into the hereafter. Many apparently believed that the bringing of the *viaticum* to the dying was more important and meritorious than the celebration of the mass itself. Foreign visitors to Spain were often surprised by the devotion shown to the *viaticum* in the streets, which seemed unusually intense to some of them. This fervor extended to the royal family: Emperor Charles V and King Philip II routinely humbled themselves in the presence of these eucharistic processions, even to the point of kneeling in muddy puddles. . . . Finally, at the very last possible moment, just before death but while the dying remained conscious, the priest administered the sacrament of extreme unction, reciting prescribed prayers and anointing the five senses of the dying with sacred oil as these began to fade away in the final stages of the separation of soul and body. This last sacrament, which was believed to guarantee entrance at least to purgatory, was approached with some trepidation, for it was also widely believed that those who recovered after receiving it had to lead a semimonastic existence for the remainder of their lives and, among other things, abstain from sex and refrain from walking barefoot. . . .

Popular and official belief in the presence of demons at the deathbed was apparently quite strong, and helped shape much of the death ritual. As the body of the *moriens* deteriorated and its five senses began to fail, it was believed the soul now could catch glimpses of the spirit world. Because the soul was now nearly out of the body, literally at the door to the hereafter, but the *moriens*'s reason remained unimpaired, the devil would make one final terrifying assault and turn the final hours of life into a pitched battle. This contest, or *agonía* (a term derived from the Greek word for struggle, *agon*), was described in graphic detail in the devotional literature of the day, not only in regard to the appearance of the demons but also in regard to specific areas of temptation. The typology of these temptations varied little in *Ars Moriendi* handbooks. One such author, Alejo Venegas, numbered the chief temptations at seven: desire for a longer life, impatience with suffering, attachment to one's family, attachment to riches and honors, false confidence in one's merits, fear of hell and punishment, and denial of one's faith. Medina numbered them at nine, but his list was nearly identical. According to one spiritual writer, these temptations were so powerful, especially the temptation to be angry with God for one's death, that it was better to lose consciousness immediately after receiving extreme unction.

Prayer was the most immediate recourse against this onslaught. This is where the assistance of the priest, of the confraternities, and of one's relatives and neighbors was crucial: it was their responsibility to recite the prescribed prayers and to encourage the *moriens* to resist the devil's temptations. Reciting the creed over and over, and invoking the power of "the sacrosanct union of the Holy Mother Catholic Church militant" was recommended as one of the most efficient means of driving off the devils who hovered around the deathbed "like bees around a hive." Acts of charity were another recourse: poor adults and children were invited to the bedside, given alms by the dying person, and asked to remain there, praying for him or her, until the struggle ended in death. These final charitable gestures might even affect the testament itself and further engage the notary in adding alms and pious bequests not previously ordered, either in a codicil or hastily inserted, out of place, at the very end of the will.

At the moment of death, which was believed to be the instant when the soul was decisively sundered from the body, the soul of the *moriens* was taken by his or her guardian angel to the hereafter. . . .

In the midst of all of this, one could say near the very center, stood the writing of the will, for it was a document that not only helped one prepare for the struggle of death but also could ostensibly ensure that one's stay in purgatory would be substantially shortened. It was a passport to the afterlife, drawn up by a notary as the dying person stood on the rim of eternity, poised between heaven and hell. It was filled with instructions for the *moriens*'s executors and heirs and was dutifully filed away for safekeeping. The surviving documents give us, centuries later, the privilege of peering into the hearts and minds of those who knew they were about to die.

. . .

Medieval and early modern Catholicism made detachment from the world one of the principal Christian virtues. Avarice was a very broadly defined vice: any desire for or attachment to temporal wealth as good in itself was frowned upon. The monastic ethic of poverty, embraced most rigorously by the mendicant orders . . . , was not only commended to those who took vows but also to all Christians. It was, after all, one of the counsels of perfection prescribed by Jesus himself when he said: "If you would be perfect, go sell what you possess and give it to the poor," and "Truly, I say to you, it will be hard for a rich man to enter the kingdom of heaven."

In a very real sense, the will functioned as an extension of the counsel of poverty to all Christians. Although it would hardly seem meritorious to part with one's belongings at death—since it is an involuntary and ultimately unavoidable divestment for all human beings, whether heathen or baptized, godly or reprobate—the act of voluntarily redistributing one's earthly possessions in the will came to be regarded as a demonstration of the proper detachment required from those who hoped to join the saints in heaven.

. . . According to Philippe Ariès, the will became a way of combining wealth with the work of salvation: "It was an insurance policy contracted between the individual and God, through the intermediary of the Church." As "insurance," the will guaranteed two benefits. First, as Jacques LeGoff has indicated, it served as a "passport to heaven." Second, it guaranteed eternal wealth in the hereafter in exchange for premiums paid in temporal currency, that is, the pious bequests.

The will was also a permit for use of one's temporal goods in this life. Of course, for those who wrote wills on their deathbeds— often the majority of all testators—this was a moot point. Still, for all testators, whether deathly ill or healthy, the will seemed to legitimize and condone the fact that one acquired and used temporal wealth throughout one's lifetime. Possessions that would normally be suspect were sanctified, in effect, at the moment in which they became provisionally detached from their owner. For those who were close to death, the will legitimized their enjoyment of earthly goods retroactively; for those who still had time remaining in this world, the will rehabilitated the continued enjoyment of their temporal fortune.

PART 5

DEATH
ISSUES

Death is inevitable, but its setting and pace are more than ever before open to choice. The exponential increase in the medical capacity to mediate death—to postpone it with machines, to relieve its sting with drugs, and even to deliver death itself swiftly and without pain to those suffering with terminal illness—has made medical dying a subject of public debate. Judgments regarding the prolongation or termination of life are now called for which fall outside the province of physicians and sometimes, according to law, outside the province of patients and their families.

To whom should such decisions belong? And faced with such a decision, how does one begin? In the sections that follow, legal philosopher Ronald Dworkin proposes an answer for today, while historian Michael Burleigh describes the warped logic of terminating "life unworthy of life" in Nazi and pre-Nazi Germany. In Timothy Quill's brief parable against painful and invasive medical treatment for terminal patients, and in Anne Munley's description of hospice care, we find two advocates of "comfort care" and death with dignity as alternative to the prolong-life-at-all-costs ethos that often obtains in the treatment of terminal patients.

Beyond the clinical management of life's end, economics now plays a greater part in the politics of death than ever before. The highest-cost medical treatments now accrue in the terminal stages of care, and with fewer Americans finding health coverage (current estimates are between 40 and 60 million uninsured) who will pay? Former H.E.W. Secretary Joseph A. Califano explores the troubling options we face. In George Orwell's "How the Poor Die," we find an unforgettable and perhaps cautionary description of what we might call an unenlightened approach to terminal care for the poor.

FINAL CARE

Shall I find comfort, travel-sore and weary?
Of labour you shall find the sum.
Will there be beds for me and all who seek?
Yea, beds for all who come?

CHRISTINA ROSETTI
"Uphill"

❧

> ". . . it is a great thing to die in your own bed,
> though it is better still to die in your boots."

GEORGE ORWELL

HOW THE POOR DIE

Eric Blair, better known as George Orwell (1903–50), was still in his twenties when he coughed up blood for the first time. He was living in Paris and, as he put it in the title of a novel, "down and out" there. He resorted to a nearby hospital and was admitted, after much questioning, to a public ward. The squalor, the medical primitiveness, the unrelieved suffering and uncomforted dying Orwell witnessed there horrified his memory for twenty years: the following account was written in the late forties. Orwell's plain-dealing style is reminiscent of a tinted photograph: the colors of sympathy are transparently present, softening but not disguising the sharp gray reality that elicited it. Orwell does not mention in this essay the nature of his illness. He was, apparently, given a sputum test for tuberculosis at this time, and on many subsequent occasions, but always the results were negative until 1947, three years before Orwell died of the disease in a London hospital.

In the year 1929 I spent several weeks in Hôpital X, in the fifteenth *arrondissement* of Paris. The clerks put me through the usual third-degree at the reception desk, and indeed I was kept answering questions for some twenty minutes before they would let me in. If you have ever had to fill up forms in a Latin country you will know the kind of questions I mean. For some days past I had been unequal to translating Réaumur into Fahrenheit, but I know that my temperature was round about 103, and by the end of the interview I had some difficulty in standing on my feet. At my back a resigned little knot of patients, carrying bundles done up in coloured handkerchiefs, waited their turn to be questioned.

After the questioning came the bath—a compulsory routine for all newcomers, apparently, just as in prison or the workhouse. My clothes were taken away from me, and after I had sat shivering for some minutes in five inches of warm water I was given a linen night-shirt and a short blue flannel dressing-gown—no slippers, they had none big enough for me, they said—and led out into the open air. This was a night in February and I was suffering from pneumonia. The ward we were going to was 200 yards away and it seemed that to get to it you had to cross the hospital grounds. Someone stumbled in front of me with a lantern. The gravel path was frosty underfoot, and the wind whipped the nightshirt round my bare calves. When we got into the ward I was aware of a strange feeling of familiarity whose origin I did not succeed in pinning down till later in the night. It was a long, rather low, ill-lit room, full of murmuring voices and with three rows of beds surprisingly close together. There was a foul smell, faecal and yet sweetish. As I lay down I saw on a bed nearly opposite me a small, round-shouldered, sandy-haired man sitting half naked while a doctor and a student performed some strange operation on him. First the doctor produced from his black bag a dozen small glasses like wine glasses, then the student burned a match inside each glass to exhaust the air, then the glass was popped on to the man's back or chest and the vacuum drew up a huge yellow blister. Only after some moments did I realise what they were doing to him. It was something called cupping, a treatment which you can read about in old medical text-books but which till then I had vaguely thought of as one of those things they do to horses.

The cold air outside had probably lowered my temperature, and

I watched this barbarous remedy with detachment and even a certain amount of amusement. The next moment, however, the doctor and the student came across to my bed, hoisted me upright and without a word began applying the same set of glasses, which had not been sterilised in any way. A few feeble protests that I uttered got no more response than if I had been an animal. I was very much impressed by the impersonal way in which the two men started on me. I had never been in the public ward of a hospital before, and it was my first experience of doctors who handle you without speaking to you, or, in a human sense, taking any notice of you. They only put on six glasses in my case, but after doing so they scarified the blisters and applied the glasses again. Each glass now drew out about a dessert-spoonful of dark-coloured blood. As I lay down again, humiliated, disgusted and frightened by the thing that had been done to me, I reflected that now at least they would leave me alone. But no, not a bit of it. There was another treatment coming, the mustard poultice, seemingly a matter of routine like the hot bath. Two slatternly nurses had already got the poultice ready, and they lashed it round my chest as tight as a strait jacket while some men who were wandering about the ward in shirt and trousers began to collect round my bed with half-sympathetic grins. I learned later that watching a patient have a mustard poultice was a favourite pastime in the ward. These things are normally applied for a quarter of an hour and certainly they are funny enough if you don't happen to be the person inside. For the first five minutes the pain is severe, but you believe you can bear it. During the second five minutes this belief evaporates, but the poultice is buckled at the back and you can't get it off. This is the period the onlookers most enjoy. During the last five minutes, I noted, a sort of numbness supervenes. After the poultice had been removed a waterproof pillow packed with ice was thrust beneath my head and I was left alone. I did not sleep and to the best of my knowledge this was the only night of my life—I mean the only night spent in bed—in which I have not slept at all, not even a minute.

During my first hour in the Hôpital X, I had had a whole series of different and contradictory treatments, but this was misleading, for in general you got very little treatment at all, either good or bad, unless you were ill in some interesting and instructive way. At five in the morning the nurses came round, woke the patients and took their temperatures, but did not wash them. If you were well enough you washed yourself, otherwise you depended on the kindness of some walking patient. It was generally patients, too, who carried the bed-bottles and the grim bed-pan, nicknamed *la casserole*. At eight break-fast arrived, called army-fashion *la soupe*. It was soup, too, a thin vegetable soup with slimy hunks of bread floating about in it. Later in the day the tall, solemn, black-bearded doctor made his rounds, with an *interne* and a troop of students following at his heels, but there were about sixty of us in the ward and it was evident that he had other wards to attend to as well. There were many beds past which he walked day after day, sometimes followed by imploring cries. On the other hand if you had some disease with which the students wanted to familiarise themselves you got plenty of attention of a kind. I myself, with an exceptionally fine specimen of a bronchial rattle, sometimes had as many as a dozen students queueing up to listen to my chest. It was a very queer feeling—queer, I mean, because of their intense interest in learning their job, together with a seeming lack of any perception that the patients were human beings. It is strange to relate, but sometimes as some young student stepped forward to take his turn at manipulating you he would be actually tremulous with excite-ment, like a boy who has at last got his hands on some expensive piece of machinery. And then ear after ear—ears of young men, of girls, of Negroes—pressed against your back, relays of fingers sol-emnly but clumsily tapping, and not from any one of them did you get a word of conversation or a look direct in your face. As a non-paying patient, in the uniform nightshirt, you were primarily a *speci-men,* a thing I did not resent but could never quite get used to.

After some days I grew well enough to sit up and study the surrounding patients. The stuffy room, with its narrow beds so close together that you could easily touch your neighbour's hand, had every sort of disease in it except, I suppose, acutely infectious cases. My right-hand neighbour was a little red-haired cobbler with one leg shorter than the other, who used to announce the death of any other patient (this happened a number of times, and my neighbour was always the first to hear of it) by whistling to me, exclaiming "*Numéro 43!*" (or whatever it was) and flinging his arms above his head. This man had not much wrong with him, but in most of the other beds within my angle of vision some squalid tragedy or some plain horror was being enacted. In the bed that was foot to foot with mine there lay, until he died (I didn't see him die—they moved him to another bed), a little weazened man who was suffering from I do not know what disease, but something that made his whole body so intensely sensitive that any movement from side to side, sometimes even the weight of the bed-clothes, would make him shout out with pain. His worst suffering was when he urinated, which he did with the greatest difficulty. A nurse would bring him the bed-bottle and then for a long time stand beside his bed, whistling, as grooms are said to do with horses, until at last with an agonised shriek of "*Je pisse!*" he would get started. In the bed next to him the sandy-haired man whom I had seen being cupped used to cough up blood-streaked mucus at all hours. My left-hand neighbour was a tall, flaccid-looking young man who used periodically to have a tube inserted into his back and astonishing quantities of frothy liquid drawn off from some part of his body. In the bed beyond that a veteran of the war of 1870 was dying, a handsome old man with a white imperial, round whose bed, at all hours when visiting was allowed, four elderly female relatives dressed all in black sat exactly like crows, obviously scheming for some pitiful legacy. In the bed opposite me in the further row was an old bald-headed man with drooping moustaches and greatly swollen face and body, who was suffering from some disease that made him urinate almost incessantly. A huge glass receptacle stood always beside his bed. One day his wife and daughter came to visit him. At the sight of them the old man's bloated face lit up with a smile of surprising sweetness, and as his daughter, a pretty girl of about twenty, approached the bed I saw that his hand was slowly working its way from under the bed-clothes. I seemed to see in advance the gesture that was coming—the girl kneeling beside the bed, the old man's hand laid on her head in his dying blessing. But no, he merely handed her the bed-bottle, which she promptly took from him and emptied into the receptacle.

About a dozen beds away from me was *numéro* 57—I think that was his number—a cirrhosis of the liver case. Everyone in the ward knew him by sight because he was sometimes the subject of a medical lecture. On two afternoons a week the tall, grave doctor would lecture in the ward to a party of students, and on more than one occasion old *numéro* 57 was wheeled on a sort of trolley into the middle of the ward, where the doctor would roll back his nightshirt, dilate with his fingers a huge flabby protuberance on the man's belly—the diseased liver, I suppose—and explain solemnly that this was a disease attributable to alcoholism, commoner in the wine-drinking countries. As usual he neither spoke to his patient nor gave him a smile, a nod or any kind of recognition. While he talked, very grave and upright, he would hold the wasted body beneath his two hands, sometimes giving it a gentle roll to and fro, in just the attitude of a man handling a rolling-pin. Not that *numéro* 57 minded this kind of thing. Obviously he was an old hospital inmate, a regular exhibit at lectures, his liver long since marked down for a bottle in some pathological museum. Utterly uninterested in what was said about him, he would lie with his colourless eyes gazing at nothing, while the doctor showed him off like a piece of antique china. He was a man of about sixty, astonishingly shrunken. His face, pale as vellum, had shrunken away till it seemed no bigger than a doll's.

One morning my cobbler neighbour woke me by plucking at my pillow before the nurses arrived. "*Numéro* 57!"—he flung his arms above his head. There was a light in the ward, enough to see by. I could see old *numéro* 57 lying crumpled up on his side, his face sticking out over the side of the bed, and towards me. He had died some time during the night, nobody knew when. When the nurses came they received the news of his death indifferently and went about their work. After a long time, an hour or more, two other nurses marched in abreast like soldiers, with a great clumping of sabots, and knotted the corpse up in the sheets, but it was not removed till some time later. Meanwhile, in the better light, I had had time for a good look at *numéro* 57. Indeed I lay on my side to look at him. Curiously enough he was the first dead European I had seen. I had seen dead men before, but always Asiatics and usually people who had died violent deaths. *Numéro* 57's eyes were still open, his mouth also open, his small face contorted into an expression of agony. What most impressed me however was the whiteness of his face. It had been pale before, but now it was little darker than the sheets. As I gazed at the tiny, screwed-up face it struck me that this disgusting piece of refuse, waiting to be carted away and dumped on a slab in the dissecting room, was an example of "natural" death, one of the things you pray for in the Litany. There you are, then, I thought, that's what is waiting for you, twenty, thirty, forty years hence: that is how the lucky ones die, the ones who live to be old. One wants to live, of course, indeed one only stays alive by virtue of the fear of death, but I think now, as I thought then, that it's better to die violently and not too old. People talk about the horrors of war, but what weapon has man invented that even approaches in cruelty some of the commoner diseases? "Natural" death, almost by definition, means something slow, smelly and painful. Even at that, it makes a difference if you can achieve it in your own home and not in a public institution. This poor old wretch who had just flickered out like a candle-end was not even important enough to have anyone watching by his deathbed. He was merely a number, then a "subject" for the students' scalpels. And the sordid publicity of dying in such a place! In the Hôpital X the beds were very close together and there were no screens. Fancy, for instance, dying like the little man whose bed was for a while foot to foot with mine, the one who cried out when the bed-clothes touched him! I dare say *Je pisse!* were his last recorded words. Perhaps the dying don't bother about such things—that at least would be the standard answer: nevertheless dying people are often more or less normal in their minds till within a day or so of the end.

. . .

When I had got back my clothes and grown strong on my legs I fled from the Hôpital X, before my time was up and without waiting for a medical discharge. . . . I have no doubt that the Hôpital X was quite untypical of French hospitals even at that date. But the patients, nearly all of them working men, were surprisingly resigned. Some of them seemed to find the conditions almost comfortable, for at least two were destitute malingerers who found this a good way of getting through the winter. The nurses connived because the malingerers made themselves useful by doing odd jobs. But the attitude of the majority was: of course this is a lousy place, but what else do you expect? It did not seem strange to them that you should be woken at five and then wait three hours before starting the day on watery soup, or that people should die with no one at their bedside, or even that your chance of getting medical attention should depend on catching the doctor's eye as he went past. According to their traditions that was what hospitals were like. If you are seriously ill, and if you are too poor to be treated in your own home, then you must go into hospital, and once there you must put up with harshness and discomfort, just as you would in the army. But on top of this I was interested to find a lingering belief in the old stories that have now almost faded from memory in England—stories, for instance, about doctors cutting you open out of sheer curiosity or thinking it funny to start operating before you were properly "under." There were dark tales about a little operating room said to be situated just beyond the bathroom. Dreadful screams were said to issue from this room. I saw nothing to confirm these stories and no doubt they were all nonsense, though I did see two students kill a sixteen-year-old boy, or nearly kill him (he appeared to be dying when I left the hospital, but he may have recovered later) by a mischievous experiment which they probably could not have tried on a paying patient. Well within living memory it used to be believed in London that in some of the big hospitals patients were killed off to get dissection subjects. I didn't hear this tale repeated at the Hôpital X but I should think some of the men there would have found it credible. For it was a hospital in which not the methods, perhaps, but something of the atmosphere of the nineteenth century had managed to survive, and therein lay its peculiar interest.

During the past fifty years or so there has been a great change in the relationship between doctor and patient. If you look at almost any literature before the later part of the nineteenth century, you find that a hospital is popularly regarded as much the same thing as a prison, and an old-fashioned, dungeon-like prison at that. A hospital is a place of filth, torture and death, a sort of antechamber to the tomb. No one who was not more or less destitute would have thought of going into such a place for treatment. And especially in the early part of the last century, when medical science had grown bolder than before without being any more successful, the whole business of doctoring was looked on with horror and dread by ordinary people. Surgery, in particular, was believed to be no more than a peculiarly gruesome form of sadism, and dissection, possible only with the aid of body-snatchers, was even confused with necromancy. From the nineteenth century you could collect a large horror-literature connected with doctors and hospitals. Think of poor old George III, in his dotage, shrieking for mercy as he sees his surgeons approaching to "bleed him till he faints"! Think of the conversations of Bob Sawyer and Benjamin Allen, which no doubt are hardly parodies, or the field hospitals in *La Débacle* and *War and Peace,* or that shocking description of an amputation in Melville's *Whitejacket*! Even the names given to doctors in nineteenth-century English fiction, Slasher, Carver, Sawyer, Fillgrave and so on, and the generic nickname "sawbones," are about as grim as they are comic. The antisurgery tradition is perhaps best expressed in Tennyson's poem, "The Children's Hospital," which is essentially a pre-chloroform document though it seems to have been written as late as 1880. Moreover, the outlook which Tennyson records in this poem had a lot to be said for it. When you consider what an operation without anaesthetics must have been like, what it notoriously was like, it is difficult not to suspect the motives of people who would undertake such things. For these bloody horrors which the students so eagerly looked forward to ("A magnificent sight if Slasher does it!") were admittedly more or less useless: the patient who did not die of shock usually died of gangrene, a result which was taken for granted. Even now doctors can be found whose motives are questionable. Anyone who has had much illness, or who has listened to medical students talking, will know what I mean. But anaesthetics were a turning-point, and disinfectants were another. Nowhere in the world, probably, would you now see the kind of scene described by Axel Munthe in *The Story of San Michele,* when the sinister surgeon in top-hat and frock-coat, his starched shirtfront spattered with blood and pus, carves up patient after patient with the same knife and flings the severed limbs into a pile beside the table. Moreover, national health insurance has partly done away with the idea that a working-class patient is a pauper who deserves little consideration. Well into this century it was usual for "free" patients at the big hospitals to have their teeth extracted with no anaesthetic. They didn't pay, so why should they have an anaesthetic—that was the attitude. That too has changed.

And yet every institution will always bear upon it some lingering memory of its past. A barrack-room is still haunted by the ghost of Kipling, and it is difficult to enter a workhouse without being reminded of *Oliver Twist*. Hospitals began as a kind of casual ward for lepers and the like to die in, and they continued as places where medical students learned their art on the bodies of the poor. You can still catch a faint suggestion of their history in their characteristically gloomy architecture. I would be far from complaining about the treatment I have received in any English hospital, but I do know that it is a sound instinct that warns people to keep out of hospitals if possible, and especially out of the public wards. Whatever the legal position may be, it is unquestionable that you have far less control over your own treatment, far less certainty that frivolous experiments will not be tried on you, when it is a case of "accept the discipline or get out." And it is a great thing to die in your own bed, though it is better still to die in your boots. However great the kindness and the efficiency, in every hospital death there will be some cruel, squalid detail, something perhaps too small to be told but leaving terribly painful memories behind, arising out of the haste, the crowding, the impersonality of a place where every day people are dying among strangers.

The dread of hospitals probably still survives among the very poor and in all of us it has only recently disappeared. It is a dark patch not far beneath the surface of our minds. I have said earlier that, when I entered the ward at the Hôpital X, I was conscious of a strange feeling of familiarity. What the scene reminded me of, of course, was the reeking, pain-filled hospitals of the nineteenth century, which I had never seen but of which I had a traditional knowledge. And something, perhaps the black-clad doctor with his frowsy black bag, or perhaps only the sickly smell, played the queer trick of unearthing from my memory that poem of Tennyson's, "The Children's Hospital," which I had not thought of for twenty years. It happened that as a child I had had it read aloud to me by a sick-nurse whose own working life might have stretched back to the time when Tennyson wrote the poem. The horrors and sufferings of the old-style hospitals were a vivid memory to her. We had shuddered over the poem together, and then seemingly I had forgotten it. Even its name would probably have recalled nothing to me. But the first glimpse of the ill-lit, murmurous room, with the beds so close together, suddenly roused the train of thought to which it belonged, and in the night that followed I found myself remembering the whole story and atmosphere of the poem, with many of its lines complete.

꩜

"During a death watch, touch can
be more effective than words."

ANNE MUNLEY

THE HOSPICE ALTERNATIVE

*In the Middle Ages, the hospice, precursor to our modern hospital, was a
place of welcome for poor or sick wayfarers, a blend of guesthouse and
infirmary, mostly managed by religious orders. The modern hospice largely
began with the work of Dr. Cicely Saunders in Britain in the 1960s, when
she opened St. Christopher's Hospice in London. The hospice movement has
taken as its objective the reforming of terminal care. Distinct from the
medical monitoring and prolonging of biological processes, the hospice goal
is to meet the physical, psychological, social, and spiritual needs of the
dying.*

    *Anne Munley, a nun, sociologist, and hospice activist, provides a
vivid picture of the hospice in this excerpt from her book* The Hospice
Alternative. *Munley here describes a hospice she pseudonymously calls
"Pennwood," where she worked for six months as a participant-observer. It
is exclusively for cancer patients, and the average inpatient stay is fifteen
days.*

It is never true that "nothing more can be
done" for a patient. It may be useless to
continue treatment with curative drugs or
surgery but one can still give attention and
friendship, relief and comfort.

RICHARD LAMERTON

Hospice care is appropriate at the stage of an illness when active
treatment is becoming irrelevant to the needs of a particular patient. It
is appropriate when radical efforts to bring about cure have been
exhausted and death is felt to be certain and not far off. Hospice care
is for dying persons who, though beyond cure, are still living and
need human warmth, concern and quality medical care to reduce the
distress of dying. Hospices do not seek to hurry death; they help
patients to live life fully until death arrives of its own accord. Hospices
do not view death as a failure. They acknowledge that death is natural
to human existence, and offer the dying safe passage in their journey
from life to death—a passage in which dignity and important relationships are preserved, patients and families have a voice in planning
care, and death is as pain-free and as meaningful as possible.

THE DEATH WATCH

Hospice caregivers use the term *death watch* to describe a period of
active dying—the days or hours immediately preceding a patient's
death. This is a time for an intensified focus on details of physical
comfort and for consistent caregiver and family presence to assure a
patient that he or she will not be abandoned.

Staff members at Pennwood have acute sensitivity to signs that
death is approaching—for example, fever, cold hands and feet, respiratory change, lapsing into coma. When such signs are present, caregivers do practical things to keep a patient comfortable. They provide
water and crushed ice for thirst, cool cloths for feverish foreheads,

alcohol rubdowns, and lotion massages and note when morphine injections need to be substituted for oral medications. Caregivers are
careful not to disturb patients unnecessarily at this time by frequent
taking of temperature, pulse, respiration, or blood pressure, and are
gentle in changing bedding, keeping the patients clean and moving
them into comfortable positions. While administering physical care,
Pennwood staff members speak softly to patients, even to ones who
appear to be in a coma.

    During a death watch, touch can be more effective than words.
At Pennwood, patients who cannot communicate otherwise are highly
responsive to touch. When caregivers stroke hands, faces, and arms,
even anxious patients appear to relax. Affectionate gestures—hugs,
kisses, handshakes—are also a part of many death watches. Such gestures are initiated by patients, family members, or caregivers to express love and farewell. Whether there is an exchange of affectionate
gestures during a death watch varies with the personality style, the
ethnic background, and customary ways in which family members
relate to one another.

    Staff members are never intrusive, nor do they impose affection
on powerless patients. For example, if anyone got too close to one
salty old man, he used to hold up a fan with "stop" written on it. His
wishes and "death style" were the product of his life. Staff members
related to him during his death watch according to his signals. From
time to time when he needed support, he reached out and caught a
nurse's hand.

    At Pennwood, family members are often actively involved with a
death watch. At the time of their admissions interview, relatives are
asked if they wish to be present at the time of death. Most family
members say they do, and the staff makes every effort to summon
them when a patient's condition deteriorates. Patients are never
moved from the room that has become home to them. What frequently happens is that additional chairs are brought in so that family
members can be present. Some relatives continue to help with their
patient's care right up to the end, as they did during the death watch
of a beautiful Hispanic woman.

    The day of Maria's death, her husband of fifty-eight years sat

next to her bed in his wheelchair holding her hand. Maria kept looking at her family, but it was hard to tell if she recognized them. She
could no longer take oral medications and had been receiving injections all day. She was not ravaged by disease. She had beautiful white
hair and smooth skin. Her husband stroked her arm and cried softly.
Nurses came in regularly to check on her and to see that she was dry
and comfortable. Maria seemed relaxed; she looked almost regal. Occasionally she turned toward her son and daughter-in-law. When it
became necessary to change her bedding, her daughter-in-law and I
stayed to help two of the nurses.

After the bed was freshened, the nurses placed pillows under
Maria's legs and all around her head and arms. Before Maria's husband and son came back into the room, her daughter-in-law knelt
by the bed, cried softly, kissed Maria, and spoke to her in Spanish.
Maria had been at home for a while before coming back into the
hospice. There was familiarity and great tenderness in her daughter-
in-law's caregiving. She was very much at home in administering
direct care.

Some staff members at Pennwood give advice to family members who do not know how to help a patient during a death watch.
The social worker, for example, told two grade-school boys that their
dying father who had lapsed into coma would probably hear them if
they wanted to speak to him. Another poignant incident involved a
nurse and a man who had been with his dying wife for hours and had
to go home. The nurse described the scene:

> He came to me at the desk and said he had to leave her but that
> he would be back. He said he didn't know why she was hanging
> on. I told him to tell her that he was going and when he would
> be back. I also said that sometimes the dying are waiting for
> permission to die from those they love. We went to her room,
> and he told her that he had to go home for a while. He also said
> that he loved her very much and that it was O.K. for her to die
> and that he would be all right. Then he took her in his arms.
> She opened her eyes, smiled at him, and died. Since then that
> man and I have been very close. That sometimes happens here.

We become significant others to people because we share something deep and personal with them.

Staff members offered the most inclusive, complex, and ideological definitions of hospice. Five themes dominated their explanations: supportiveness on multiple levels; allowing patients to make their own decisions; hospice as an affirming, open, and peaceful environment; the importance of creating community; and freedom from technological efforts to prolong life. Staff members at Pennwood viewed the hospice as a support network that tries to reach out to all needs of patients and families at the last stage of illness and during death and bereavement, and perceives the pains of the dying as spiritual and emotional as well as physical.

A nurses' aide focused on the importance of gentleness in relating to the dying:

You have to be extra careful about not being harsh with these people. You have to be kind and patient, then they gain confidence in you.

Although several caregivers emphasized the patient's role as primary decision maker ("Here people are allowed to die their way"), it was a medical student who was most struck by the hospice's focus on patient participation:

Medical care here is directed toward symptom control not toward curative or diagnostic measures. The way pain is treated is different. The patient is the guide here; he determines the nature of his care.

Other staff members attempted to capture in words their powerful but elusive sense of hospice ambiance as accepting and affirming. They saw hospice as confirming death as a natural part of life and spoke of special characteristics of the hospice environment: "It's O.K. to die here." "It's O.K. to have feelings about death here." "It's O.K. to grieve with and for another human being here." "It's O.K. to continue to support family members of patients who have died here." A young registered nurse expressed several of these themes:

> Here the idea is that life includes death. There are so many cultural attitudes that make death a more fearful thing than it need be. Hospice is a place with a lot of love and a lot of life going on where people can learn to die. Death is as much a part of life as breathing. It's natural, and why not treat it that way? Here we try to do that. It's a place for people to live instead of just waiting to die.

For the hospice maintenance man, living while dying requires presence and community rather than abandonment:

> This is a place where dedicated people try to do the most they can to help the person with pain until the last second, and a place to say, "My friend, I did the best I could. I'm here and I'll be with you."

A home-care nurse emphasized that presence to family members is also important during the period of bereavement:

> We try to make the family's recovery from the experience as easy as possible. A lot of problems people have stem from an inability to face pain and loss. This is important not just for this point but for the rest of their lives.

Also present in staff interpretations of the hospice concept is a view that the quality of a patient's life is enhanced when invasive life-prolonging technology is not used. As another medical student put it:

> Hospice is a place where terminal patients can go to end their lives in a comfortable atmosphere, dying at their own pace without nasogastric feeding tubes and monitors. It's also a place where families can learn to take care of the patients so they can go home for a while and possibly be able to die at home.

Staff sentiments for "natural death" echoed those of some patients and family members. It was, for example, a conviction that "there is a time for dying" that led this wife to promise her husband that she would not let him die surrounded by technological devices:

> Death is natural, and we both signed papers that we didn't want machines and all those things keeping us alive. We're not afraid of death. I tell my children we're all like leaves on the trees. In the spring they are green and then in the fall they drop off the trees and die, but in the spring there are green leaves again.

. . .

If surrogate extended family is an apt sociological interpretation of hospice, why has such a form emerged at this particular time? One reason is, as I have said, that hospice is a reaction to the dominant pattern of bureaucratic, technological death. It is a manifestation of a shifting consciousness of death and of shifting ideas that relate death to issues of dignity and human rights. Hospice strikes a responsive chord in people who lament the gradual erosion of the many modes of support once provided by family and community. Smaller families, higher divorce rates, geographic mobility, greater involvement of women in the labor force, the breakdown of ethnic neighborhoods and small communities, and the development of sprawling megalopolises have all eroded traditional bases of support for modern American families.

In contemporary American society, small nuclear families have become the prime satisfiers of the individual's emotional needs. At crises such as death, pressures on the nuclear family can be overwhelming. Furthermore, growing numbers of Americans are entering old age without nuclear or extended family ties. Hospice affords these old people a means of social support. At the same time, it provides a work environment for caregivers interested in community and in responding to the many needs of dying patients and their families.

". . . Uncle Sam will soon be playing King Solomon
with our fathers and mothers and with us."

JOSEPH A. CALIFANO

DEATH MANAGEMENT

*Joseph A. Califano served as Secretary of Health, Education and Welfare
under Jimmy Carter, from 1977 to 1979. He has worked for and written
widely on health-care reform. Characterizing the battle over reform, where
interests are so many and varied, Califano has observed, "Think of health-
care reform as throwing a trillion-dollar pot of gold up for grabs."*

This excerpt from America's Health Care Revolution: Who Lives?
Who Dies? *(1986) zeroes in on the frightening inevitability, as Califano
sees it, of health-care rationing, particularly for the elderly, and of what he
calls "death management."*

America is at the dawn of the first four-generation society in the
history of the world. That dawn can be the start of a brilliant era in
which great-grandfathers pass on a rich, living inheritance of love and
wisdom to their great-grandchildren, or it can be the era of death
control.

———————

As the twentieth century makes way for the twenty-first, we will become a society in which it will be common to have two generations of
the same family in retirement, on Social Security, on Medicare, in the
hospital. When a seventy-six-year-old patient of Jeanne Lynn, a Washington, D.C., geriatrician, died, she commented, "The real tragedy is
that he'd been taking care of his ninety-five-year-old mother at home
and now she has no one." Increasingly, those who take care of the
elderly, particularly at home, will be elderly themselves.

   The implications of this demographic transformation for our
nation are stunning in every aspect: voting patterns, shifts of political
power, demands on economic resources and social service systems,
housing, income redistribution. But nowhere is the aging of the American population more freighted with opportunity and danger than in
the area of health care.

. . .

Three dramatic and inexorable trends etch the aging of America:
   *First, life expectancy has increased by almost twelve years since
1940.* In that year, the average life expectancy at birth was just over
sixty-three years, lower than Social Security's retirement age of sixty-
five. In 1985 life expectancy for all Americans is about seventy-five
years: almost seventy-two for men, seventy-nine for women. In 1985
three-quarters of our population will reach age sixty-five. Once there,
they will live, on the average, for another seventeen years to age
eighty-two. By the year 2050, we are told, life expectancy will increase
only another four years for men and five for women. But healthier
habits, better public health, biomedical advances, and increased access to health care have consistently rendered projections of life expectancy far too low.
   *Second, the postwar baby boom will result, early in the twenty-first
century, in a senior boom.* In 1940 roughly 7 percent of our people
were sixty-five or over; today the proportion is about 12 percent,

some 28 million. After 2010 the percentage of the elderly will soar, as the children of the baby boom grow old. By the year 2030, at least 21 percent of our population—66 million citizens—will be sixty-five or older.

Third, America's older population is itself aging. In 1940, less than 30 percent of people over sixty-five were seventy-five or older. By the year 2000, 50 percent of those over sixty-five will be seventy-five or older; more than 1 million Americans will be over ninety. Even in 1985, almost 12 million people, approximately 40 percent of Americans over sixty-five, are seventy-five or older.

The impact of this historically unprecedented aging of a nation acquires magnum force as a result of simultaneous trends in our society. Though people are living longer, they are retiring earlier; the birth rate is stabilizing at a lower level, and Americans are waiting to have babies at an older age. The erosion of the tax and support base is ominous. Thirty years ago, nearly one-half of all men sixty-five and over worked; in 1984, less than one man in five (and one woman in twelve) worked after age sixty-five. As babyboomers swell the ranks of the elderly, the ratio of active workers to retired citizens will slip from about six to one in 1985 to about three to one in 2030.

The shift in the total dependent population—those under eighteen and over sixty-four—signals the menace ahead. In 1965, with the baby boom, there were almost four children under eighteen for each person over sixty-four. In 1985 the ratio is two children to each senior. By 2030 the ratio will be one to one, and shortly thereafter the number of elderly will exceed the youth population. For the health care system, this means fewer of the lowest-cost, lowest-intensity users of medical services, and lots more high-cost, high-intensity consumers—against the background of a shrinking proportion of active workers to pay the bills.

In 1984 Americans sixty-five and over used more than a third of the money we spent on personal health care, even though they comprised only 12 percent of the population. At almost twice that proportion of the population in the year 2030, if we go along as we have, those sixty-five and older will use two-thirds of the vastly increased dollars we'll spend for health care. Not only do basic medical costs rise, so does the need for home health assistance and nursing-home care. Only one out of twenty people between the ages of sixty-five and seventy-four needs help walking, while eight out of twenty people eighty-five years and older need such help.

. . .

These monumental liabilities, the health care needs of a multiplying elderly population, and the potential cost of technology make it imperative to create an efficient health care delivery system. We can't keep going the way we are. We simply don't have the money. That stark fact presages a terrifying question of triage for the American people and an ugly debate over death control.

In *The Painful Prescription*, Henry Aaron and Dr. William Schwartz argue that, like Great Britain, America will soon ration health care. America has always had rationing, of course, related to individual economic wealth. But with Medicare and the Veterans Administration, government becomes the rationer for those who use and need acute care most. This role is reinforced by the fact that the federal government controls virtually all the basic biomedical research in America and, together with state and local governments, pays most hospital bills.

Bluntly put, Uncle Sam will soon be playing King Solomon with our fathers and mothers and with us.

Without the most energetic pursuit of efficiencies, America will soon be a nation in which there is no kidney dialysis for people over fifty-five and no hip operations (or artificial hips) for those over sixty-five; a nation in which eligibility for expensive anticancer therapy will be based on statistical assessments of success, and key organ transplants will be severely limited to special cases of virtually certain recovery—all as defined in pages and pages of government regulations and as understood in quiet compacts among bureaucrats and health care providers.

That seems a grim vision for the future of a country with the most miraculous medical complex in history. But in Great Britain that future is now. That is just about what the British have been doing.

Rationing started in Great Britain largely because its stagnant economy could not absorb major increases in health care costs. With virtually all hospitals owned by the government and virtually all doctors on government salaries, the British government is the only source of health care for most of its citizens. Although apparently on the rise, private spending pays for less than 5 percent of physician and hospital expenses and less than 12 percent of total health care. As the government weighs demands for health services against other public needs, such as defense, highways, education, and police protection, its decisions determine for most Britons what medical services they receive. Each of Britain's fourteen health regions (and each of their hospitals) gets a specific amount of money. If a region exceeds its budget in one period, the excess is subtracted from what it gets for the next. If prices go up more than expected, individual hospitals must make do within their budgets, if necessary postponing or even eliminating medical procedures and laying off doctors and nurses. Unless a case is urgent, a patient can wait weeks or months to see a specialist, months or even years to be admitted to a hospital. Of patients admitted to hospitals, one-third wait three months, 6 percent wait more than a year.

So the British National Health Service, which provides free health care, also rations what it provides, making choices about who will live and who will die. The British government treats less than half the cases of chronic kidney failure in England. Although kidney transplants take place at about the same rate as in the United States, kidney dialysis is performed at less than one-third the U.S. rate, and in substantially fewer cases than in other European countries. Since kidney failure is terminal, the decision not to provide dialysis is a sentence of death.

In Britain that decision, though not stated explicitly, is clearly related to the age of the patient. For its citizens up to age forty-four, Britain provides about the same level of treatment as France, West Germany, and Italy do, but for patients forty-five through fifty-four the rate of treatment slips to about two-thirds. British patients fifty-five through sixty-four receive treatment at only one-third the rate of treatment in the other three countries, and those over sixty-five are treated at less than one-tenth the rate. In the United States, virtually everyone with chronic kidney failure is treated, mostly under Medicare.

The British perform hip replacements at almost 80 percent of the U.S. rate, but patients wait an average of fourteen months, with some in line for years. Effectively, most over sixty-five are denied hip replacements. While there is a consensus that coronary bypass surgery is performed too often here in the United States, it is performed only one-tenth as often in Britain.

There's no point in saying it can't happen in America. It already is happening. In the early years of Medicare and Medicaid, government decisions invariably gave the old and the poor more medical services than had previously been available to them. In the early 1980s, spiraling health care costs collided with federal and state budgets hobbled by recession-driven deficits and, in the case of the federal budget, the people's desire for massive tax cuts. The old and the poor learned that the hand that caresses can also choke. The government started reducing medical services.

Predictably, rationing hit the poor first and hardest. Between 1981 and 1984, an estimated 700,000 children and 567,000 senior citizens lost Medicaid benefits. Some states sharply curtailed the number of hospital days, physician visits, and prescription drugs they would pay for.

. . .

The problem is as fundamental as ensuring that our towering technical brilliance has decent and not destructive effects, and as immediate as the last son or daughter who just told the doctor to disconnect a father or mother from the tubes through which the parent was breathing and eating. The urgency of informing our health care system with efficiency, or wringing from it billions of dollars of unnecessary hospitalization and waste, has far deeper roots than bankrupting Medicare, gobbling up larger shares of our gross national product, imposing higher taxes on our working population. The tap root of urgency goes to the morality and political civility of our society. Our failure as a people to confront and conquer the health care cost Goliath threatens all of us—and particularly the elderly—with a system of death control.

. . .

Organ transplants that can make the difference between life and death have become a form of political patronage, with congressmen, governors, and even the President of the United States intervening to find organs and get Medicare and Medicaid to pay for operations. In actions that render the popular entertainment *Coma*—in which individuals were placed in a deep sleep and warehoused so their organs would be available for sale—something of a prophetic experience, Congress authorized the federal government to keep a computer file of available organs, and in 1985 New York State passed a law requiring hospitals to ask next of kin for organs of relatives at or near death. Patients and doctors are quarreling over the right to die and responsibilities to support life. The New Jersey Supreme Court first found that extraordinary means need not be deployed to sustain life, and later included nasogastric feeding, a common procedure, among the medical practices that could be discontinued for a terminally ill patient.

. . .

The sagas of artificial heart recipients like Dr. Barney Clark and William Schroeder alert us to the probability that the geniuses of modern medicine and bioengineering will some day perfect for us a workable, artificial heart. But do we have the geniuses to decide who should be eligible to have such a marvelous, life-sustaining—and incredibly expensive—device?

EUTHANASIA AND ASSISTED SUICIDE

In life's unhappier end games, there
can be no "safe side" to err on.

JOEL FEINBERG
Harm to Self

TIMOTHY QUILL

THE BURDENS OF
AGGRESSIVE
MEDICAL TREATMENT

In 1991 Timothy E. Quill, physician and former director of a hospice program, published an article in the New England Journal of Medicine *describing in frank detail his cooperation in the suicide of a patient who, diagnosed with acute leukemia, had declined treatment. Dr. Quill had prescribed barbiturates for her, and after her suicide, he reported her cause of death as acute leukemia, rather than suicide. Following publication of this article, the case was put before a grand jury, which refused to indict him. This brief excerpt is taken from the book he wrote following his legal ordeal,* Death and Dignity: Making Choices and Taking Charge *(1993).*

A frightening, very dark parable has passed through the halls of many medical centers. It captures a disturbing, torturous process that can contaminate the medical care of dying patients. The actual metaphor may vary, but the invasive treatment described, with its deep loss of meaning for all concerned, rings true to health-care providers who are on the front lines providing medical care in the United States today. The parable goes as follows:

Three sailors are shipwrecked on a remote island, and captured by a primitive tribe. They are tied up by the tribesmen and brought before a tribunal of elders. The elders gave the first sailor a choice: "What would you rather have, death or Chi-Chi?" The sailor hesitated only a moment. "I know what death is, and I surely don't want it. I will take Chi-Chi." The sailor was then slowly skinned alive by the tribesmen, and had his heart cut out while he was still conscious, after which he died.

After watching this horrible ritual, the second sailor was brought before the tribunal. He was much more circumspect, and thought very carefully before giving his answer. "I certainly don't want to die, but I also don't want to be tortured and die anyway. But maybe Chi-Chi changes. Maybe it's a relative phenomenon. Maybe it won't happen to me. Given these limited choices, I guess I will take Chi-Chi." The second sailor was then subjected to the same ordeal, skinned alive, after which his heart was cut out while it was still beating.

The third sailor was then offered the same choice. His perspective was radically altered by the disturbing ritual he had witnessed. "Maybe death isn't all that bad. I certainly don't want Chi-Chi. I guess I will take death." The elders looked a bit surprised, and said, "Okay, but first Chi-Chi."

❧

"None of us wants to end our lives out of character."

RONALD DWORKIN

LIFE'S DOMINION

Philosopher and professor of jurisprudence Ronald Dworkin has written widely on the law and our rights in matters of life and death. In this excerpt from Life's Dominion *(1993), Dworkin argues that the state should leave decisions about terminating life support in the hands of family members and those most intimate with the priorities and values of the patient. He shows how "people's views about how to live color their convictions about when to die," and how no general or abstract standard can determine when a life is no longer worth living.*

We must . . . begin by asking: how does it matter to the critical success of our whole life how we die? We should distinguish between two different ways that it might matter: because death is the far boundary of life, and every part of our life, including the very last, is important; and because death is special, a peculiarly significant event in the narrative of our lives, like the final scene of a play, with everything about it intensified, under a special spotlight. In the first sense, when we die is important because of what will happen to us if we die later; in the second, how we die matters because it is how we *die*.

Let us begin with the first, less theatrical, of these ideas. Sometimes people want to live on, even though in pain or dreadfully crippled, in order to do something they believe important to have done. They want to finish a job, for example, or to learn something they have always wanted to know. Gareth Evans, a brilliant philosopher who died of cancer at the age of thirty-four, struggled to work on his unfinished manuscript as long as medicine could keep him in a condition in which he could work at all. Many people want to live on, as long as they can, for a more general reason: so long as they have any sense at all, they think, just being alive is *something*. Though Philip Roth had persuaded his eighty-six-year-old father to sign a living will, he hesitated when his father was dying and the doctors asked whether Roth wanted him put on a respirator. Roth thought, "How could I take it on myself to decide that my father should be finished with life, life which is ours to know just once?"

On the other hand, people often think they have strong reasons of a comparable kind for *not* staying alive. The badness of the experiences that lie ahead is one: terrible pain or constant nausea or the horror of intubation or the confusions of sedation. When Roth thought about the misery to come, he whispered, "Dad, I'm going to have to let you go." But people's reasons for wanting to die include critical reasons as well; many people, as I said, think it undignified or bad in some other way to live under certain conditions, however they might feel if they feel at all. Many people do not want to be remembered living in those circumstances; others think it degrading to be wholly dependent, or to be the object of continuing anguish. These feelings are often expressed as a distaste for causing trouble, pain, or expense to others, but the aversion is not fully captured in that other-regarding preference. It may be just as strong when the burden of physical care is imposed on professionals whose career is precisely in providing such care, and when the financial burden falls on a public eager to bear it. At least part of what people fear about dependence is its impact not on those responsible for their care, but on their own dignity.

I must emphasize that this is *not* a belief that every kind of dependent life under severe handicaps is not worth living. That belief is disproved not only by dramatic examples, like the brilliant life of Stephen Hawking, the almost wholly paralyzed cosmologist, but by the millions of ordinary people throughout the world who lead engaged, valuable lives in spite of appalling handicaps and dependencies. It is, however, plausible, and to many people compelling, that total dependence is in itself a very bad thing, quite apart from the pain or discomfort it often but not invariably entails. Total or near-total dependence with nothing positive to redeem it may seem not only to add nothing to the overall quality of a life but to take something important from it. That seems especially true when there is no possibility even of understanding that care has been given, or of being grateful for it. Sunny von Bulow still lies wholly unconscious in a hospital room in Manhattan; every day she is turned and groomed by people willing and paid to do it. She will never respond in any way to that care. It would not have been odd for her to think, before she fell into her coma, that this kind of pointless solicitude was insulting, itself an affront to her dignity.

When patients remain conscious, their sense of integrity and of the coherence of their lives crucially affects their judgment about whether it is in their best interests to continue to live. Athletes, or others whose physical activity was at the center of their self-conception, are more likely to find a paraplegic's life intolerable. When Nancy B., the Canadian woman who won the right to have her respirator turned off, said that all she had in her life was television, she was saying not that watching television was painful, but that a wholly passive life, which watching television had come to symbolize, was worse than none. For such people, a life without the power of motion is unacceptable, not for reasons explicable in experiential terms, but because it is stunningly inadequate to the conception of self around which their own lives have so far been constructed. Adding decades of immobility to a life formerly organized around action will for them leave a narrative wreck, with no structure or sense, a life worse than one that ends when its activity ends.

Others will have radically different senses of self, of what has been critically important to their own lives. Many people, for example, would want to live on, almost no matter how horrible their circumstances, so long as they were able to read, or understand if read to them, the next day's newspaper. They would want to hear as many chapters as possible of the many thousands of stories about science and culture and politics and society that they had been following all their lives. People who embrace that newspaper test have assumed, and cannot easily disown, that part of the point of living is to know and care how things are turning out.

So people's views about how to live color their convictions about when to die, and the impact is intensified when it engages the second way in which people think death is important. There is no doubt that most people treat the manner of their deaths as of special, symbolic importance: they want their deaths, if possible, to express and in that way vividly to confirm the values they believe most important to their lives. That ancient hope is a recurrent theme of Shakespearean drama. (Siward, for example, learning that Macbeth has killed Young Siward at Dunsinane in that poor boy's first battle, says: "Had I as many sons as I have hairs, I would not wish them to a fairer death.") When the great British political columnist Peter Jenkins realized on his deathbed that any conversation might be his last, he insisted on talking, though his nurses warned him not to, and on talking about political philosophy and the latest threats to free speech.

The idea of a good (or less bad) death is not exhausted by how one dies—whether in battle or in bed—but includes timing as well. It explains the premium people often put on living to "see" some particular event, after which the idea of their own death seems less tragic to them. A woman dying of cancer, whose life can be prolonged though only in great pain, might think she had good reason to live until the birth of an expected grandchild, or a long-awaited graduation, or some other family milestone. The aim of living not just until, but actually for an event has very great expressive power. It confirms, in a fashion much exploited by novelists and dramatists, the critical importance of the values it identifies to the patient's sense of his own integrity, to the special character of his life. If his has been a life rooted in family, if he has counted, as among the high peaks of his life, family holidays and congresses and celebrations, then stretching his life to include one more such event does not merely add to a long list of occasions and successes. Treating the next one as salient for death confirms the importance of them all.

Many people have a parallel reason for wanting to die if an unconscious, vegetable life were all that remained. For some, this is an understandable worry about how they will be remembered. But for most, it is a more abstract and self-directed concern that their death, whatever else it is like, express their conviction that life has had value because of what life made it possible for them to do and feel. They are horrified that their death might express, instead, the opposite idea, which they detest as a perversion: that mere biological life—just hanging on—has independent value. Nietzsche said, "In a certain state it is indecent to live longer. To go on vegetating in cowardly dependence on physicians and machinations, after the meaning of life, the right to life, has been lost, that ought to prompt a profound contempt in society." He said he wanted "to die proudly when it is no longer possible to live proudly." That concern might make no sense for unconscious patients in a world where everyone treated the onset of permanent unconsciousness as itself the event of death, the final curtain after which nothing else is part of the story. But in such a world, no one would be kept alive in permanent unconsciousness anyway. No one would need worry, as many people in our world do, that others will feed or care for his vegetating body with what he believes the ultimate insult: the conviction that they do it for *him*.

The relatives I mentioned, who visit permanently unconscious patients regularly, and feel uncomfortable or anxious when they cannot, do not necessarily have that conviction. They come because they cannot bear not to see and touch someone they love so long as that is possible and not bad for him, and because they think that closing the final door before he is biologically dead and buried or cremated—before they can mourn him—would be a terrible betrayal, a declaration of indifference rather than the intense concern they still feel. There is no contradiction, but great force and sense, in the views of parents who fight, in court if necessary, to have life support terminated but who will not leave their child's side until it is. But some people do believe . . . that it is in a patient's best interests to be kept alive as long as possible, even in an unconscious state. For such people, contemplating themselves in that position, integrity delivers a very different command. The struggle to stay alive, no matter how hopeless or how thin the life, expresses a virtue central to their lives, the virtue of defiance in the face of inevitable death. It is not just a matter of taste on which people happen to divide, as they divide about surfing or soccer. None of us wants to end our lives out of character.

Now we can better answer the question of why people think what they do about death, and why they differ so dramatically. Whether it is in someone's best interests that his life end in one way rather than another depends on so much else that is special about him—about the shape and character of his life and his own sense of his integrity and critical interests—that no uniform collective decision can possibly hope to serve everyone even decently. So we have that reason of beneficence, as well as reasons of autonomy, why the state should not impose some uniform, general view by way of sovereign law but should encourage people to make provision for their future care themselves, as best they can, and why if they have made no provision the law should so far as possible leave decisions in the hands of their relatives or other people close to them whose sense of their best interests—shaped by intimate knowledge of everything that makes up where their best interests lie—is likely to be much sounder than some universal, theoretical, abstract judgment born in the stony halls where interest groups maneuver and political deals are done.

"There could be no doubt that some lives were a 'burden'
upon state and society as well as to
the individuals themselves."

MICHAEL BURLEIGH

"EUTHANASIA"
IN GERMANY

*In the last years of the nineteenth century and the early decades of the
twentieth, the most malignant of all ideas—that of the primacy of race—
found new opportunity in the scientific interests of the day, especially those
concerned with evolution and genetics. These it distorted with a bravado
that might have proved as laughable as any other venture in the history of
pseudoscience, except that in this case the ludicrous and often willful fallacy
resulted in the deaths of millions.*

*The name for this pseudoscience, "eugenics," had been coined in
1908 by an Englishman, Francis Galton, who promoted it as a "merciful"
alternative to the "suffering" brought about by natural selection, though he
was very ready to imagine a time when, if natural selection proved lacka-
daisical, those who "continued to procreate children inferior in moral, intellectual and physical qualities would be considered enemies of the state, and
to have forfeited all claims to kindness." Even where politeness forbids
asserting it, the philosophy of "good breeding" (for that is what "eugenics"*

means) sooner or later admits to the view that genetic imperfection is a capital crime.

At the heart of the doctrine lies a notion not at all scientific: that health is a single, holistic condition, uniformly affecting all the systems of the body and the intellect and emotions as well. More irrational still, individual health furnishes a suitable metaphor for the well-being of entire populations. "Races," like individuals, can be more or less wholesome, more or less degenerate, and "scientists" can foster and select them with the focused judgment of breeders of livestock. The details, the ethical niceties, would have to be worked out among the enlightened.

Such ideas were widely disseminated in England and America, in the Soviet Union, and throughout Europe, although their monstrous application during the Nazi period gives their circulation in pre-Hitler Germany special historical importance. Tracing the growing credibility of eugenic doctrines among German medical and social "thinkers," historian Michael Burleigh's Death and Deliverance *offers a painstaking account of the fortunes of the thing grotesquely misnamed "euthanasia" from the turn of the century through the Nazi period, when fantasy became policy and patients institutionalized for congenital and acquired illnesses, physical and mental, were systematically taken from their white beds and sanitary rooms and led somewhere to be killed. Amid his teeming catalog of despicable ideas and murderous acts, Burleigh manages to locate the residue of bad conscience, or at least of public shame, in even the most zealous proponent of racial hygiene and unnatural selection.*

We offer two passages here. The first provides a view of the ideological background to the idea of "euthanasia"; the second a picture of a single patient, Helene, an epileptic, who knew that she was marked for the kill.

I.

. . . By far the most influential contribution to the debate on euthanasia was a tract published in 1920 and entitled "Permission for the Destruction of Life Unworthy of Life," by Karl Binding (1841–1920) and Alfred Hoche (1856–1944). The subject was no longer merely a matter of academic contemplation; millions of people had died in the recent war, and hard choices about resources had been made. The fact that one of those choices involved the mass starvation of mental patients not only went unmentioned, but was consciously denied. It is difficult to decide whether the tract was prescriptive or an uneasy and evasive ethical rationalisation of what had already taken place. Building, at least in Binding's case, upon a series of unimpeachably liberal premises, the tract systematically rehearsed a series of illiberal and crudely materialistic arguments in favour of involuntary euthanasia. Binding was the senior partner, although he did not actually live to see the fruits of his cogitations beyond proof stage. One of Germany's leading specialists in constitutional and criminal jurisprudence, Binding had retired to Freiburg after distinguished appointments at the universities of Heidelberg, Freiburg, Strassburg and Leipzig. His positivistic theory of legal norms based on social requirements and historical precedents accorded the state paramount rights, overriding the claims of individuals or morality. Alfred Hoche was a more mediocre figure, a professor of psychiatry at Freiburg, better known for his sharp critical interventions and stylistic elegance than for the scientific import of his neuropathological studies of how electricity was conducted by the spinal cords of people who had been decapitated.

He lost his only son at Langemark and wrote rather bad poetry about the experience of grief. He was clearly a difficult character, and a number of his obituarists took the opportunity to speak ill of the dead. Because of his marriage to a Jew, he took early retirement from his post at Freiburg when the National Socialists came to power. Ironically, he was privately critical of the National Socialist eugenic laws, pointing out that they would have precluded the birth of (inter aliis) Goethe, Schopenhauer and Beethoven; and he opposed the "euthanasia" programme, after it claimed one of his relatives, even though much of its rationale derived from his own writings.

Binding's starting point was the idea that every individual had sovereign powers to dispose of his or her own life as he or she saw fit; specifically, to commit suicide. The only argument he could muster against the legality of suicide was the loss to society of potentially valuable members. Legal problems inevitably multiplied when people tried to assign this sovereign right to third parties in the case of assisted suicide or voluntary euthanasia. He had no problems with euthanasia in its "pure" form, regarding it as an "act of healing" for the doctor to use artificial means to bring about a person's death, if it spared that person protracted suffering. Only a "pedant" would regard this as curtailing a person's life in any meaningful sense; rather it was merely a question of substituting a painless, shorter-term death for longer terminal suffering. Since the person dying was often unconscious, Binding apparently regarded questions of consent as being academic and marginal. Pointing to others . . . active in rolling back the state's monopolistic and limited control of killing (i.e. war and capital punishment), Binding finally broached the question which transparently most exercised him: "Is there human life which has so far forfeited the character of something entitled to enjoy the protection of the law, that its prolongation represents a perpetual loss of value, both for its bearer and for society as a whole?" He invited the reader to compare battlefields littered with the corpses of young soldiers, or a mine after a terrible accident, with the profligate care allegedly currently expended upon "idiots" in institutions, described here as "not merely worthless, but actually existences of negative value." There could be no doubt that some lives were a "burden" upon state and society as well as to the individuals themselves. Should one protect such life or license its destruction?

Temporarily recovering his liberal respect for the rights of individuals, Binding introduced the rather feeble caveat that such measures would have to be consensual, or would be prohibited in the case of feebleminded persons who appeared to enjoy their lives. Three groups of people would be affected by the new legal measures he was proposing. First, terminally ill or mortally wounded individuals who unequivocally expressed the wish to accelerate the act of dying. Hopelessness would augment the more customary criterion of unendurable pain. Secondly, "incurable idiots"—for there was little concern with precise categories, regardless of whether the idiocy was congenital or of relatively recent provenance. Since these people allegedly had no will to live, killing them could not be regarded as an infringement of their will. "Their life is absolutely pointless, but they do not regard it as being unbearable. They are a terrible, heavy burden upon their relatives and society as a whole. Their death would not create even the smallest gap—except perhaps in the feelings of their mothers or loyal nurses." They were a "travesty of real human beings, occasioning disgust in anyone who encounters them." In more heroic times, the state would have had no qualms in doing away with them. In a footnote, Binding actually claims that death would spare idiots the humiliation of "having to run the gauntlet of other people's cruel jokes and obloquy." The third and final group consisted of mentally healthy people who, having been rendered unconscious through accident of battle, would be appalled to see their own condition in the event of their regaining consciousness. Others should simply anticipate their wishes for them, by the dubious method of projecting what their own rational response to such a condition might be. Who were these "others," and indeed, how did Binding view the practicalities of extending the range of permissible killing? Proceedings were to be instigated either by the person concerned, or his or her relatives or doctor. A state authority would then determine whether that person was dying or incurably mentally ill. In the first case this body—which was to consist of a doctor, a lawyer and a psychiatrist under a non-voting chairman—would also ascertain whether the person was articulating a genuine and sustained wish or giving voice to temporary despair. This panel would then recommend that nothing stood in the way of killing the supplicant; the act of killing would be done by a doctor with the aid of powerful drugs. The "permitting committee" would be obliged to keep detailed records. The possibility of error was brushed aside with the remark: "what is good and reasonable must happen despite every risk of error . . . humanity loses so many of its members on account of error, that one more or less hardly counts in the balance."

Hoche, arguing from decades of practical experience—presumably other than with the spinal columns of executed criminals—began his "medical comments" by highlighting the virtual absence of an accessible body of work on medical ethics which could constitute a "code of practice." Instruction in medical ethics was *ad hoc* and informal, a matter of gleaning pearls of wisdom from one's superiors during the long medical apprenticeship. There were inevitably exceptions to the Hippocratic oath, of which the most obvious was abortion when the mother's survival was at stake. Everything was relative, including codes of medical ethics "which are not to be regarded as something which remains the same for eternity."

Like his colleague, Hoche turned quickly to the subject of the incurably mentally ill. Hoche distinguished between those whose mental defects were congenital and those who acquired them later in life. The former resembled a scattering of stones which had never been shaped by a creative hand; the latter the rubble of a building that had suddenly collapsed. The first group had no emotional ties either with their surroundings or with others; the second group could exert a very considerable emotional purchase upon other people. "Full idiots" represented a considerable burden for the community, their relatives and the state. They were "mentally dead," without human personality or self-consciousness, "on an intellectual level which we only encounter way down in the animal kingdom." Pity was a totally misplaced emotion in these cases, since "where there was no suffering, there can also be no pity." . . .

He next moved swiftly from questions of personality to the question of cost and numbers. These vulgar economistic arguments should not be confused with philosophical utilitarianism. Hoche claimed to have contacted every German asylum in order to establish an average annual cost of 1,300RMS for the care of each idiot. Although he did not bother to do the arithmetic, Hoche claimed that 20–30 idiots with an average life expectancy of fifty represented "a massive capital in the form of foodstuffs, clothing and heating, which is being subtracted from the national product for entirely unproductive purposes." This was before one started calculating such indirect costs as wages and salaries for the personnel in asylums, interest payments in the case of private establishments, and so on. The question of "ballast existences" had become acute in these times of national crisis. The nation resembled a difficult expedition, in which there was no room for "half, quarter, or eighth forces."

In a key passage, Hoche claimed that people had allegedly ceased to think of the state in organic terms, with the corollary that any single part of the "body" that had become either useless or harmful ought to be removed. It would take time for these new ethical

perspectives to become general currency. Only a few exceptional individuals were at present capable of thinking in those terms. The sort of
sentiments which would have to become general were exemplified by
the examples of the explorer Greely, who shot a fellow member of his
expedition in the back of the head because by surreptitiously taking
more than his fair share of food, he was growing stronger than the
rest; or Scott, who watched stoically as one member too many of his
expedition walked out of a tent to a death in the snow in the interests
of his fellows. These examples of extreme choices in situations in
which the explorers had entered voluntarily were supposed to sanc-
tion throwing overboard dead "ballast" from the Ship of Fools. Speaking very much *de haut en bas,* Hoche claimed that only a layman
would be concerned about the potential for serious error of the sort
that can occur in capital cases. Doctors would be in no doubt that
there was "one hundred per cent certainty in selection." He concluded
with Goethe's metaphor of civilisation ascending in the manner of
steadily ascending spirals. Just as the present time condemned as barbaric earlier eras in which killing defective infants was allegedly customary, so future epochs would regard the over-exaggerated notions
of humanity and over-estimation of the "value of existence" in the
present as their own barbaric past. Rather like critics of the "rational-
totalitarian" aspiration represented by modern prisons, Hoche evidently believed the progression lay in regression to simpler times.

. . .

II.

Although the first patients to be transferred may have believed the
story that they were being taken on an outing, with some of those
transferred first from Stetten acting out courtly farewells and kissing
hands while others felt aggrieved not to be going too, people destined
for subsequent transports were often under no illusions about their
ultimate destination. Consider a letter dated 1 October 1940 from
Helene M. to her father:

Dearest, beloved father!

Unfortunately it cannot be otherwise. Today I must write these words of farewell as I leave this earthly life for an eternal home. This will cause you and yours much, much heartache. But think that I must die as a martyr, and that this is not happening without the will of my heavenly redeemer, for whom I have longed for many years. Father, good father, I do not want to part from you without asking you and all my dear brothers and sisters once more for forgiveness, for all that I have failed you in throughout my whole life. May the dear Lord God accept my illness and this sacrifice as a penance for this.

Best of fathers, don't hold anything against your child, who loved you so very profoundly; always think that I am going to heaven, where we will all be reunited together with God and our deceased dear ones. Dear father, I am going with firm resolve and trust in God, never doubting in his good deeds, which he tests us with, but which unfortunately we do not comprehend when we are here. We will reap our reward on judgement day. Decreed by God! Please, tell this to my dear brothers and sisters. I won't lament, but shall be happy. I send you this little picture by way of a memento, your child will be meeting the saints in this way too.

I embrace you in undying love and with the firm promise I made when we last said our goodbyes, that I will persevere with fortitude.

Your child Helene.

On 2 October 1940. Please pray a lot for the peace of my soul. See you again, good father, in heaven.

This was the second of two letters which Helene, an epileptic, had managed to smuggle out of the asylum. Since the first spoke of patients being transferred and killed, her brother (the father, a retired doctor, had a weak heart) had gone to the Stuttgart health authorities to establish what was happening. He was reassured that if there were such steps being taken (!), epileptics would not be affected. The father visited the asylum and was advised to contact the authorities in the interests of having his daughter struck off the transfer list. He succeeded, but a little too late. A letter confirming that Helene should not be transferred arrived shortly after a letter informing the family of her death in Brandenburg because of "breathing problems."

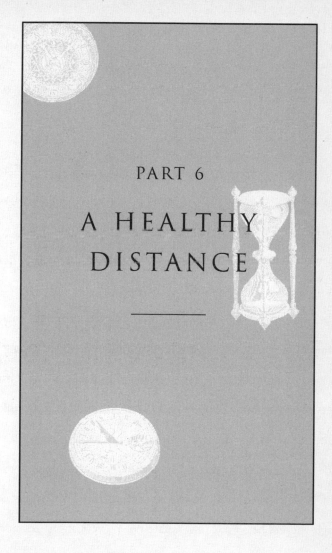

PART 6

A HEALTHY
DISTANCE

It is extraordinary, when you consider it, that a human being has the capacity to be consoled, comforted, even enlightened, by the words of another like himself. Extraordinary that, despite our common fate, we can, through the communication of knowledge, intelligence, or mere sympathy supply a deep need. That there is such a thing as consolation among the practices of mankind is testimony to the ingenuity and audacity of the human spirit; for consolation is also, in a way, absurd. It is people in the same boat trying to save one another from sinking. Laughter is a primary tool in this long and hapless effort. It's not wanted in the immediate precincts of death, nor is it proper there. But it is in its way a genuine mode of consolation, a way of demonstrating through wit and brashness that we are not powerless just because we are not omnipotent. Comedy doesn't exactly lead to transcendence, but it does magnify the moment and create a small infinity on earth. While we are laughing, we feel no limit to our might: we are using a uniquely human power to hedge out forces greater than ourselves. Perhaps we can't hold them off long, but while we are managing it, time stops. And when it is back to mortal business as usual, we can still relive the joke.

That's what hell must be like, small chat to the babbling of Lethe about the good old days when we wished we were dead.

SAMUEL BECKETT
Embers

❧

"It's vague, life and death."

SAMUEL BECKETT

MALONE DIES

The ever-solid antithesis of life and death dissolves at last in the novels and plays of Samuel Beckett (1906–89), whose characters run the gamut from those who wish they were dead, through those who think they might be, to those who see no difference between the states. We offer here one of the long-dying Malone's many reflections on the subject.

I was speaking then was I not of my little pastimes and I think about to say that I ought to content myself with them, instead of launching forth on all this ballsaching poppycock about life and death, if that is what it is all about, and I suppose it is, for nothing was ever about anything else to the best of my recollection. But what it is all about exactly I could no more say, at the present moment, than take up my bed and walk. It's vague, life and death. I must have had my little private idea on the subject when I began, otherwise I would not have begun, I would have held my peace, I would have gone on peacefully being bored to howls, having my little fun and games with the cones and cylinders, the millet grains beloved of birds and other panics, until someone was kind enough to come and coffin me. But it is gone clean out of my head, my little private idea. No matter, I have just had another. Perhaps it is the same one back again, ideas are so alike, when you get to know them. Be born, that's the brainwave now, that is to say live long enough to get acquainted with free carbonic gas, then say thanks for the nice time and go.

" 'Saint Peter,' Ellerbee said . . . , 'I'm Ellerbee.'
'I'm Saint Peter,' Saint Peter said."

STANLEY ELKIN

THE BEGINNING
OF THE (LIVING) END

*The American novelist Stanley Elkin (1930–95) was a great comic master,
yet suffering and mortality are his most powerful themes, and no tragedian
addresses them with greater passion or penetration. The Living End is a
kind of modern Divine Comedy. The reader visits both heaven and hell
and has a chance to observe God's mysterious ways at uncomfortably close
range. The selection offered here comes from the first chapter of the book.
Ellerbee, the public-spirited proprietor of a liquor store, is shot by two men
during a holdup along with his clerk, Kroll, while a third man stands by
without intervening. Our scene opens as Ellerbee pleads with this complacent stranger to call for help.*

"Where's Kroll? The other man, my manager?"

"Kroll's all right."

"He is?"

"There, right beside you."

He tried to look. They must have blasted Ellerbee's throat away, half his spinal column. It was impossible for him to move his head. "I can't see him," he moaned.

"Kroll's fine." The man cradled Ellerbee's shoulders and neck and shifted him slightly. "There. See?" Kroll's eyes were shut. Oddly, both were blackened. He had fallen in such a way that he seemed to lie on both his arms, retracted behind him into the small of his back like a yogi. His mouth was open and his tongue floated in blood like meat in soup. A slight man, he seemed strangely bloated, and one shin, exposed to Ellerbee's vision where the trouser leg was hiked up above his sock, was discolored as thundercloud.

The man gently set Ellerbee down again. "Call an ambulance," Ellerbee wheezed through his broken throat.

"No, no. Kroll's fine."

"He's not conscious." It was as if his words were being mashed through the tines of a fork.

"He'll be all right. Kroll's fine."

"Then for me. Call one for me."

"It's too late for you," the man said.

"For Christ's sake, will you!" Ellerbee gasped. "I can't move. You could have grabbed that hoodlum's gun when he set it down. All right, you were scared, but some of this is your fault. You didn't lift a finger. At least call an ambulance."

"But you're dead," he said gently. "Kroll will recover. You passed away when you said move."

"Are you crazy? What are you talking about?"

"Do you feel pain?"

"What?"

"Pain. You don't feel any, do you?" Ellerbee stared at him. "Do you?"

He didn't. His pain was gone. "Who are you?" Ellerbee said.

"I'm an angel of death," the angel of death said.

"You're—"

"An angel of death."

Somehow he had left his body. He could see it lying next to Kroll's. "I'm dead? But if I'm dead—you mean there's really an after-life?"

"Oh boy," the angel of death said.

. . .

They went to Heaven.

Ellerbee couldn't have said how they got there or how long it took, though he had the impression that time had passed, and distance. It was rather like a journey in films—a series of quick cuts, of montage. He was probably dreaming, he thought.

"It's what they all think," the angel of death said, "that they're dreaming. But that isn't so."

"I could have dreamed you said that," Ellerbee said, "that you read my mind."

"Yes."

"I could be dreaming all of it, the holdup, everything."

The angel of death looked at him.

"Hobgoblin . . . I could . . ." Ellerbee's voice—if it was a voice—trailed off.

"Look," the angel of death said, "I talk too much. I sound like a cabbie with an out-of-town fare. It's an occupational hazard."

"What?"

"What? Pride. The proprietary air. Showing off death like a booster. Thanatopography. 'If you look to your left you'll see where . . . Julius Caesar de dum de dum . . . Shakespeare da da da . . . And dead ahead our Father Adam heigh ho—' The tall buildings and the four-star sights. All that Baedeker reality of plaque place and high history. The Fields of Homer and the Plains of Myth. Where whosis got locked in a star and all the Agriculture of the Periodic Table—the South Forty of the Universe, where Hydrogen first bloomed, where Lithium, Berylium, Zirconium, Niobium. Where Lead failed and Argon came a cropper. The furrows of gold, Bismuth's orchards. . . . Still think you're dreaming?"

"No."

"Why not?"

"The language."

"Just so," the angel of death said. "When you were alive you had a vocabulary of perhaps seventeen or eighteen hundred words. Who am I?"

"An eschatological angel," Ellerbee said shyly.

"One hundred percent," the angel of death said. "Why do we do that?"

"To heighten perception," Ellerbee said, and shuddered.

The angel of death nodded and said nothing more.

When they were close enough to make out the outlines of Heaven, the angel left him, and Ellerbee, not questioning this, went on alone. From this distance it looked to Ellerbee rather like a theme park, but what struck him most forcibly was that it did not seem—for Heaven—very large. He traveled as he would on Earth, distance familiar again, volume, mass, and dimension restored, ordinary. (Quotidian, Ellerbee thought.) Indeed, now that he was convinced of his death, nothing seemed particularly strange. If anything, it was all a little familiar. He began to miss May. She would have learned of his death by this time. Difficult as the last year had been, they had loved each other. It had been a good marriage. He regretted again that they had been unable to have children. Children—they would be teenagers now—would have been a comfort to his widow. She still had her looks. Perhaps she would remarry. He did not want her to be lonely.

He continued toward Heaven and now, only blocks away, he was able to perceive it in detail. It looked more like a theme park than ever. It was enclosed behind a high milky fence, the uprights smooth and round as the poles in subway trains. Beyond the fence were golden streets, a mixed architecture of minaret-spiked mosques, great cathedrals, the rounded domes of classical synagogues, tall pagodas like holy vertebrae, white frame churches with their beautiful steeples, even what Ellerbee took to be a storefront church. There were many mansions. But where were the people?

Just as he was wondering about this he heard the sound of a gorgeous chorus. It was making a joyful noise. "Oh dem golden slippers," the chorus sang, "Oh dem golden slippers." It's the Heavenly

Choir, Ellerbee thought. They've actually got a Heavenly Choir. He went toward the fence and put his hands on the smooth posts and peered through into Heaven. He heard laughter and caught a glimpse of the running heels of children just disappearing around the corner of a golden street. They all wore shoes.

Ellerbee walked along the fence for about a mile and came to gates made out of pearl. The Pearly Gates, he thought. There are actually Pearly Gates. An old man in a long white beard sat behind them, a key attached to a sort of cinch that went about his waist.

"Saint Peter?" Ellerbee ventured. The old man turned his shining countenance upon him. "Saint Peter," Ellerbee said again, "I'm Ellerbee."

"I'm Saint Peter," Saint Peter said.

"Gosh," Ellerbee said, "I can't get over it. It's all true."

"What is?"

"Everything. Heaven. The streets of gold, the Pearly Gates. You. Your key. The Heavenly Choir. The climate."

A soft breeze came up from inside Heaven and Ellerbee sniffed something wonderful in the perfect air. He looked toward the venerable old man.

"Ambrosia," the Saint said.

"There's actually ambrosia," Ellerbee said.

"You know," Saint Peter said, "you never get tired of it, you never even get used to it. He does that to whet our appetite."

"You eat in Heaven?"

"We eat manna."

"There's actually manna," Ellerbee said. An angel floated by on a fleecy cloud playing a harp. Ellerbee shook his head. He had never heard anything so beautiful. "Heaven is everything they say it is," he said.

"It's paradise," Saint Peter said.

Then Ellerbee saw an affecting sight. Nearby, husbands were reunited with wives, mothers with their small babes, daddies with their sons, brothers with sisters—all the intricate blood loyalties and enlisted loves. He understood all the relationships without being told—his heightened perception. What was most moving, however, were the old people, related or not, some just lifelong friends, people who had lived together or known one another much the greater part of their lives and then had lost each other. It was immensely touching to Ellerbee to see them gaze fondly into one another's eyes and then to watch them reach out and touch the patient, ancient faces, wrinkled and even withered but, Ellerbee could tell, unchanged in the loving eyes of the adoring beholder. If there were tears they were tears of joy, tears that melded inextricably with tender laughter. There was rejoicing, there were Hosannas, there was dancing in the golden streets. "It's wonderful," Ellerbee muttered to himself. He didn't know where to look first. He would be staring at the beautiful flowing raiments of the angels—There are actually raiments, he thought, there are actually angels—so fine, he imagined, to the touch that just the caress of the cloth must have produced exquisite sensations not matched by anything in life, when something else would strike him. The perfectly proportioned angels' wings like discrete Gothic windows, the beautiful halos—There are actually halos—like golden quoits, or, in the distance, the lovely green pastures, delicious as fairway—all the perfectly banked turns of Heaven's geography. He saw philosophers deep in conversation. He saw kings and heroes. It was astonishing to him, like going to an exclusive restaurant one has only read about in columns and spotting, even at first glance, the celebrities one has read about, relaxed, passing the time of day, out in the open, up-front and sharing their high-echelon lives.

"This is for keeps?" he asked Saint Peter. "I mean it goes on like this?"

"World without end," Saint Peter said.

"Where's . . ."

"That's all right, say His name."

"God?" Ellerbee whispered.

Saint Peter looked around. "I don't see Him just . . . Oh, wait. There!" Ellerbee turned where the old Saint was pointing. He shaded his eyes. "There's no need," Saint Peter said.

"But the aura, the light."

"Let it shine."

He took his hand away fearfully and the light spilled into his

eyes like soothing unguents. God was on His throne in the green
pastures, Christ at His right Hand. To Ellerbee it looked like a picture
taken at a summit conference.

"He's beautiful. I've never . . . It's ecstasy."

"And you're seeing Him from a pretty good distance. You should
talk to Him sometime."

"People can talk to Him?"

"Certainly. He loves us."

There were tears in Ellerbee's eyes. He wished May no harm, but
wanted her with him to see it all. "It's wonderful."

"We like it," Saint Peter said.

"Oh, I do too," Ellerbee said. "I'm going to be very happy here."

"Go to Hell," Saint Peter said beatifically.

※

"If you hadn't nailed it to the perch,
it would be pushing up the daisies."

MONTY PYTHON

THE DEAD PARROT

Comedy may change the tone, but not the subject. It finds hilarity in the very same matters that are treated seriously in the other parts of this book. The following selection, one of the most popular sketches of the British ensemble Monty Python's Flying Circus, finds humor in the unfamiliarity of the dead body, for instance, and the indignity perhaps that it lingers on awhile after the self is extinguished. A chapter of this book puts the question "What words are there?" In this sketch we are offered a thorough lexicon of death's plain language and its euphemisms, and much of the joke depends upon our recognizing the lengths to which we go both to comprehend death in words and to avoid it with their help.

The text is taken from the original script, which includes character-names not actually spoken. The parts were played by John Cleese and Michael Palin.

Mr. PRALINE walks into the shop carrying a dead parrot in a cage. He walks to counter where SHOPKEEPER tries to hide below cash register.

PRALINE (JOHN)   Hello, I wish to register a complaint . . . Hello? Miss?

SHOPKEEPER (MICHAEL)   What do you mean, miss?

PRALINE   Oh, I'm sorry, I have a cold. I wish to make a complaint.

SHOPKEEPER   Sorry, we're closing for lunch.

PRALINE   Never mind that, my lad, I wish to complain about this parrot what I purchased not half an hour ago from this very boutique.

SHOPKEEPER   Oh yes, the Norwegian Blue. What's wrong with it?

PRALINE   I'll tell you what's wrong with it. It's dead, that's what's wrong with it.

SHOPKEEPER   No, no it's resting, look!

PRALINE   Look, my lad, I know a dead parrot when I see one and I'm looking at one right now.

SHOPKEEPER   No, no sir, it's not dead. It's resting.

PRALINE   Resting?

SHOPKEEPER   Yeah, remarkable bird the Norwegian Blue, beautiful plumage, innit?

PRALINE   The plumage don't enter into it—it's stone dead.

SHOPKEEPER   No, no—it's just resting.

PRALINE   All right then, if it's resting I'll wake it up. [Shouts into cage] Hello, Polly! I've got a nice cuttlefish for you when you wake up, Polly Parrot!

SHOPKEEPER [jogging cage]   There, it moved.

PRALINE   No, he didn't. That was you pushing the cage.

SHOPKEEPER   I did not.

PRALINE   Yes, you did. [Takes parrot out of cage, shouts] Hello, Polly,

Polly. [*Bangs it against counter*] Polly Parrot, wake up. Polly. [*Throws it in the air and lets it fall to the floor*] Now that's what I call a dead parrot.

SHOPKEEPER   No, no it's stunned.

PRALINE   Look, my lad, I've had just about enough of this. That parrot is definitely deceased. And when I bought it not half an hour ago you assured me that its lack of movement was due to it being tired and shagged out after a long squawk.

SHOPKEEPER   It's probably pining for the fiords.

PRALINE   Pining for the fiords, what kind of talk is that? Look, why did it fall flat on its back the moment I got it home?

SHOPKEEPER   The Norwegian Blue prefers kipping on its back. Beautiful bird, lovely plumage.

PRALINE   Look, I took the liberty of examining that parrot, and I discovered that the only reason that it had been sitting on its perch in the first place was that it had been nailed there.

SHOPKEEPER   Well of course it was nailed there. Otherwise it would muscle up to those bars and voom.

PRALINE   Look, matey [*Picks up parrot*], this parrot wouldn't voom if I put four thousand volts through it. It's bleeding demised.

SHOPKEEPER   It's not, it's pining.

PRALINE   It's not pining, it's passed on. This parrot is no more. It has ceased to be. It's expired and gone to meet its maker. This is a late parrot. It's a stiff. Bereft of life, it rests in peace. If you hadn't nailed it to the perch, it would be pushing up the daisies. It's rung down the curtain and joined the choir invisible. This is an ex-parrot.

SHOPKEEPER   Well, I'd better replace it then.

PRALINE [*to camera*]   If you want to get anything done in this country you've got to complain till you're blue in the mouth.

SHOPKEEPER   Sorry, guv, we're right out of parrots.

PRALINE   I see. I see. I get the picture.

SHOPKEEPER   I've got a slug.

PRALINE   Does it talk?

SHOPKEEPER   Not really, no.

PRALINE   Well, it's scarcely a replacement, then, is it?

SHOPKEEPER   Listen, I'll tell you what [*handing over a card*], tell you what, if you go to my brother's pet shop in Bolton he'll replace your parrot for you.

PRALINE   Bolton eh?

SHOPKEEPER   Yeah.

PRALINE   All right.

[*He leaves, holding the parrot*]

Caption: "A Similar Pet Shop in Bolton Lancs"

Close-up of sign on door reading "Similar Pet Shops Ltd." Pull back from sign to see same pet shop. SHOPKEEPER *now has moustache.* PRALINE *walks into shop. He looks around with interest, noticing the empty parrot cage still on the floor. . . .*

"He seemed to be addressing the dearly departed
as if he were hiding somewhere among them."

MILAN KUNDERA

GRAVESIDE LAUGHTER

This scene from The Book of Laughter and Forgetting *(1979), by Czech-
born writer Milan Kundera, is taken from the final chapter, "The Border."
It presents the funeral of a character whose name, aptly, is Passer. Here, as
throughout the novel, Kundera probes the sudden affective transformations
that can result from a small quake of consciousness, a tiny mental displace-
ment that can carry one suddenly across a kind of psychic fissure. Kundera
writes, "It takes so little, so infinitely little, for a person to cross the border
beyond which everything loses meaning. . . ." A sudden revelation of absurdity, Kundera suggests, can have the salutary effect of preserving us
from the self-deluded earnestness of fanaticism, but can also fling us from
the heights of heroic self-sacrifice—or the peaks of sexual ecstasy. Likewise,
it takes ridiculously little, "an insignificant breeze," to transform grief to
hilarity.*

It was windy and muddy. A straggly semicircle of mourners stood
around the open grave. They included Jan and nearly all his friends:

Jeanne the actress, the Clevises, Barbara, and, of course, the Passers—
Passer's wife and his son and daughter, both in tears.

Two men in shabby clothes were lifting the ropes the coffin
rested on when a nervous man with a piece of paper in his hand came
up to the grave, turned to the gravediggers, looked back at his paper,
and began to read. The gravediggers looked over at him, trying to
gauge whether to put the coffin down beside the grave again. Then
they began lowering it slowly into the pit, apparently having decided
to spare the corpse the torture of a fourth speech.

The sudden disappearance of the coffin caught the speaker off
guard. He had written his entire speech in the second person singular,
and as he exhorted the corpse, reassured it, agreed with it, comforted
it, thanked it, and answered the questions he had put in its mouth,
the coffin was making its way down into the grave. Finally it settled
on the bottom, and the gravediggers pulled out the ropes and stood
there trying to look unobtrusive. When they realized the speaker was
addressing his tirade right at them, they lowered their eyes in embarrassment.

The more aware the orator became of the incongruity of the
situation, the more the two sad figures attracted his attention. Finally
he tore his eyes away from them and turned toward the semicircle of
mourners. But that did not help his second-person delivery at all. He
seemed to be addressing the dearly departed as if he were hiding
somewhere among them.

Where should he have looked? In anguish he stared down at the
paper, and even though he knew the text by heart, he kept his eyes
riveted on it.

Everyone present felt a certain uneasiness. It was heightened by
the neurotic bursts of wind constantly attacking them. Papa Clevis
had pulled his hat down firmly over his temples, but the wind was so
strong it lifted it off his head and set it down halfway between the
open grave and the Passer family.

His first impulse was to make his way up to them slowly and
then dart out for the hat, but that, he realized, might make it look as
though he thought his hat was more important than the dignity of the

rites honoring his friend. Instead, he decided to stay where he was and pretend nothing had happened. It was the wrong decision. From the minute the hat landed in the no-man's-land before the grave, the assembly of mourners found it impossible to follow the orator's words. Now they were even more uneasy. Though modestly immobile, the hat was clearly disturbing the funeral more than Clevis would by taking a few steps and retrieving it. So he finally said "Excuse me" to the man standing next to him and emerged from the group. He now stood in the empty space (about the size of a small stage) between the grave and the mourners. But just as he bent down for the hat, a gust of wind moved it out of his reach and dropped it at the feet of the orator.

By then no one was thinking of anything but Papa Clevis and his hat. The orator was not aware of the hat, but even he had realized there was something disturbing his audience. When he finally lifted his eyes from the paper, he was amazed to see a stranger standing a foot or two away from him and apparently ready to jump the rest of the way. He quickly looked back down at the paper, hoping perhaps that by the time he looked up again the improbable vision would have vanished. But when he did, there was that man still standing there staring at him.

Papa Clevis could move neither forward nor back. Storming the feet of the orator seemed too daring, retreating without the hat seemed ridiculous. So he stood there, motionless, nailed to the spot by indecisiveness, trying vainly to come up with a viable way out.

Desperate for help, he looked over at the gravediggers standing motionless on the other side of the grave and staring straight at the orator's feet. But once again the wind began coaxing the hat in the direction of the grave. Clevis made up his mind. He took a few energetic steps forward, stretched out his arm, and bent over. Unfortunately, the hat slid farther out of his reach. He had finally just caught up with it when it tipped over the side and fell into the pit.

Clevis's first impulse was to stretch his arms out after it. Then he decided to act as though no hat had ever existed and he just happened to be standing there. He tried his best to be completely natural and relaxed, but with all eyes trained on him it was not easy. He contorted his face to avoid everybody's glance, and walked back to the front row next to Passer's sobbing son.

Once the dangerous specter of the man about to leap had disappeared, the man with the paper calmed down, raised his eyes to the crowd, which by now had no idea of what he was talking about, and pronounced the final sentence of his oration. Then he turned to the gravediggers and said with great pomp, "Victor Passer, those who loved you will never forget you. May the earth not weigh heavily upon you."

He bent down over a pile of dirt at the edge of the grave, picked up the small shovel sticking out of it, shoveled up some dirt, and peered down into the grave. At that moment the entire assembly of mourners was racked by a silent wave of laughter. They all knew that the orator, poised with the shovel of dirt over the grave, was staring at the coffin lying at the bottom of the pit and the hat lying on the coffin. (It was as if in a last vain plea for dignity the dead man had wished to keep his head covered in deference to the solemnity of the occasion.)

The orator managed to control himself, and threw the dirt on the coffin in such a manner as to avoid the hat, afraid, perhaps, that Passer's head actually was hiding underneath it. Then he passed the shovel to Passer's widow. Yes, they all had to drink the cup to the dregs. They all had to join the terrible battle with laughter. They all had to follow Passer's wife, daughter, and sobbing son, shovel up some dirt, and lean over into the pit where there was a coffin with a hat lying on it. It was as though the indomitably vital and optimistic Passer had stuck his head out for one last look.

Translated by Michael Henry Heim.

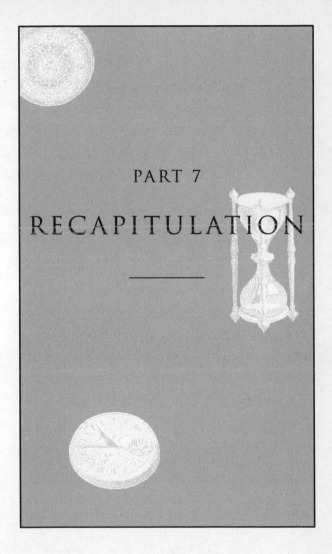

PART 7

RECAPITULATION

WILLIAM SHAKESPEARE (1564–1616)

HAMLET:
THE GRAVEYARD

CLOWN   Is she to be buried in Christian burial that wilfully seeks her own salvation?

OTHER   I tell thee she is; and therefore make her grave straight. The crowner hath sat on her, and finds it Christian burial.

CLOWN   How can that be, unless she drown'd herself in her own defence?

OTHER   Why, 'tis found so.

CLOWN   It must be *se offendendo*, it cannot be else. For here lies the point: if I drown myself wittingly, it argues an act; and an act hath three branches—it is to act, to do, and to perform. Argal, she drowned herself wittingly.

OTHER   Nay, but hear you, Goodman Delver—

CLOWN   Give me leave. Here lies the water; good. Here stands the man; good. If the man go to this water and drown himself, it is, will he nill he, he goes. Mark you that. But if the water come to him and drown him, he drowns not himself. Argal, he that is not guilty of his own life.

OTHER   But is this law?

CLOWN   Ay, marry, is't, crowner's quest law.

OTHER   Will you ha' the truth on't? If this had not been a gentle-woman, she should have been buried out of Christian burial.

CLOWN   Why, there thou sayst; and the more pity that great folk should have countenance in this world to drown or hang them-selves more than their even-Christian. Come, my spade. There is no ancient gentlemen but gardeners, ditchers, and grave-makers; they hold up Adam's profession.

OTHER   Was he a gentleman?

CLOWN   A was the first that ever bore arms.

OTHER   Why, he had none.

CLOWN   What, art a heathen? How dost thou understand the Scripture? The Scripture says Adam digged. Could he dig without arms? I'll put another question to thee. If thou answerest me not to the purpose, confess thyself—

OTHER   Go to.

CLOWN   What is he that builds stronger than either the mason, the shipwright, or the carpenter?

OTHER   The gallows-maker; for that frame outlives a thousand ten-ants.

CLOWN   I like thy wit well, in good faith. The gallows does well. But how does it well? It does well to those that do ill. Now thou dost ill to say the gallows is built stronger than the church. Argal, the gallows may do well to thee. To't again, come.

OTHER   Who builds stronger than a mason, a shipwright, or a carpenter?

CLOWN   Ay, tell me that, and unyoke.

OTHER   Marry, now I can tell.

CLOWN   To't . . .

OTHER   Mass, I cannot tell.

CLOWN   Cudgel thy brains no more about it, for your dull ass will
not mend his pace with beating. And when you are asked this
question next, say "a grave-maker." The houses that he makes lasts
till doomsday. Go, get thee to Yaughan; fetch me a stoup of liquor.

[*Exit* OTHER. *Enter* HAMLET *and* HORATIO. CLOWN *sings.*]

> In youth when I did love, did love,
> Methought it was very sweet
> To contract—O—the time for—a—my behove,
> O, methought there was nothing meet.

HAMLET   Has this fellow no feeling of his business that he sings at
grave-making?

HORATIO   Custom hath made it in him a property of easiness.

HAMLET   'Tis e'en so; the hand of little employment hath the
daintier sense.

CLOWN   [*Sings*]

> But age with his stealing steps
> Hath caught me in his clutch,
> And hath shipped me intil the land,
> As if I had never been such.

[*He throws up a skull*]

HAMLET   That skull had a tongue in it, and could sing once. How
the knave jowls it to th' ground, as if it were Cain's jaw-bone, that

did the first murder. It might be the pate of a politician which this
ass now o'er-offices, one that would circumvent God, might it not?

HORATIO   It might, my lord.

HAMLET   Or of a courtier, which could say, "Good morrow, sweet
lord. How dost thou, good lord?" This might be my Lord
Such-a-one, that praised my Lord Such-a-one's horse when he
meant to beg it, might it not?

HORATIO   Ay, my lord.

HAMLET   Why, e'en so, and now my Lady Worm's, chapless, and
knock'd about the mazard with a sexton's spade. Here's fine revolution, if we had the trick to see't. Did these bones cost no more the
breeding but to play at loggats with 'em? Mine ache to think on't.

CLOWN   [Sings]

A pickaxe and a spade, a spade,
For and a shrouding-sheet;
O, a pit of clay for to be made
For such a guest is meet.

[Throws up another skull]

HAMLET   There's another. Why, might not that be the skull of a
lawyer? Where be his quiddities now, his quillities, his cases, his
tenures, and his tricks? Why does he suffer this rude knave now to
knock him about the sconce with a dirty shovel, and will not tell
him of his action of battery?
        Hum! This fellow might be in's time a great buyer of land,
with his statutes, his recognizances, his fines, his double vouchers,
his recoveries. Is this the fine of his fines and the recovery of his
recoveries, to have his fine pate full of fine dirt? Will his vouchers
vouch him no more of his purchases, and double ones too, than
the length and breadth of a pair of indentures? The very convey-
ances of his lands will hardly lie in this box; and must the inheritor
himself have no more, ha?

HORATIO   Not a jot more, my lord.

HAMLET   Is not parchment made of sheepskins?

HORATIO   Ay, my lord, and of calf-skins too.

HAMLET   They are sheep and calves that seek out assurance in that.
I will speak to this fellow. Whose grave's this, sirrah?

CLOWN   Mine, sir. [Sings]

        O, a pit of clay for to be made
        For such a guest is meet.

HAMLET   I think it be thine indeed, for thou liest in't.

CLOWN   You lie out on't, sir, and therefore it is not yours. For my
part, I do not lie in't, and yet it is mine.

HAMLET   Thou dost lie in't, to be in't and say 'tis thine. 'Tis for the
dead, not for the quick; therefore thou liest.

CLOWN   'Tis a quick lie, sir, 'twill away again from me to you.

HAMLET   What man dost thou dig it for?

CLOWN   For no man, sir.

HAMLET   What woman, then?

CLOWN   For none neither.

HAMLET   Who is to be buried in't?

CLOWN   One that was a woman, sir; but, rest her soul, she's dead.

HAMLET   How absolute the knave is! We must speak by the card, or
equivocation will undo us. By the Lord, Horatio, these three years I
have taken note of it; the age is grown so picked that the toe of the
peasant comes so near the heel of the courtier he galls his kibe.
How long hast thou been a grave-maker?

CLOWN   Of all the days i'th' year, I came to't that day that our last
king Hamlet o'ercame Fortinbras.

HAMLET   How long is that since?

CLOWN   Cannot you tell that? Every fool can tell that. It was the very day that young Hamlet was born—he that was mad and sent into England.

HAMLET   Ay, marry. Why was he sent into England?

CLOWN   Why, because he was mad. He shall recover his wits there; or if he do not, it's no great matter there.

HAMLET   Why?

CLOWN   'Twill not be seen in him there. There the men are as mad as he.

HAMLET   How came he mad?

CLOWN   Very strangely, they say.

HAMLET   How strangely?

CLOWN   Faith, e'en with losing his wits.

HAMLET   Upon what ground?

CLOWN   Why, here in Denmark. I have been sexton here, man and boy, thirty years.

HAMLET   How long will a man lie i'th' earth ere he rot?

CLOWN   I'faith, if he be not rotten before he die—as we have many pocky corses nowadays that will scarce hold the laying in—he will last you some eight year or nine year. A tanner will last you nine year.

HAMLET   Why he more than another?

CLOWN   Why, sir, his hide is so tanned with his trade that he will keep out water a great while; and your water is a sore decayer of your whoreson dead body. Here's a skull now. This skull has lain in the earth three and twenty years.

HAMLET   Whose was it?

CLOWN   A whoreson mad fellow's it was. Whose do you think it
was?

HAMLET   Nay, I know not.

CLOWN   A pestilence on him for a mad rogue! A poured a flagon of
Rhenish on my head once. This same skull, sir, was Yorick's skull,
the King's jester.

HAMLET   This?

CLOWN   E'en that.

HAMLET   Let me see. [*Takes the skull*] Alas, poor Yorick. I knew
him, Horatio, a fellow of infinite jest, of most excellent fancy. He
hath borne me on his back a thousand times. And now how ab-
horred in my imagination it is! My gorge rises at it. Here hung
those lips that I have kissed I know not how oft. Where be your
gibes now, your gambols, your songs, your flashes of merriment
that were wont to set the table on a roar? No one now to mock
your own grinning? Quite chop-fallen? Now get you to my lady's
chamber and tell her, let her paint an inch thick, to this favour she
must come. Make her laugh at that. Prithee, Horatio, tell me one
thing.

HORATIO   What's that, my lord?

HAMLET   Dost thou think Alexander look'd o' this fashion i'th'
earth?

HORATIO   E'en so.

HAMLET   And smelt so? Pah!

[*Puts down the skull*]

HORATIO   E'en so, my lord.

HAMLET   To what base uses we may return, Horatio. Why, may not
imagination trace the noble dust of Alexander till he find it stop-
ping a bung-hole?

HORATIO   'Twere to consider too curiously to consider so.

HAMLET   No, faith, not a jot; but to follow him thither with modesty enough, and likelihood to lead it. As thus: Alexander died,
Alexander was buried, Alexander returneth into dust. The dust is
earth, of earth we make loam, and why of that loam whereto he
was converted might they not stop a beer-barrel?

[*Sings*]

> Imperial Caesar, dead and turn'd to clay,
> Might stop a hole to keep the wind away.
> O, that that earth, which kept the world in awe,
> Should patch a wall t'expel the winter's flaw.

PERMISSIONS

Awooner-Renner, Sheila: "I Desperately Needed to See My Son." *The British Medical Journal*, 1991; no. 302: 356–359. Reprinted by permission of *The British Medical Journal*.

Baldwin, James: from *Notes of a Native Son* by James Baldwin, copyright © 1955, renewed 1983, by James Baldwin. Reprinted by permission of Beacon Press, Boston.

Barthes, Roland: from *Camera Lucida: Reflections on Photography* by Roland Barthes, translated by Richard Howard. Translation copyright © 1981 by Farrar, Straus & Giroux, Inc. Reprinted by permission of Hill & Wang, a division of Farrar, Straus & Giroux, Inc.

Beauvoir, Simone de: from *A Very Easy Death* by Simone de Beauvoir. Reprinted by permission of Weidenfeld & Nicolson.

Beckett, Samuel: from *Malone Dies* by Samuel Beckett. Copyright © 1956 by Grove Press.

Boccaccio, Giovanni: from *The Decameron*. Translation copyright © 1996 by Richard Tristman.

Brecht, Bertolt: "On His Mortality" from *Bertolt Brecht: Poems 1913–1956,* translated by H. B. Mallalieux. Edited by John Willett and Ralph Manheim with the cooperation of Erich Fried. Routledge: New York and London. (Previously printed by Eyre Methuen Ltd. Copyright © 1976.) Reprinted by permission of the publisher.

Buñuel, Luis: from *My Last Sigh* by Luis Buñuel, translated by Abigail Israel. Translation copyright © 1983 by Alfred A. Knopf, Inc. Reprinted by permission of the publisher.

Burleigh, Michael: from *Death and Deliverance: Euthanasia in Germany c. 1900–1945* by Michael Burleigh, pp. 15–19, 142–143. Copyright © 1994 by Cambridge University Press. Reprinted with the permission of Cambridge University Press.

Califano, Joseph: from *America's Health Care Revolution* by Joseph A. Califano, Jr. Copyright © 1986 by Joseph A. Califano, Jr. Reprinted by permission of Random House, Inc.

Cavafy, C. P.: "The Horses of Achilles," from *The Collected Poems.* Copyright © 1975, 1992 by Edmund Keeley and Philip Sherrard. Reprinted by permission of Princeton University Press.

Colette: from *Earthly Paradise* by Colette, edited by Robert Phelps. Copyright © 1966, copyright renewed © 1994 by Farrar, Straus & Giroux, Inc.

Dickinson, Emily: letter #868 (October 1883), from *The Letters of Emily Dickinson*, edited by Thomas H. Johnson. Cambridge, Mass.: The Belknap Press of Harvard University Press, copyright © 1958, 1986 by the President and Fellows of Harvard College. Reprinted by permission of the publishers.

Dickinson, Emily: poem #586 from *The Complete Poems of Emily Dickinson*, edited by T. H. Johnson, copyright 1929 by Martha Dickinson Bianchi. Copyright © renewed 1957 by Mary L. Hampson. Reprinted by permission of Little, Brown and Company.

ABOUT THE EDITORS

Maura Spiegel teaches at Columbia University and Barnard College. She has recently completed a book on the history of emotions in the nineteenth century.

Richard Tristman was a professor of literature for twenty-eight years. He is a contributor to *The Encyclopedia of Aesthetics,* and is now writing a book on the idea of indecency.